WAR OF THE MARVELS

WRITER: *BRIAN REED*
ARTISTS: *SANA TAKEDA, SERGIO ARIÑO*
& PHILIPPE BRIONES
COLOR ART (ISSUES #43 AND #45): *IKARI STUDIOS*
COVER ARTIST: *SANA TAKEDA*
ASSISTANT EDITOR: *TOM BRENNAN*
EDITOR: *STEPHEN WACKER*

COLLECTION EDITOR: *CORY LEVINE*
ASSISTANT EDITORS: *ALEX STARBUCK & JOHN DENNING*
EDITORS, SPECIAL PROJECTS: *JENNIFER GRÜNWALD & MARK D. BEAZLEY*
SENIOR EDITOR, SPECIAL PROJECTS: *JEFF YOUNGQUIST*
SENIOR VICE PRESIDENT OF SALES: *DAVID GABRIEL*

EDITOR IN CHIEF: *JOE QUESADA*
PUBLISHER: *DAN BUCKLEY*
EXECUTIVE PRODUCER: *ALAN FINE*

PREVIOUSLY: In the wake of the Skrull Invasion, Norman Osborn, then-director of the Thunderbolts, has risen to power and installed his own Avengers team made up mostly of his old Thunderbolts. Karla Sofen, a.k.a. Moonstone, has taken the role of Ms. Marvel. She has taken a surprising shine to heroism and has set about to finish up cases the seemingly dead Ms. Marvel let fall to the wayside.

One such case was the operations of a rogue A.I.M. cell operating under the leadership of Monica Rappacini that created a new group of M.O.D.O.K.s. Using a mental link with Sofen, the creatures called for her help and she absconded with 10 of the babies.

Before Sofen could make her next move, she and the infant M.O.D.O.K.s were attacked by a woman made of pure energy. Elsewhere, Wolverine and Spider-Man were also approached by these energy creatures and discovered they were part of Carol Danvers' essence. With the other Avengers in tow, Spider-Man brought the energy beings to the A.I.M. base – and revived Carol Danvers...

MS. MARVEL VOL. 8: WAR OF THE MARVELS. Contains material originally published in magazine form as MS. MARVEL #42-46. First printing 2009. Hardcover ISBN# 978-0-7851-3840-2. Softcover ISBN# 978-0-7851-3841-9. Published by MARVEL PUBLISHING, INC., a subsidiary of MARVEL ENTERTAINMENT, INC. OFFICE OF PUBLICATION: 417 5th Avenue, New York, NY 10016. Copyright © 2009 and 2010 Marvel Characters, Inc. All rights reserved. Hardcover: $19.99 per copy in the U.S. (GST #R127032852). Softcover: $14.99 per copy in the U.S. (GST #R127032852). Canadian Agreement #40668537. All characters featured in this issue and the distinctive names and likenesses thereof, and all related indicia are trademarks of Marvel Characters, Inc. No similarity between any of the names, characters, persons, and/or institutions in this magazine with those of any living or dead person or institution is intended, and any such similarity which may exist is purely coincidental. **Printed in the U.S.A.** ALAN FINE, EVP - Office Of The Chief Executive Marvel Entertainment, Inc. & CMO Marvel Characters B.V.; DAN BUCKLEY, Chief Executive Officer and Publisher - Print, Animation & Digital Media; JIM SOKOLOWSKI, Chief Operating Officer; DAVID GABRIEL, SVP of Publishing Sales & Circulation; DAVID BOGART, SVP of Business Affairs & Talent Management; MICHAEL PASCIULLO, VP Merchandising & Communications; JIM O'KEEFE, VP of Operations & Logistics; DAN CARR, Executive Director of Publishing Technology; JUSTIN F. GABRIE, Director of Publishing & Editorial Operations; SUSAN CRESPI, Editorial Operations Manager; ALEX MORALES, Publishing Operations Manager; STAN LEE, Chairman Emeritus. For information regarding advertising in Marvel Comics or on Marvel.com, please contact Mitch Dane, Advertising Director, at mdane@marvel.com. For Marvel subscription inquiries, please call 800-217-9158. **Manufactured between 11/9/09 and 12/9/09 (hardcover), and 11/9/09 and 4/14/10 (softcover), by R.R. DONNELLEY, INC., SALEM, VA, USA.**

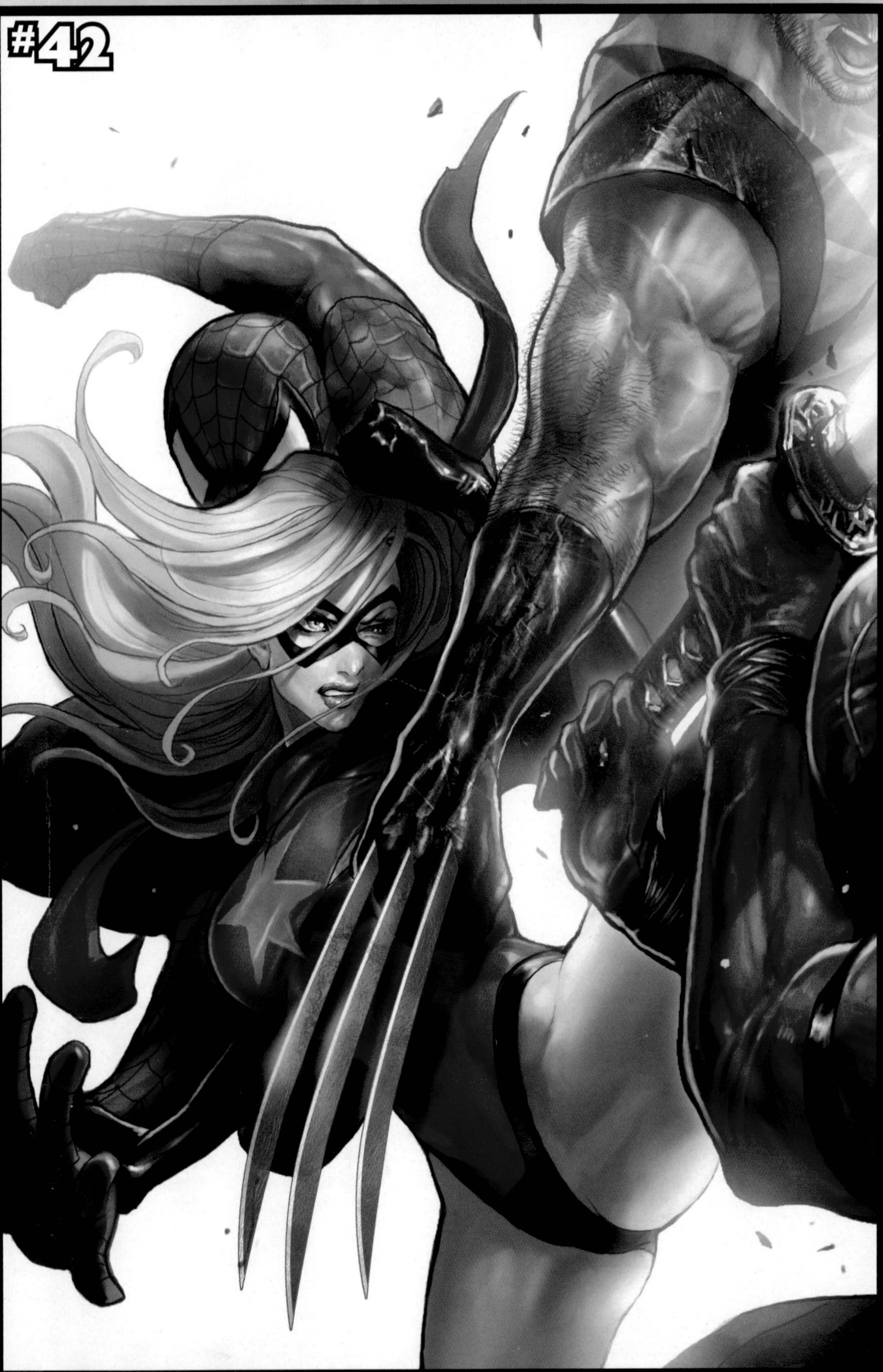
#42

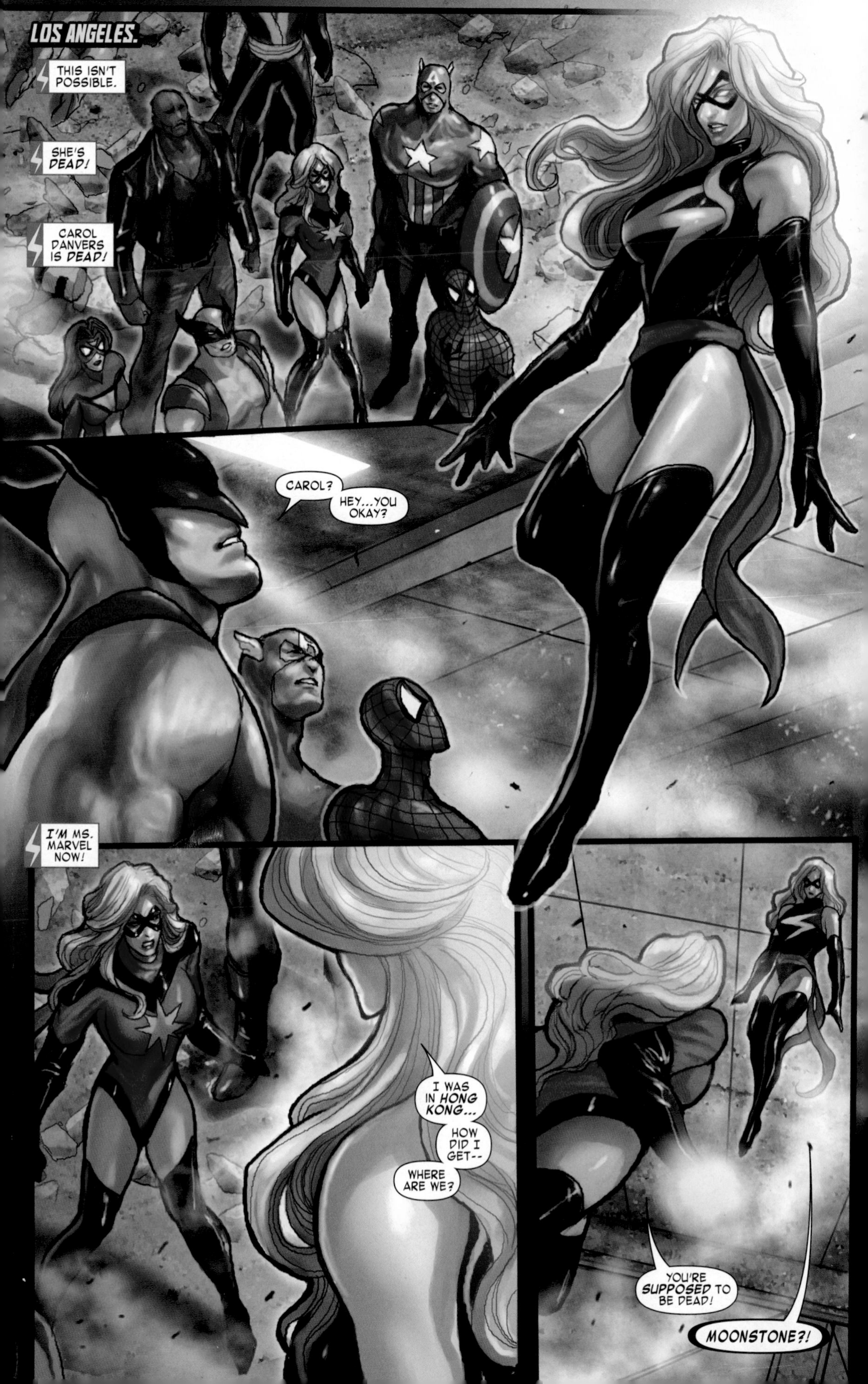
LOS ANGELES.
THIS ISN'T POSSIBLE.
SHE'S DEAD!
CAROL DANVERS IS DEAD!
CAROL?
HEY...YOU OKAY?
I'M MS. MARVEL NOW!
I WAS IN HONG KONG...
HOW DID I GET--
WHERE ARE WE?
YOU'RE SUPPOSED TO BE DEAD!
MOONSTONE?!

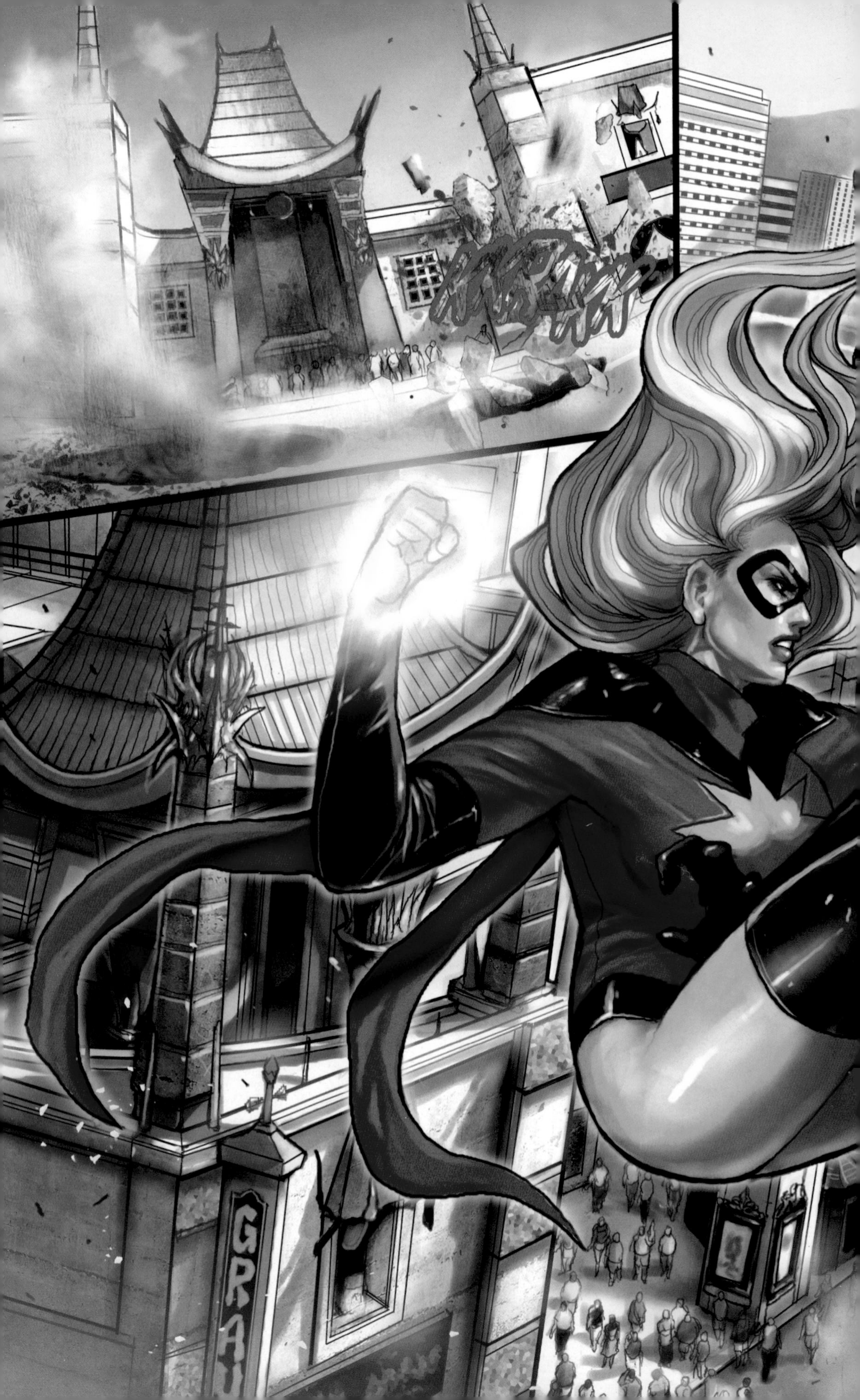
GRA

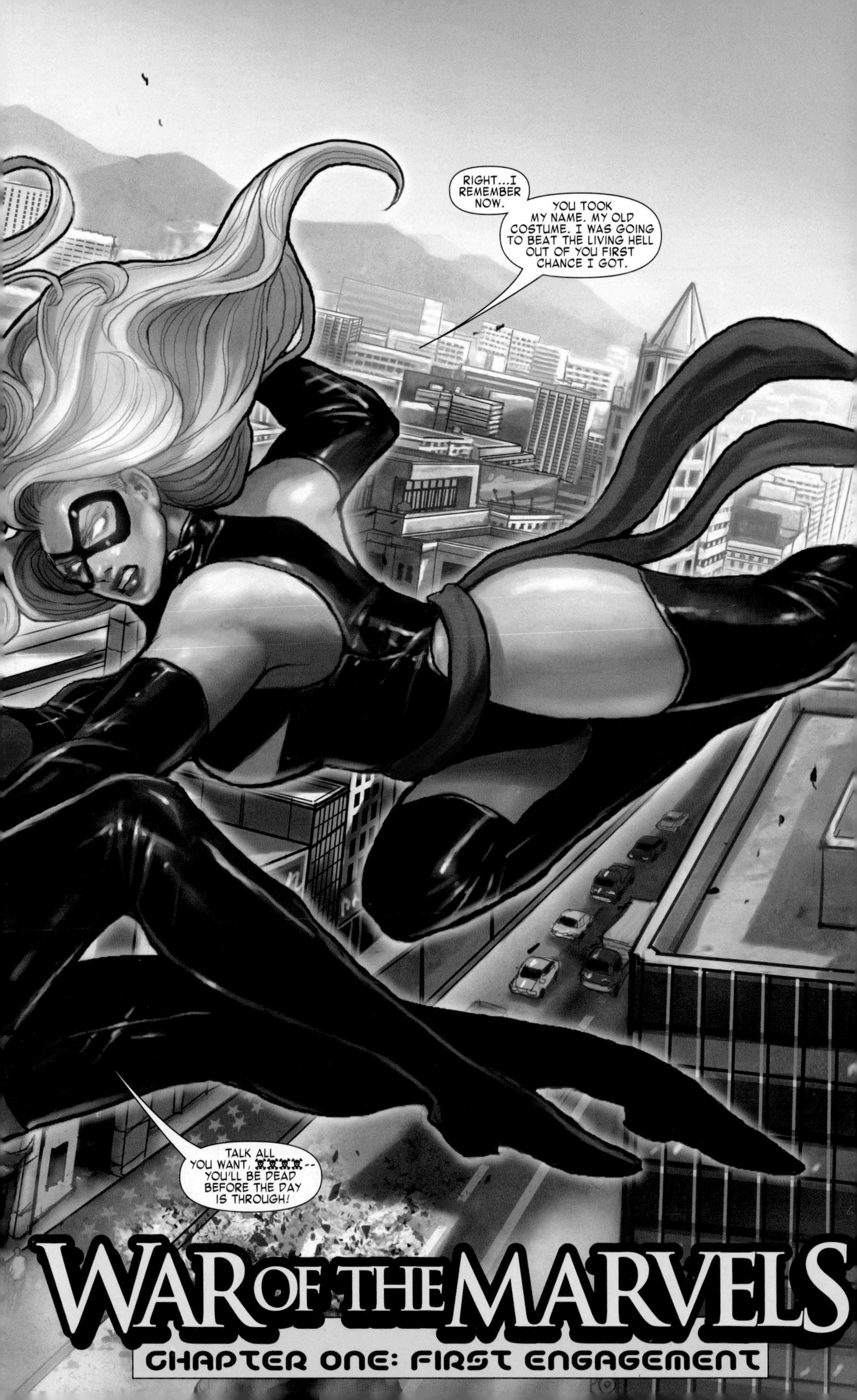
RIGHT...I REMEMBER NOW.
YOU TOOK MY NAME. MY OLD COSTUME. I WAS GOING TO BEAT THE LIVING HELL OUT OF YOU FIRST CHANCE I GOT.
TALK ALL YOU WANT, ☠☠☠☠--YOU'LL BE DEAD BEFORE THE DAY IS THROUGH!
WAR OF THE MARVELS
CHAPTER ONE: FIRST ENGAGEMENT

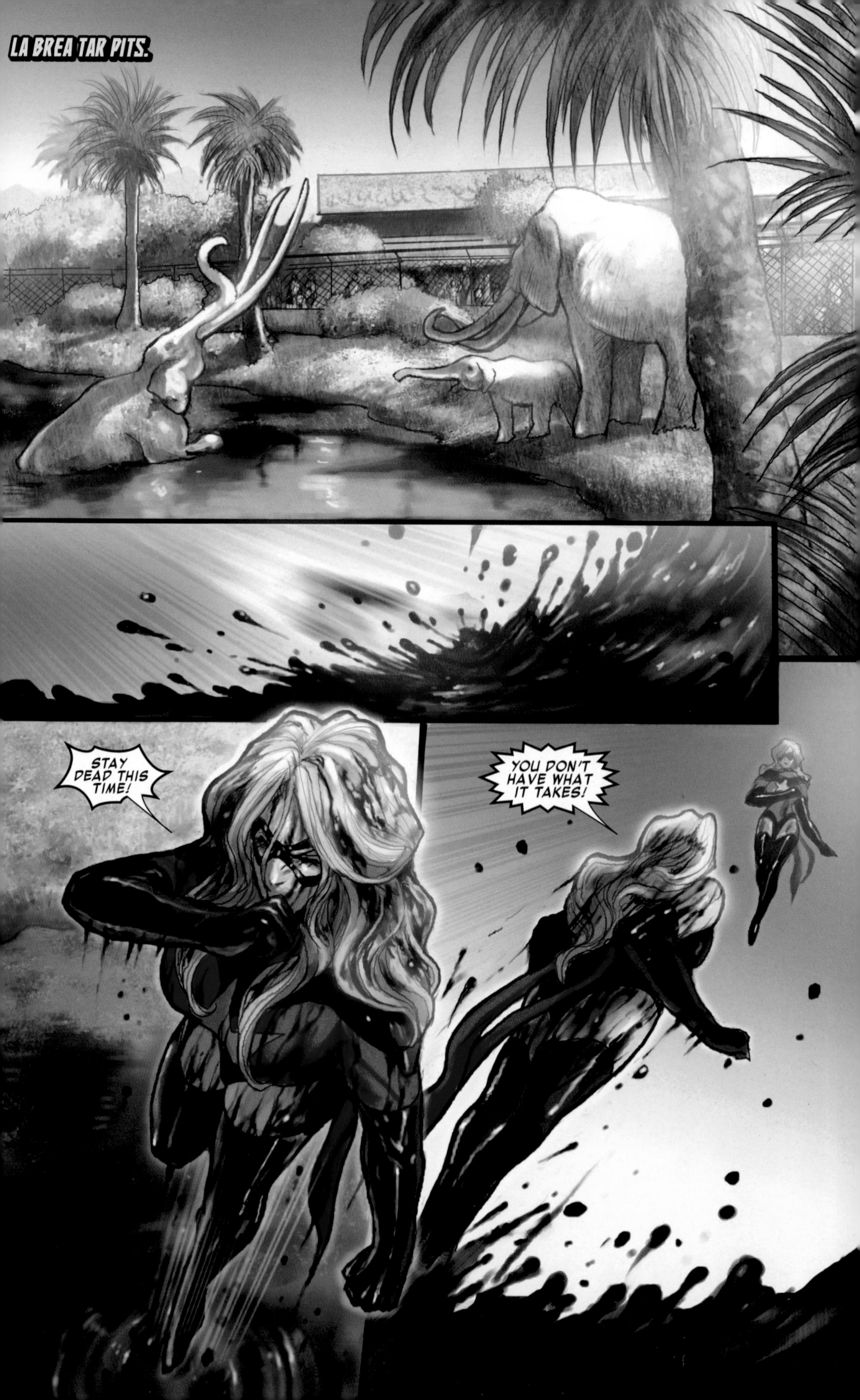
LA BREA TAR PITS.
STAY DEAD THIS TIME!
YOU DON'T HAVE WHAT IT TAKES!

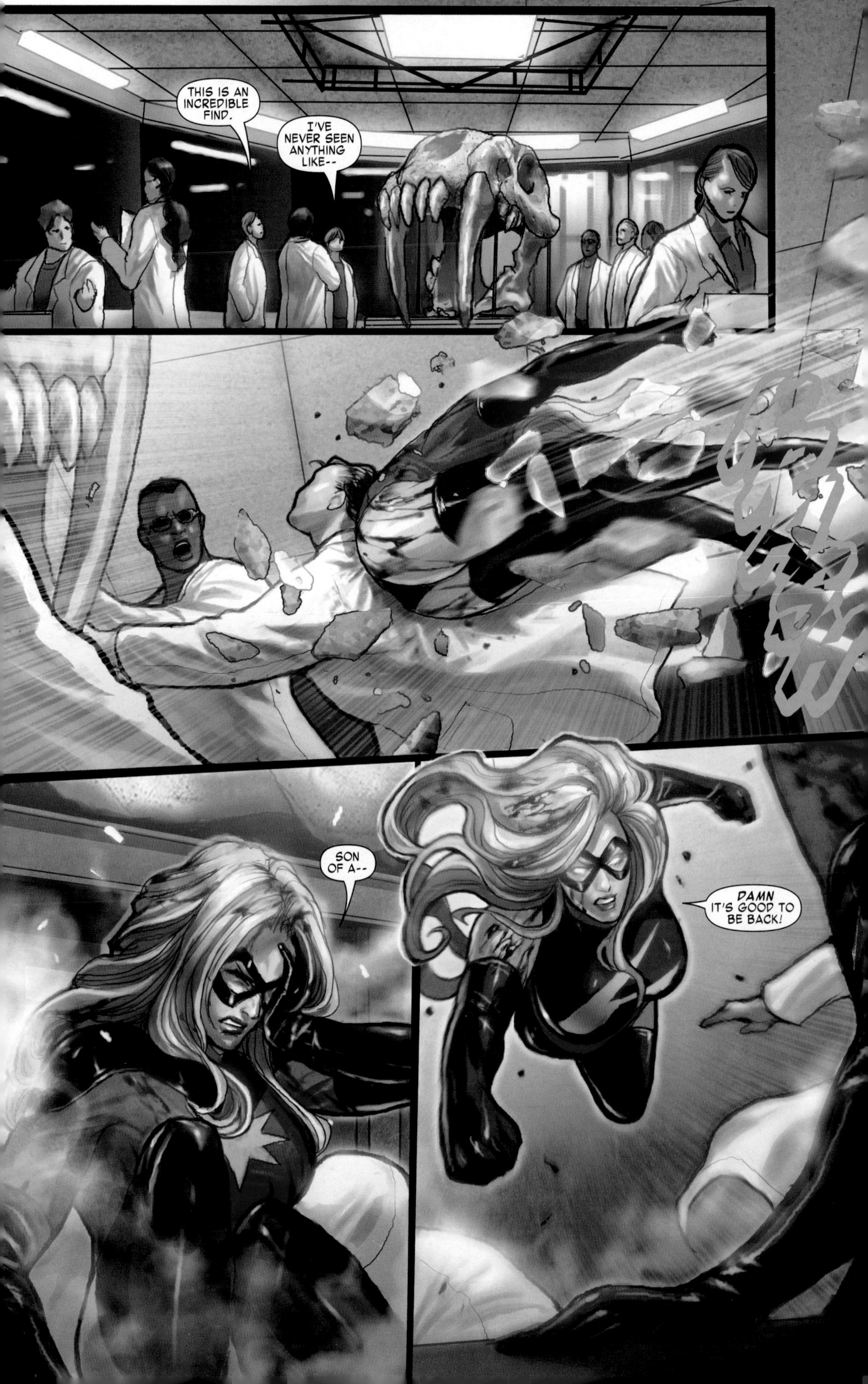

THIS IS AN INCREDIBLE FIND.
I'VE NEVER SEEN ANYTHING LIKE--
SON OF A--
DAMN IT'S GOOD TO BE BACK!

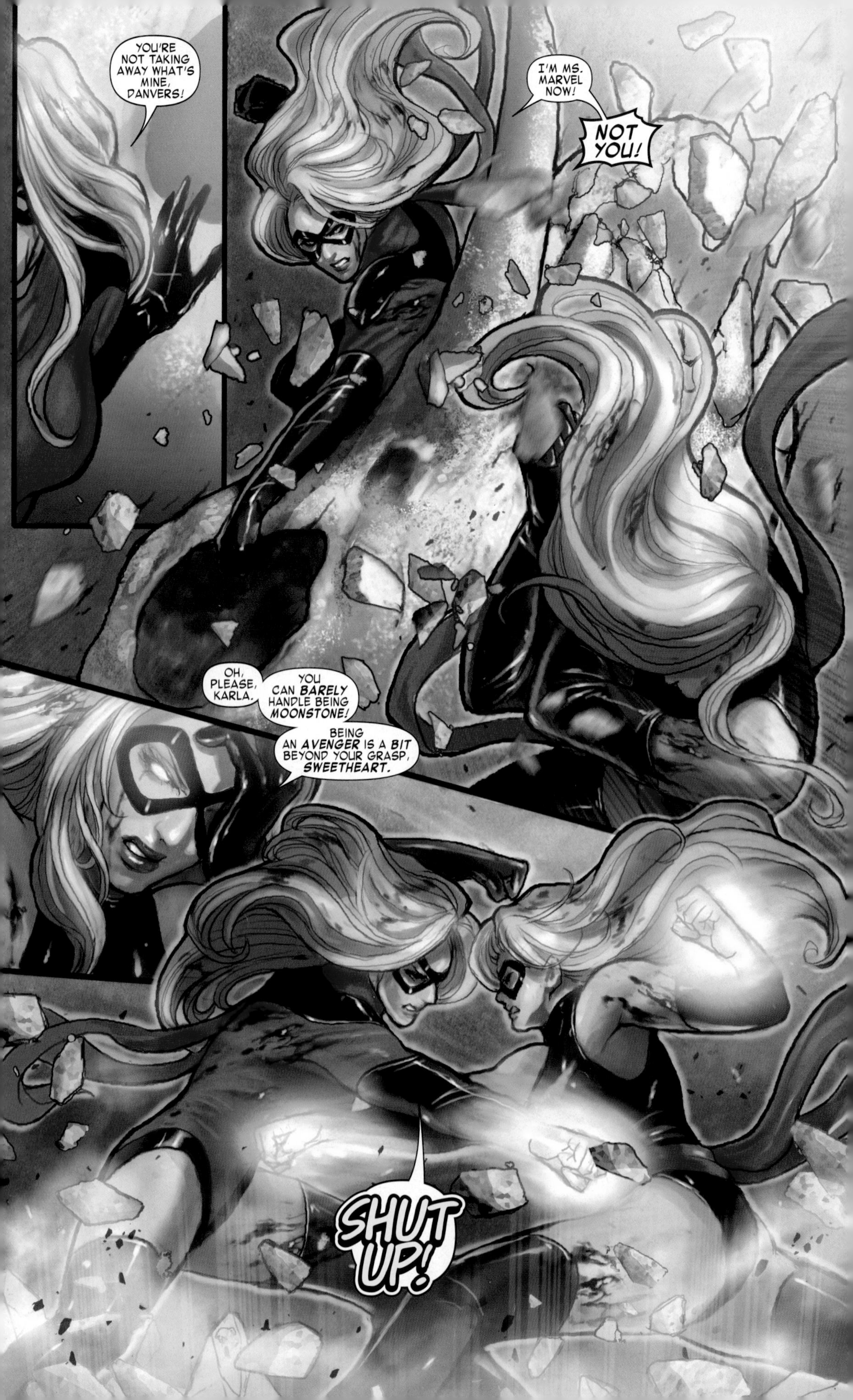

YOU'RE NOT TAKING AWAY WHAT'S MINE, DANVERS!
I'M MS. MARVEL NOW!
NOT YOU!
OH, PLEASE, KARLA.
YOU CAN BARELY HANDLE BEING MOONSTONE!
BEING AN AVENGER IS A BIT BEYOND YOUR GRASP, SWEETHEART.
SHUT UP!

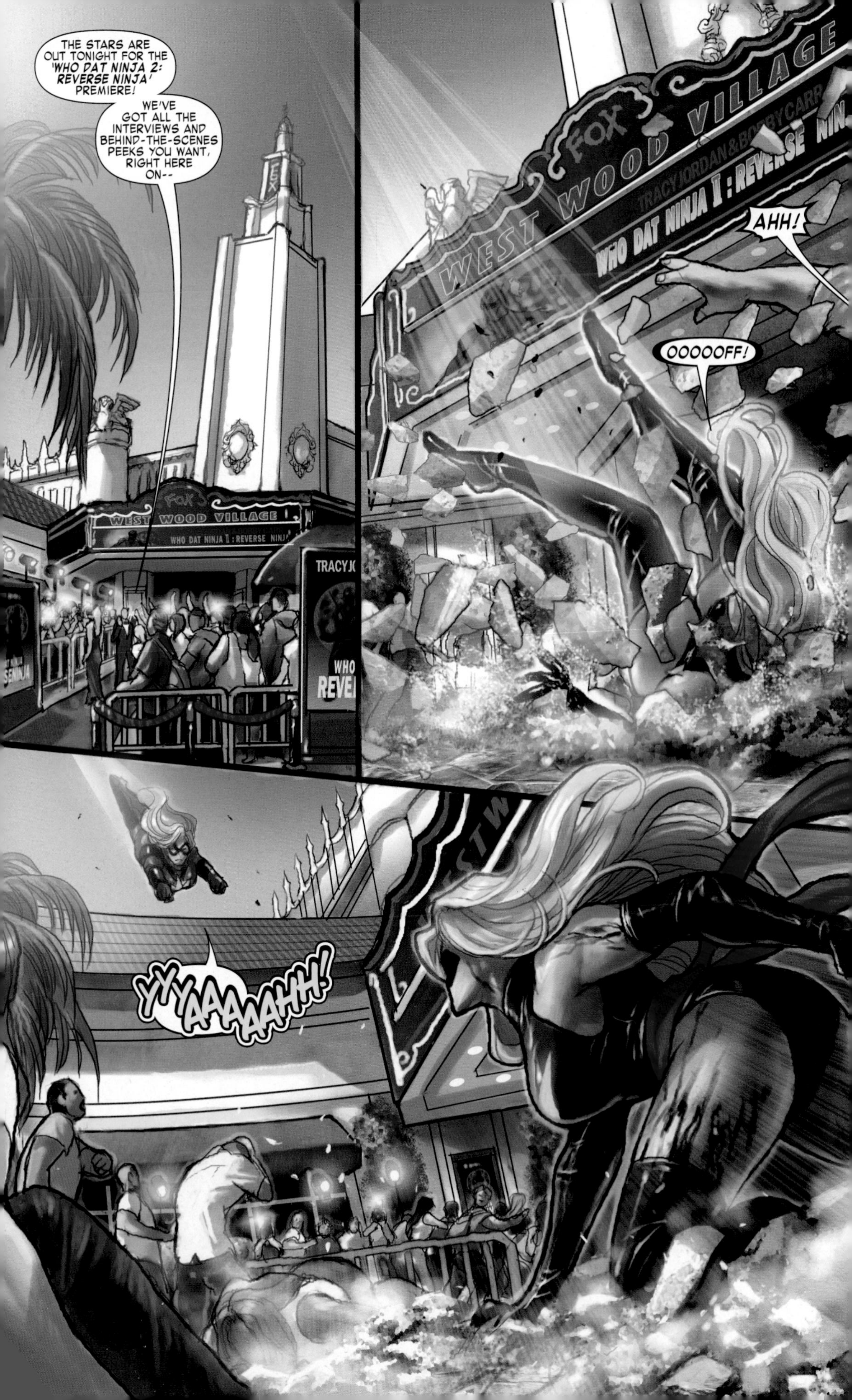
THE STARS ARE OUT TONIGHT FOR THE 'WHO DAT NINJA 2: REVERSE NINJA' PREMIERE!
WE'VE GOT ALL THE INTERVIEWS AND BEHIND-THE-SCENES PEEKS YOU WANT, RIGHT HERE ON--
FOX
WEST WOOD VILLAGE
WHO DAT NINJA II : REVERSE NINJA
TRACYJORDAN&BOBBYCARR
AHH!
OOOOOFF!
YYYAAAAAHH!

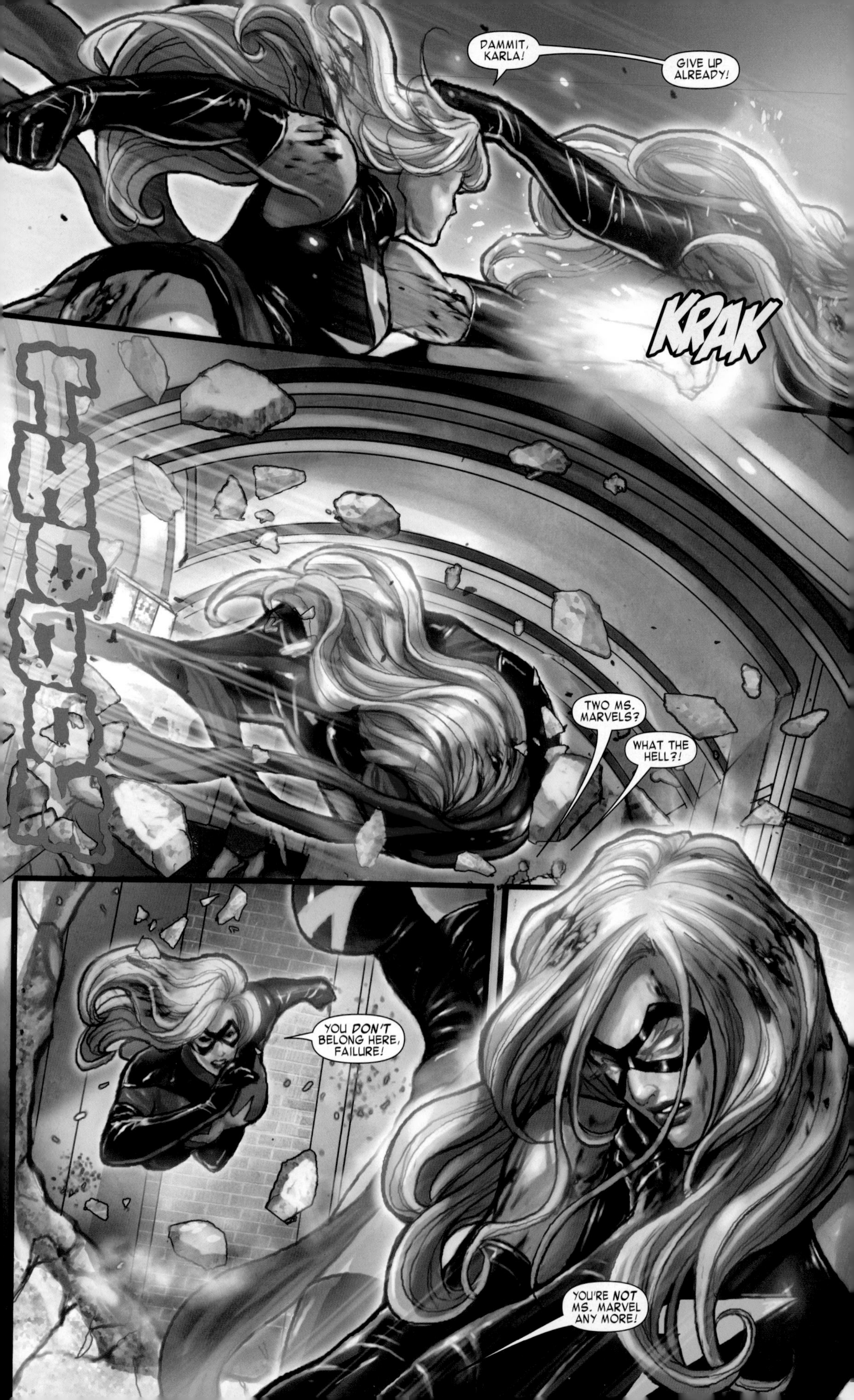
DAMMIT, KARLA!
GIVE UP ALREADY!
KRAK
THUD
TWO MS. MARVELS?
WHAT THE HELL?!
YOU DON'T BELONG HERE, FAILURE!
YOU'RE NOT MS. MARVEL ANY MORE!

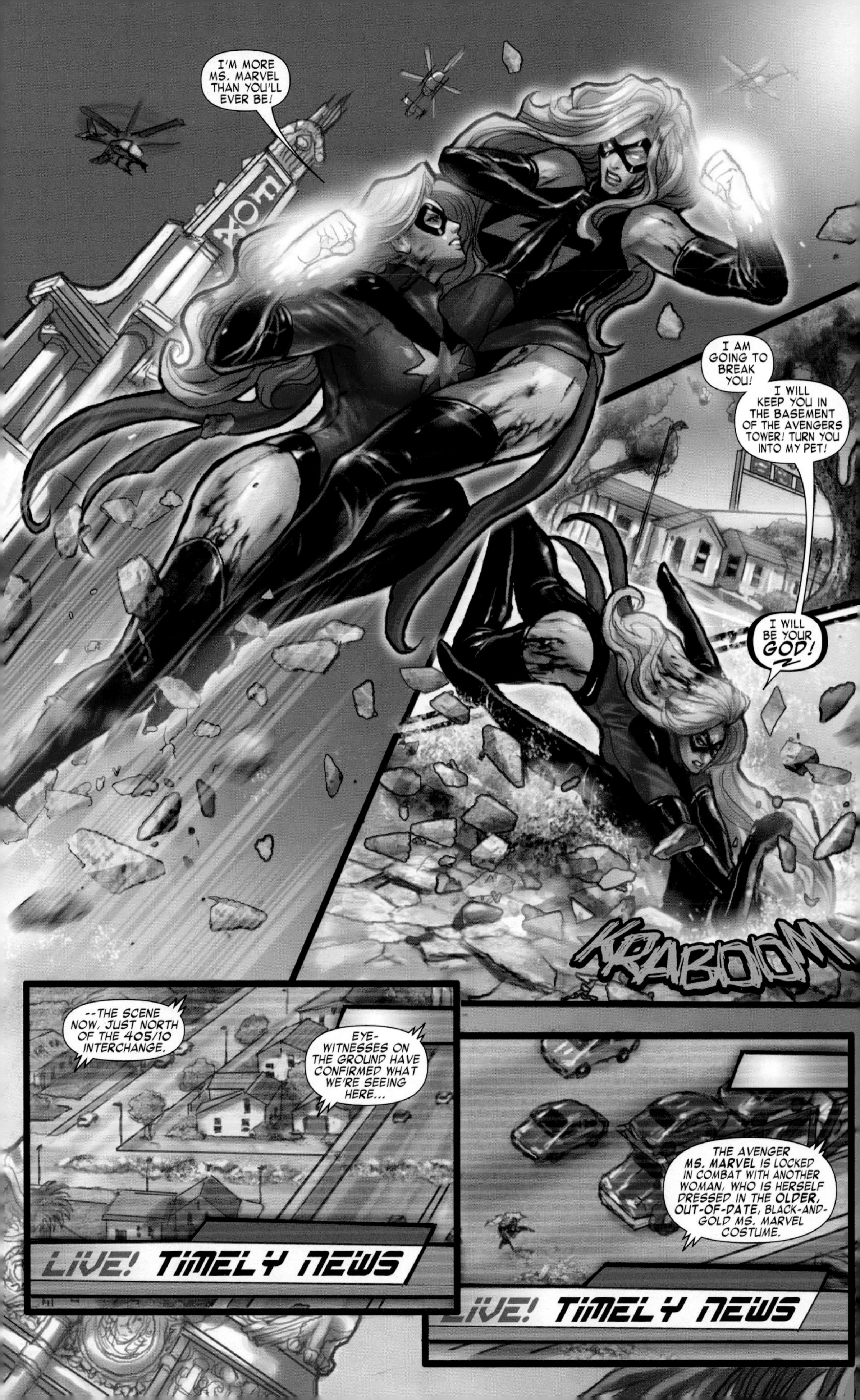
I'M MORE MS. MARVEL THAN YOU'LL EVER BE!
FOX
I AM GOING TO BREAK YOU!
I WILL KEEP YOU IN THE BASEMENT OF THE AVENGERS TOWER! TURN YOU INTO MY PET!
I WILL BE YOUR GOD!
KRABOOM
--THE SCENE NOW, JUST NORTH OF THE 405/10 INTERCHANGE.
EYE-WITNESSES ON THE GROUND HAVE CONFIRMED WHAT WE'RE SEEING HERE...
LIVE! TIMELY NEWS
THE AVENGER MS. MARVEL IS LOCKED IN COMBAT WITH ANOTHER WOMAN, WHO IS HERSELF DRESSED IN THE OLDER, OUT-OF-DATE, BLACK-AND-GOLD MS. MARVEL COSTUME.
LIVE! TIMELY NEWS

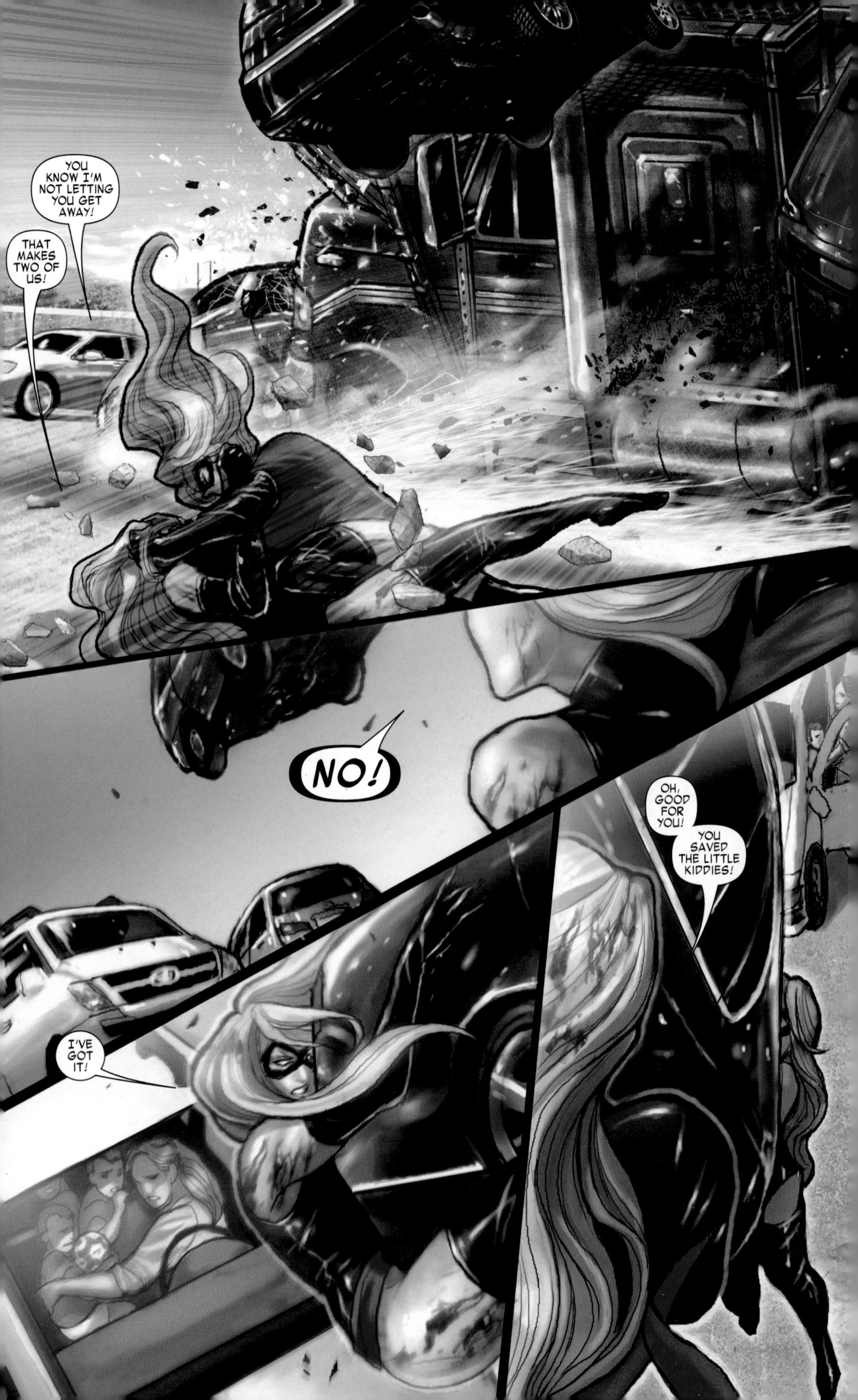
YOU KNOW I'M NOT LETTING YOU GET AWAY!
THAT MAKES TWO OF US!
NO!
I'VE GOT IT!
OH, GOOD FOR YOU!
YOU SAVED THE LITTLE KIDDIES!

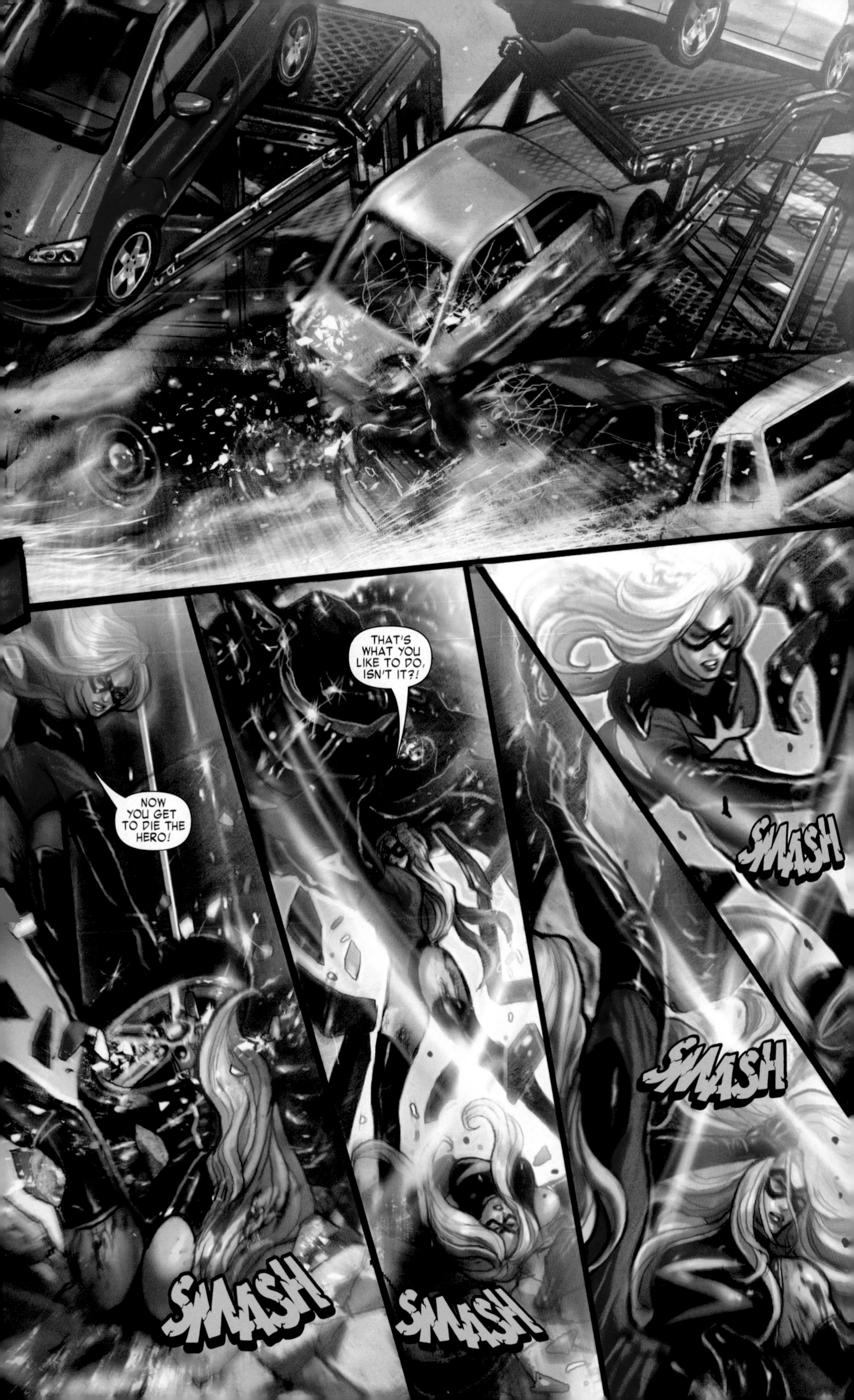
NOW YOU GET TO DIE THE HERO!
THAT'S WHAT YOU LIKE TO DO, ISN'T IT?!
SMASH
SMASH
SMASH
SMASH

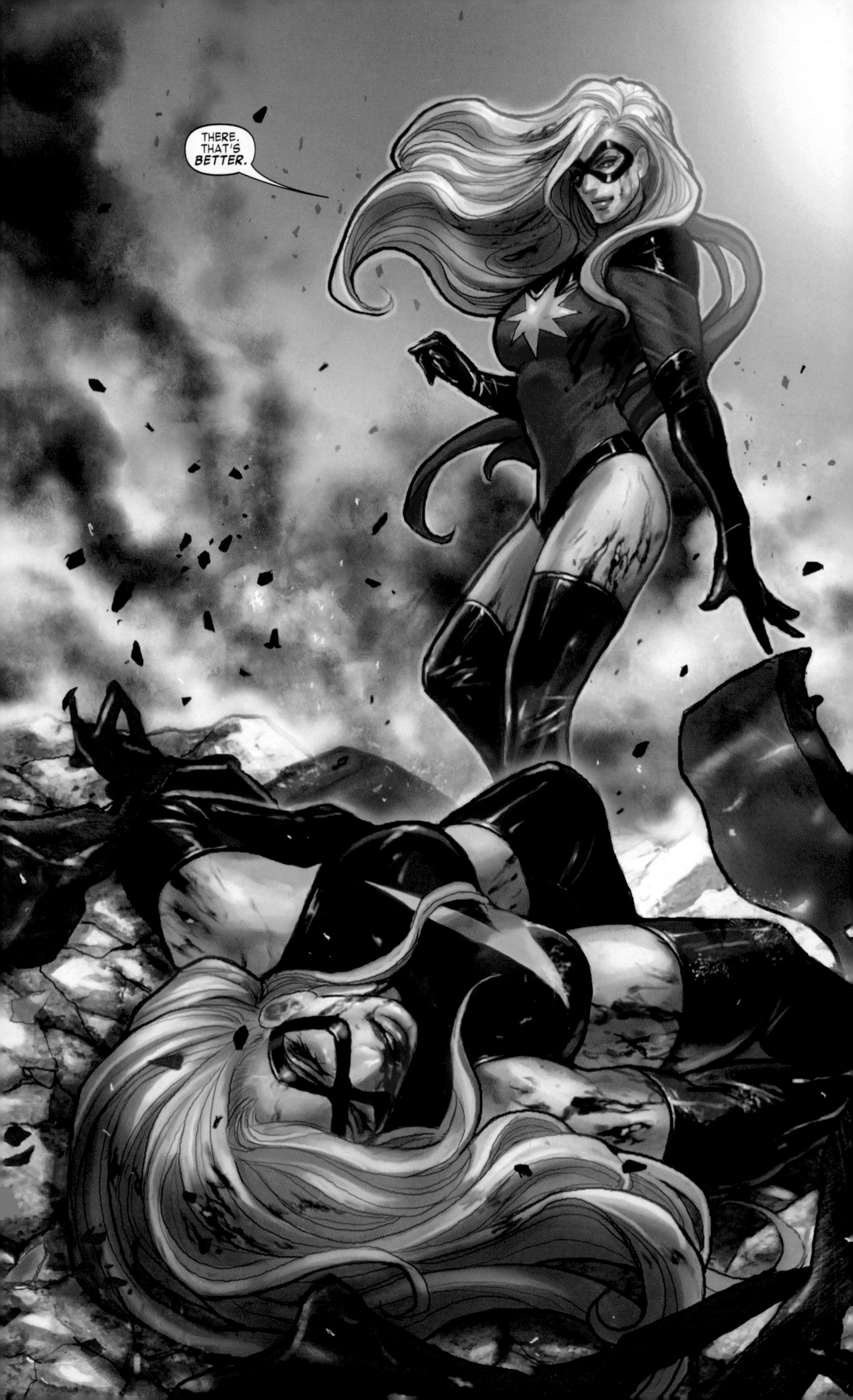
THERE. THAT'S *BETTER.*

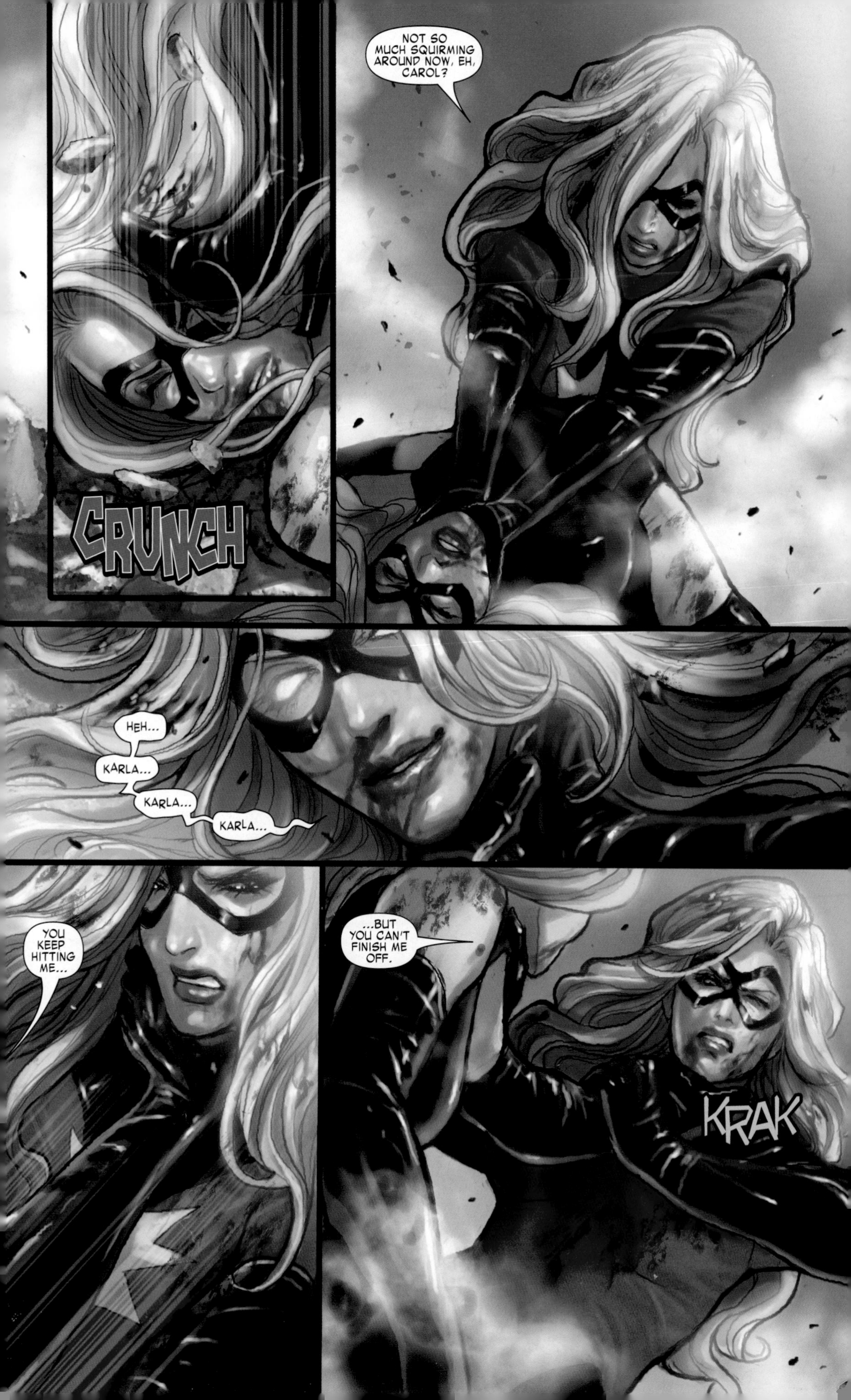
CRUNCH
NOT SO MUCH SQUIRMING AROUND NOW, EH, CAROL?
HEH...
KARLA...
KARLA...
KARLA...
YOU KEEP HITTING ME...
...BUT YOU CAN'T FINISH ME OFF.
KRAK

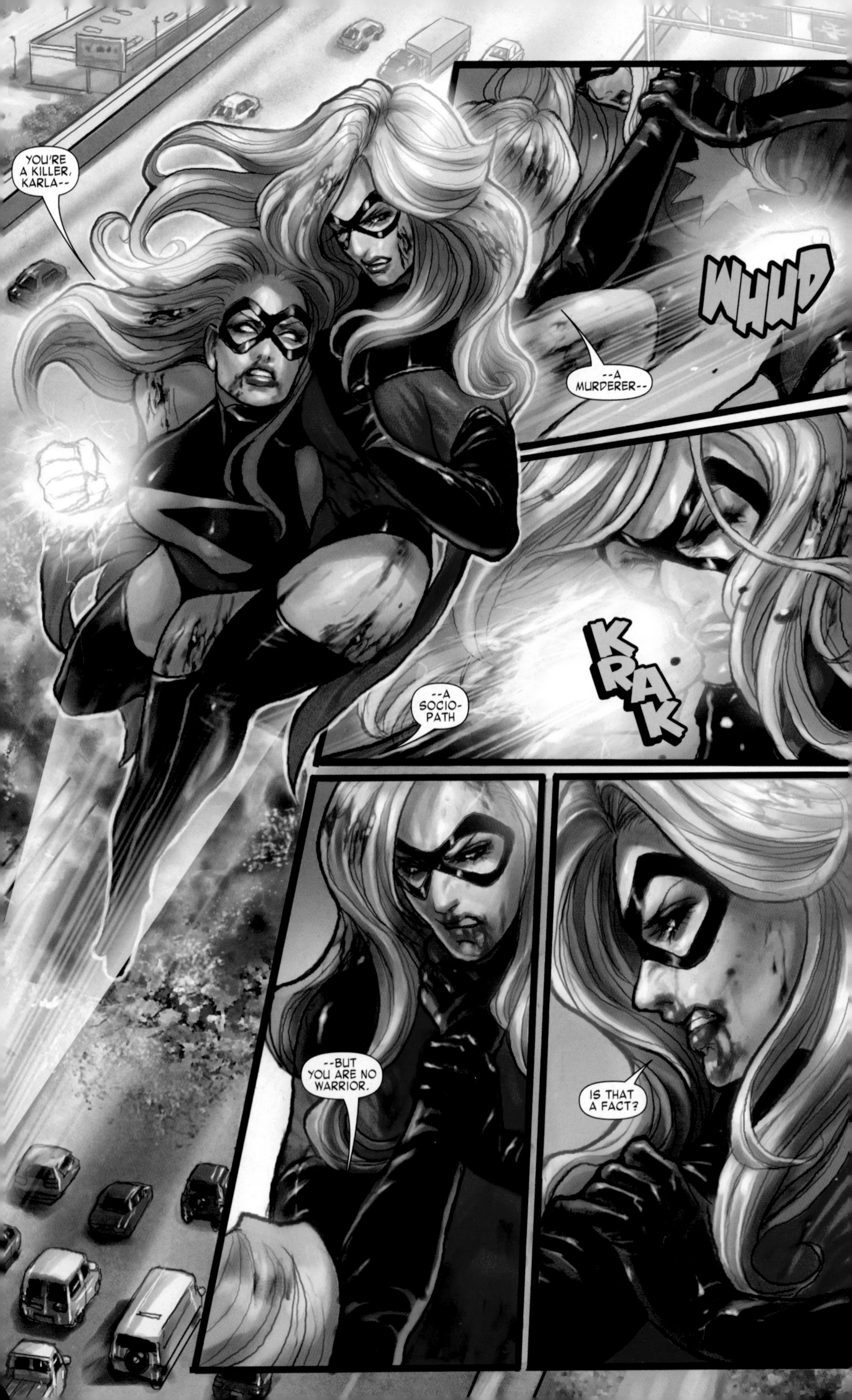
YOU'RE A KILLER, KARLA--
WHUD
--A MURDERER--
KRAK
--A SOCIO-PATH
--BUT YOU ARE NO WARRIOR.
IS THAT A FACT?

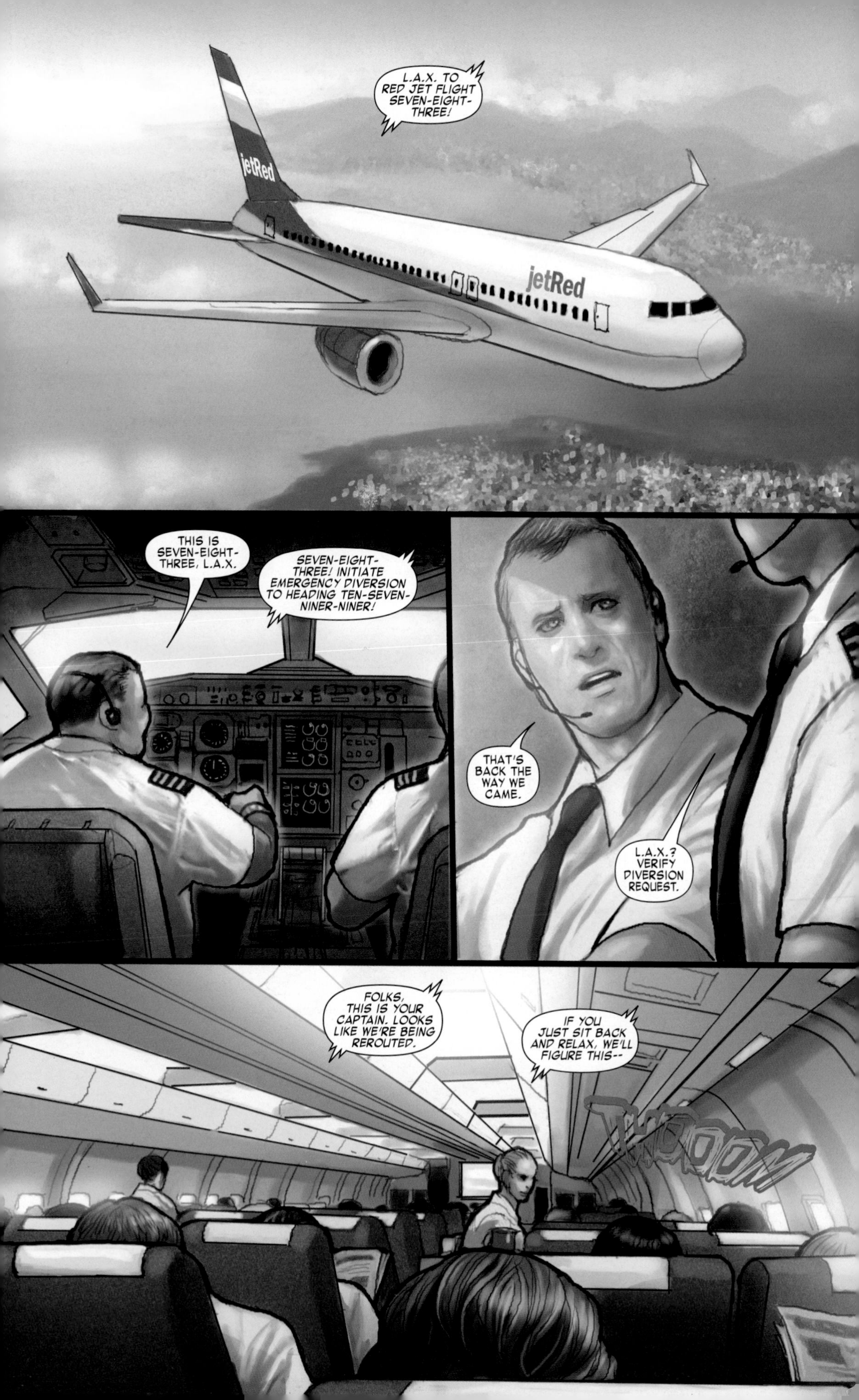
L.A.X. TO RED JET FLIGHT SEVEN-EIGHT-THREE!
jetRed
THIS IS SEVEN-EIGHT-THREE, L.A.X.
SEVEN-EIGHT-THREE! INITIATE EMERGENCY DIVERSION TO HEADING TEN-SEVEN-NINER-NINER!
THAT'S BACK THE WAY WE CAME.
L.A.X.? VERIFY DIVERSION REQUEST.
FOLKS, THIS IS YOUR CAPTAIN. LOOKS LIKE WE'RE BEING REROUTED.
IF YOU JUST SIT BACK AND RELAX, WE'LL FIGURE THIS--
THOOOOM

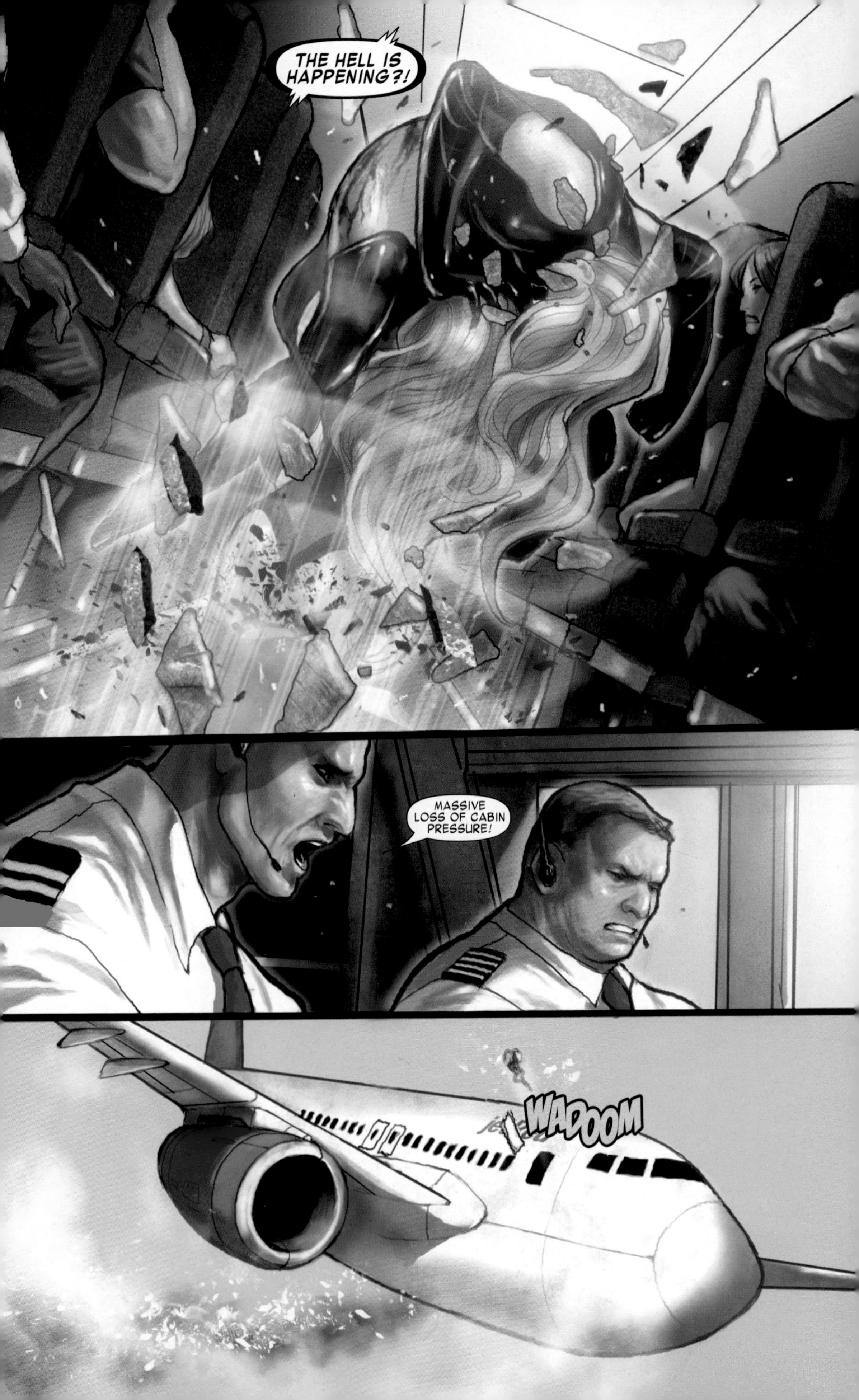
THE HELL IS HAPPENING?!
MASSIVE LOSS OF CABIN PRESSURE!
WADOOM

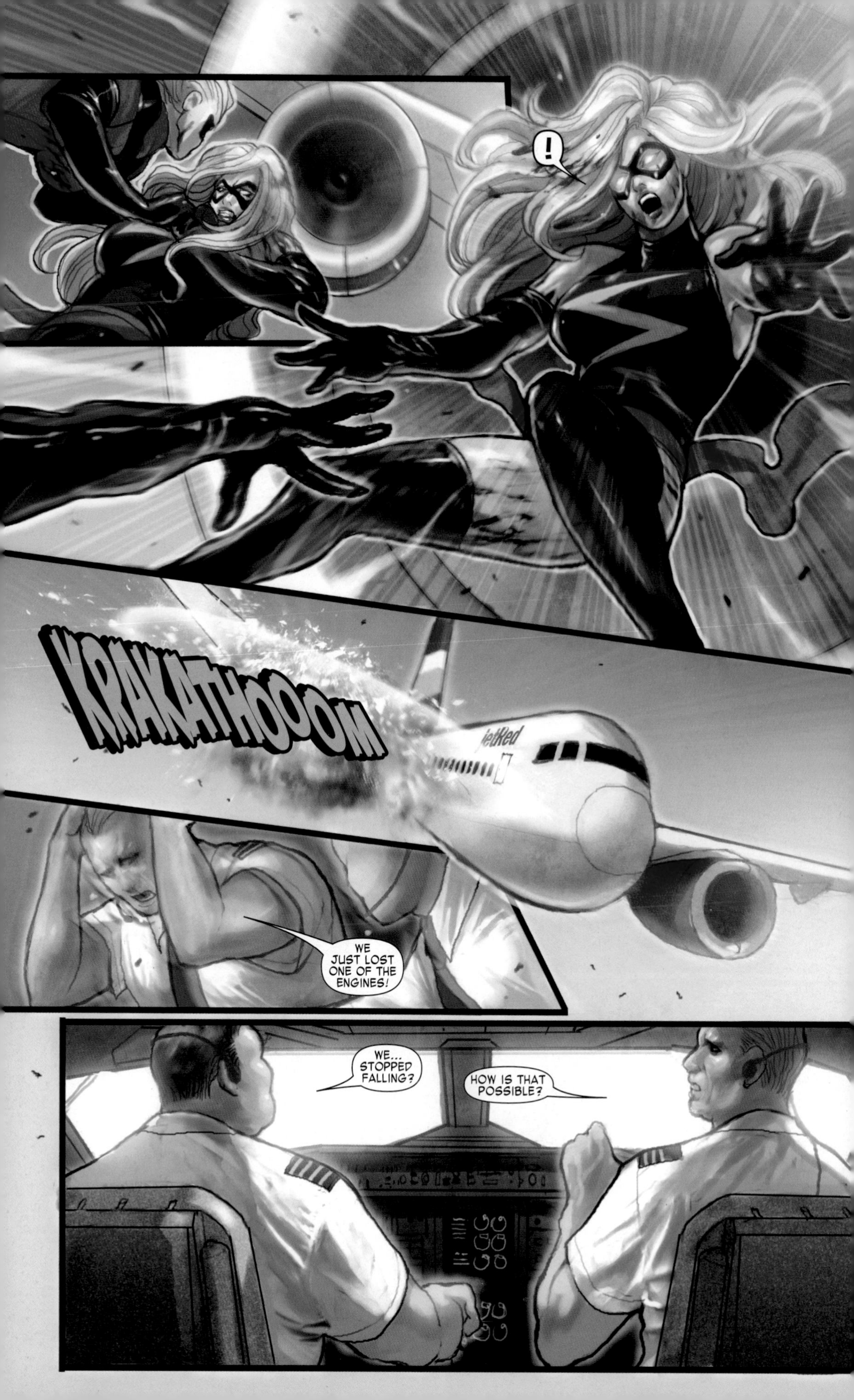
!
KRAKATHOOOM
jetRed
WE JUST LOST ONE OF THE ENGINES!
WE... STOPPED FALLING?
HOW IS THAT POSSIBLE?

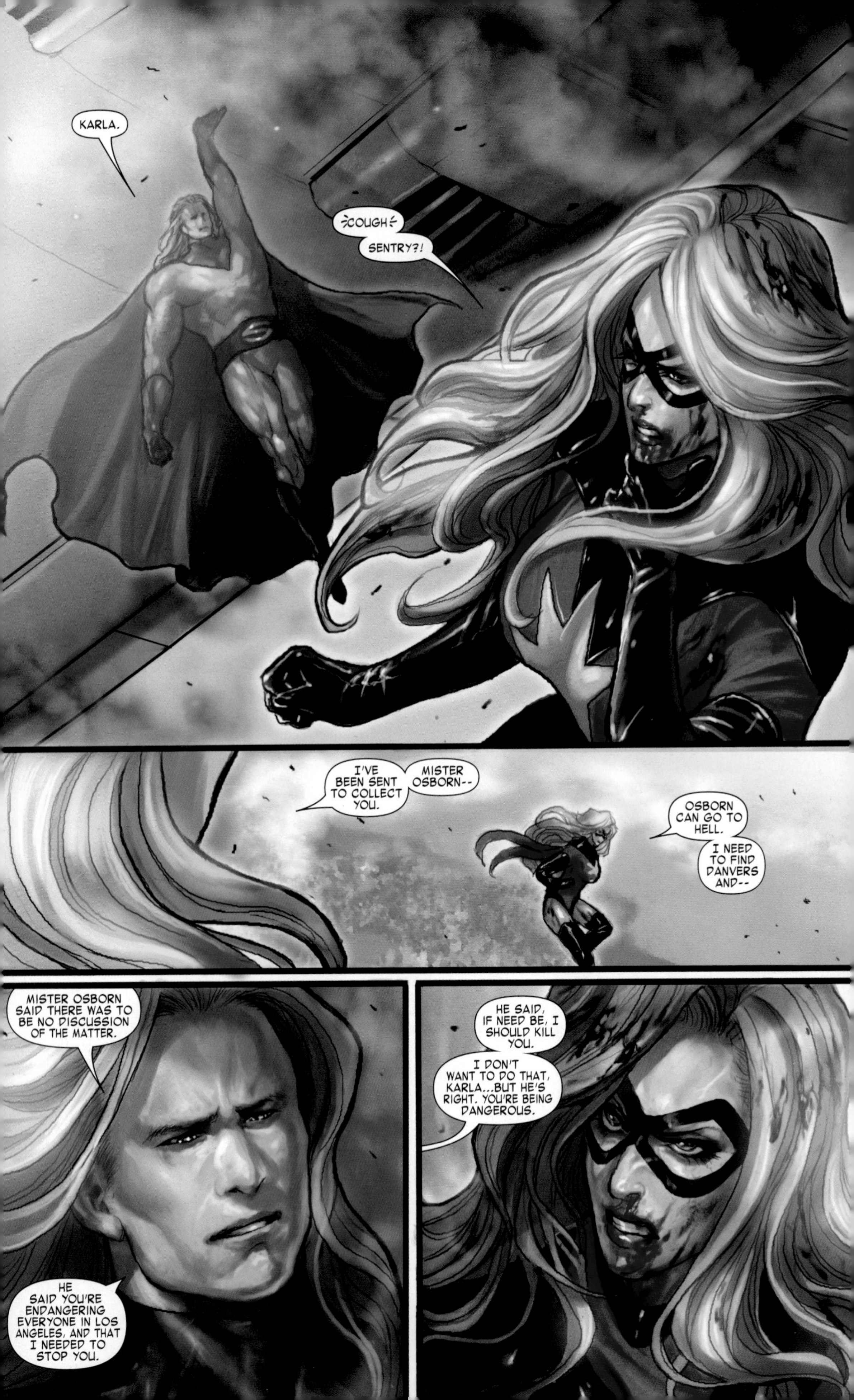
KARLA.
COUGH
SENTRY?!
I'VE BEEN SENT TO COLLECT YOU.
MISTER OSBORN--
OSBORN CAN GO TO HELL.
I NEED TO FIND DANVERS AND--
MISTER OSBORN SAID THERE WAS TO BE NO DISCUSSION OF THE MATTER.
HE SAID YOU'RE ENDANGERING EVERYONE IN LOS ANGELES, AND THAT I NEEDED TO STOP YOU.
HE SAID, IF NEED BE, I SHOULD KILL YOU.
I DON'T WANT TO DO THAT, KARLA...BUT HE'S RIGHT. YOU'RE BEING DANGEROUS.

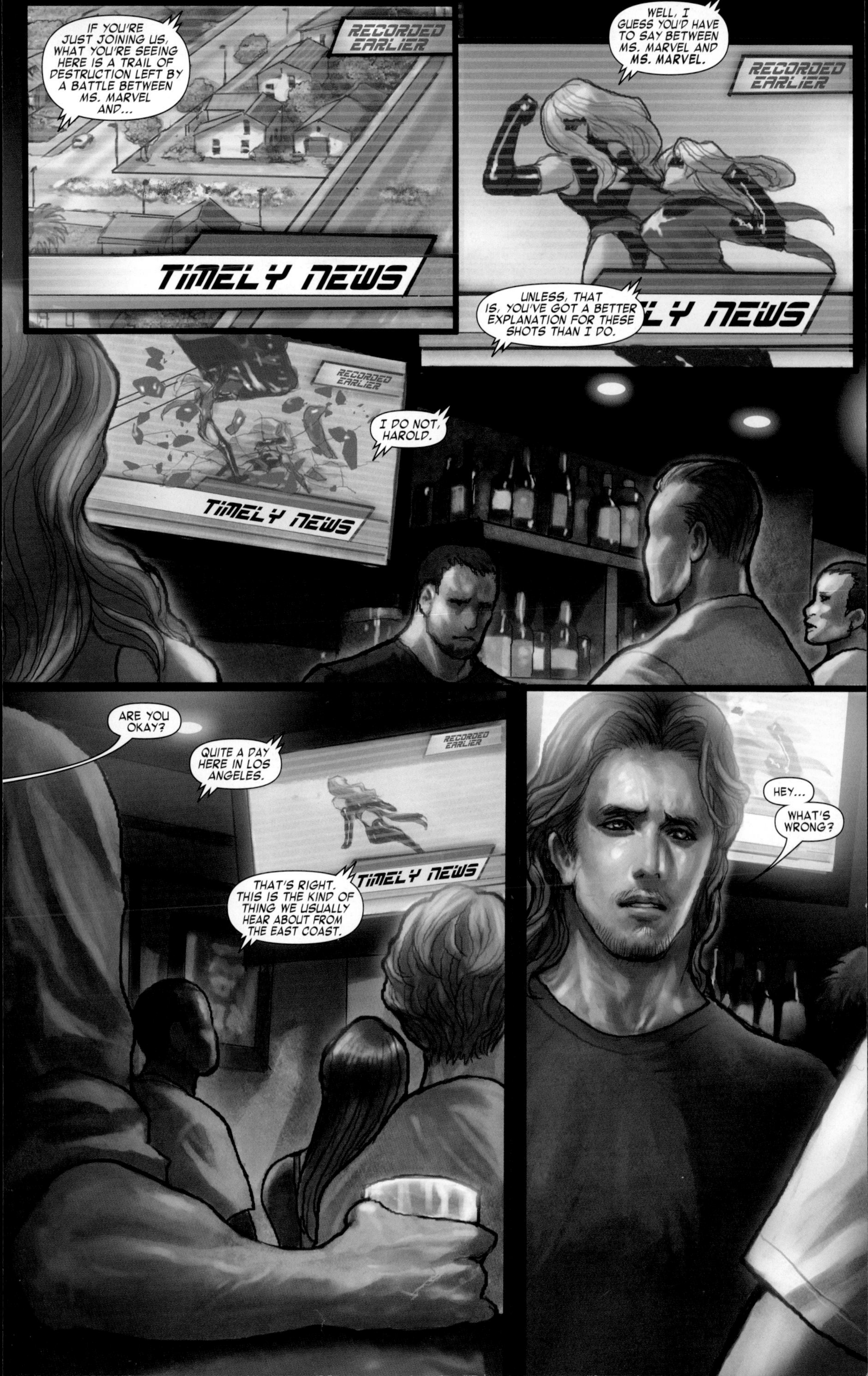
RECORDED EARLIER
IF YOU'RE JUST JOINING US, WHAT YOU'RE SEEING HERE IS A TRAIL OF DESTRUCTION LEFT BY A BATTLE BETWEEN MS. MARVEL AND...
TIMELY NEWS
WELL, I GUESS YOU'D HAVE TO SAY BETWEEN MS. MARVEL AND MS. MARVEL.
RECORDED EARLIER
UNLESS, THAT IS, YOU'VE GOT A BETTER EXPLANATION FOR THESE SHOTS THAN I DO.
RECORDED EARLIER
TIMELY NEWS
I DO NOT, HAROLD.
ARE YOU OKAY?
RECORDED EARLIER
QUITE A DAY HERE IN LOS ANGELES.
THAT'S RIGHT. THIS IS THE KIND OF THING WE USUALLY HEAR ABOUT FROM THE EAST COAST.
TIMELY NEWS
HEY...
WHAT'S WRONG?

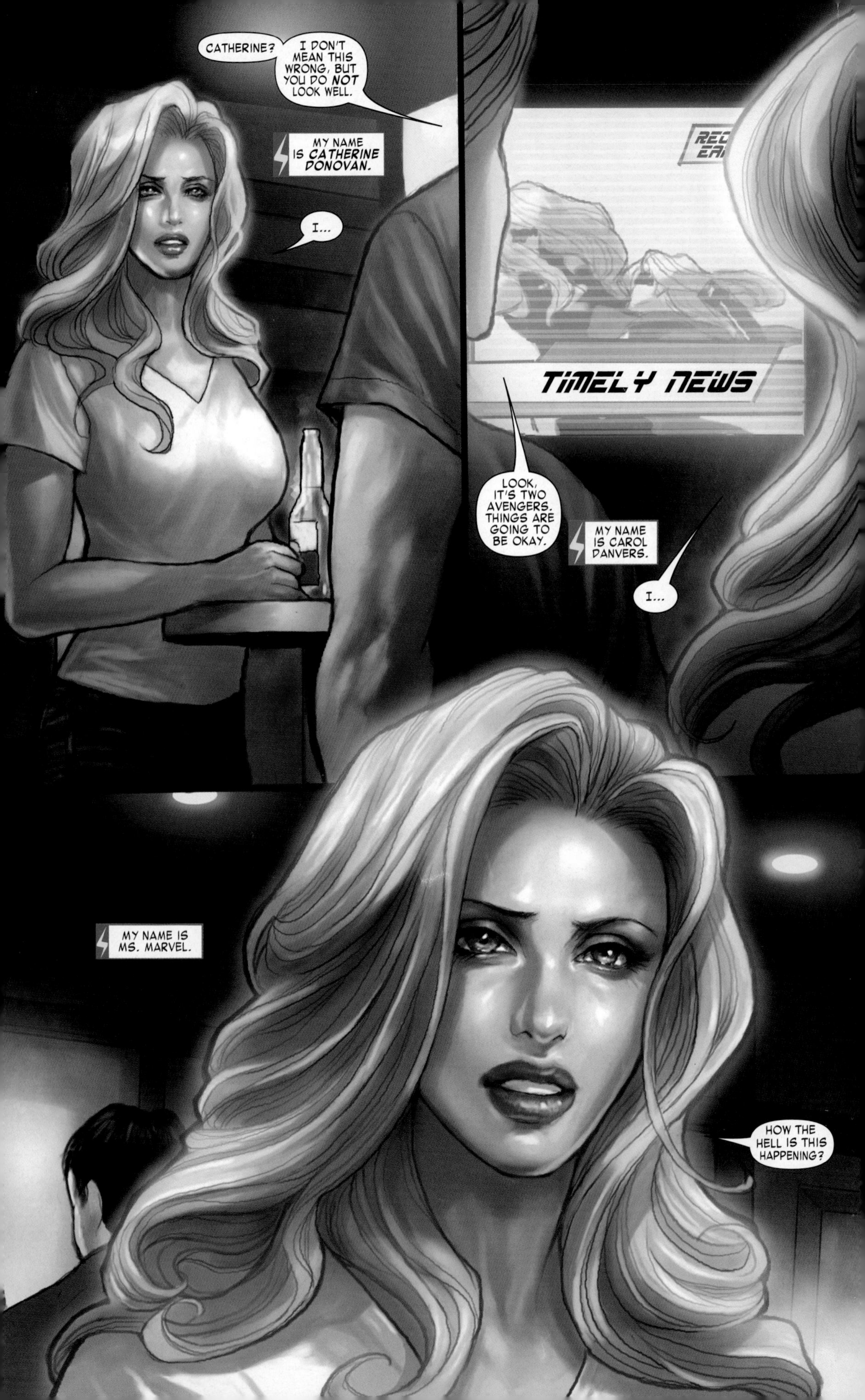
CATHERINE?
I DON'T MEAN THIS WRONG, BUT YOU DO NOT LOOK WELL.
MY NAME IS CATHERINE DONOVAN.
I...
TIMELY NEWS
LOOK, IT'S TWO AVENGERS. THINGS ARE GOING TO BE OKAY.
MY NAME IS CAROL DANVERS.
I...
MY NAME IS MS. MARVEL.
HOW THE HELL IS THIS HAPPENING?

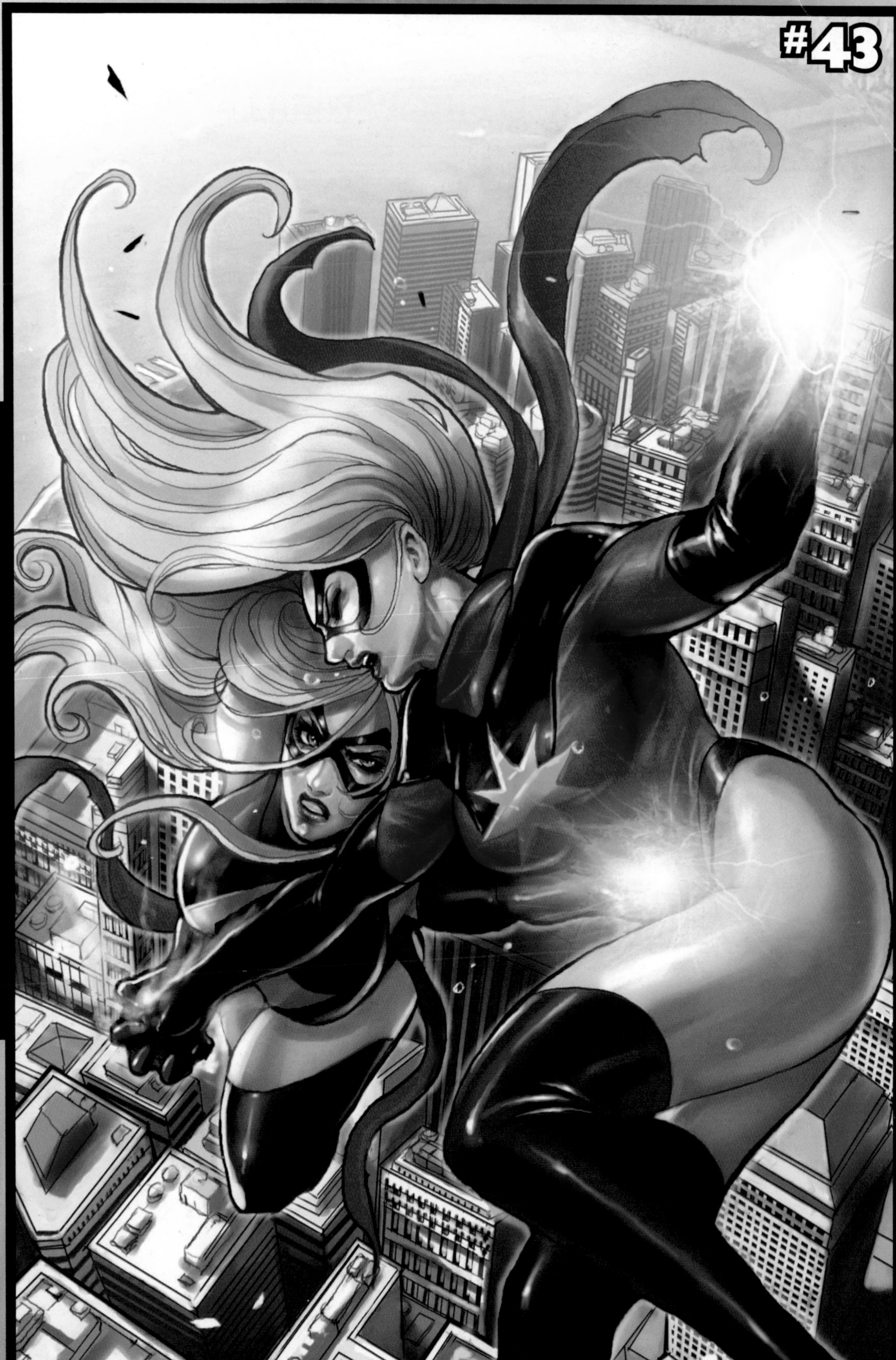
#43

#43
70th Anniversary Frame Variant
by Sana Takeda

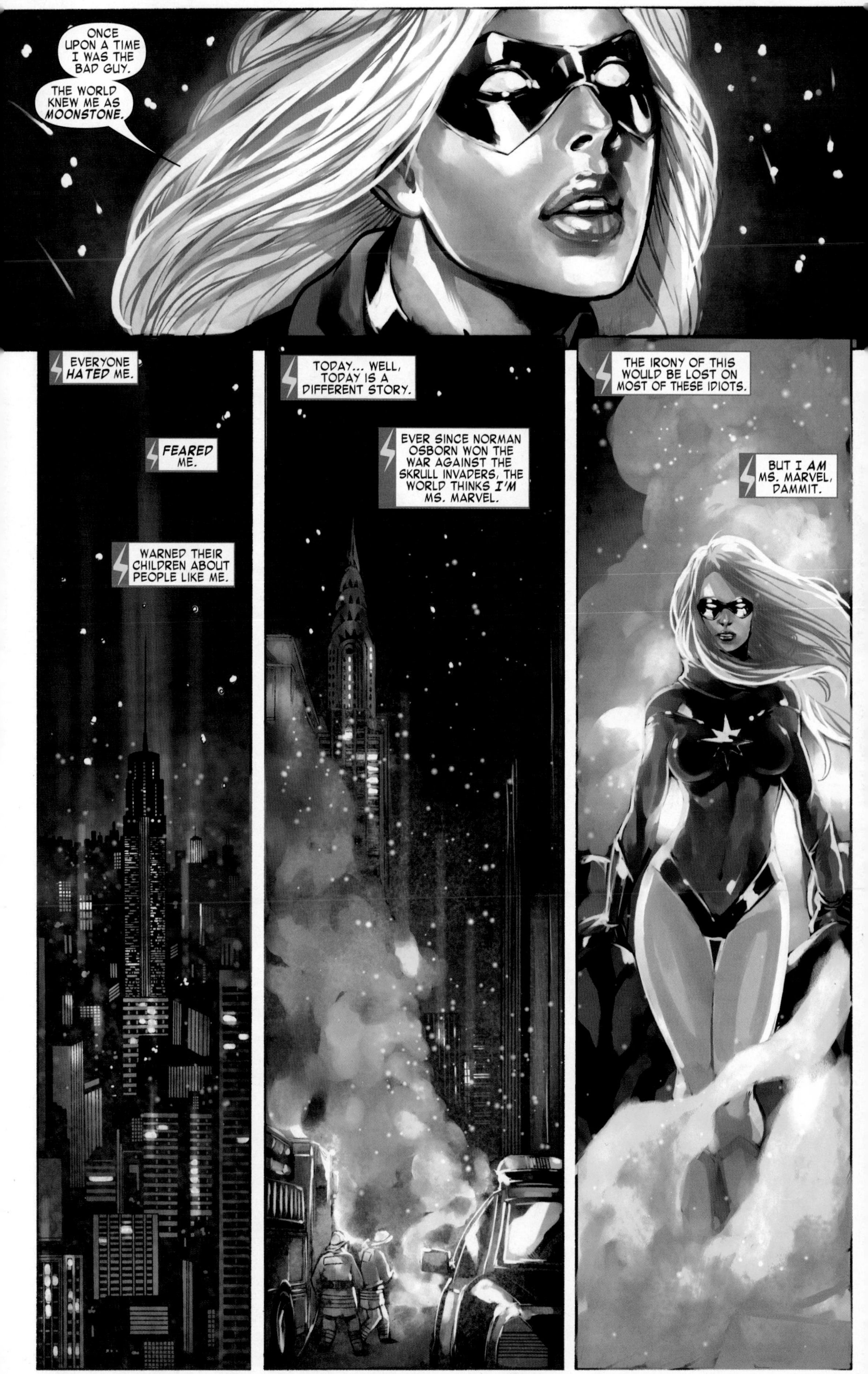
ONCE UPON A TIME I WAS THE BAD GUY.
THE WORLD KNEW ME AS MOONSTONE.
EVERYONE HATED ME.
FEARED ME.
WARNED THEIR CHILDREN ABOUT PEOPLE LIKE ME.
TODAY... WELL, TODAY IS A DIFFERENT STORY.
EVER SINCE NORMAN OSBORN WON THE WAR AGAINST THE SKRULL INVADERS, THE WORLD THINKS I'M MS. MARVEL.
THE IRONY OF THIS WOULD BE LOST ON MOST OF THESE IDIOTS.
BUT I AM MS. MARVEL, DAMMIT.

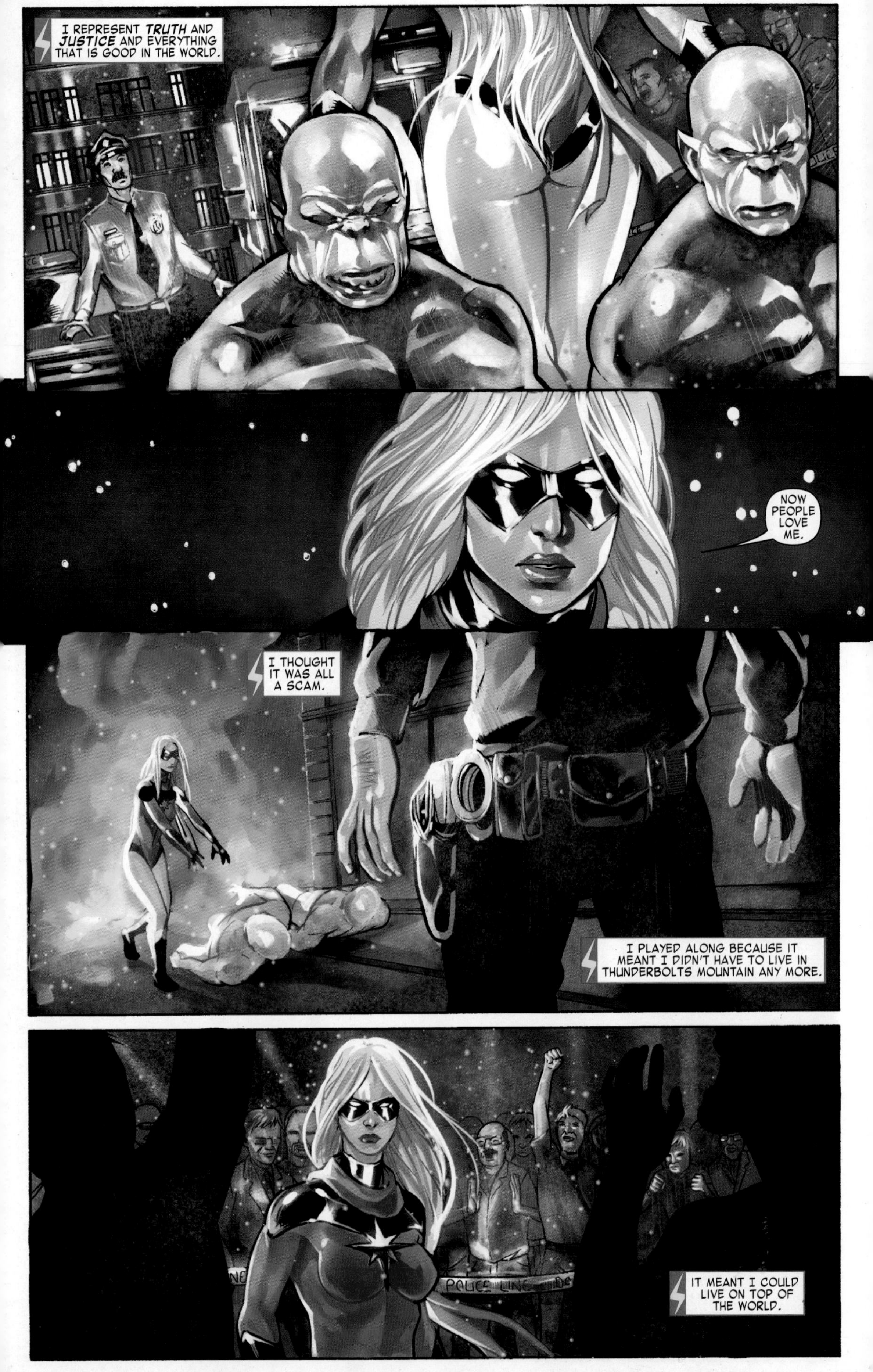

I REPRESENT TRUTH AND JUSTICE AND EVERYTHING THAT IS GOOD IN THE WORLD.
NOW PEOPLE LOVE ME.
I THOUGHT IT WAS ALL A SCAM.
I PLAYED ALONG BECAUSE IT MEANT I DIDN'T HAVE TO LIVE IN THUNDERBOLTS MOUNTAIN ANY MORE.
IT MEANT I COULD LIVE ON TOP OF THE WORLD.

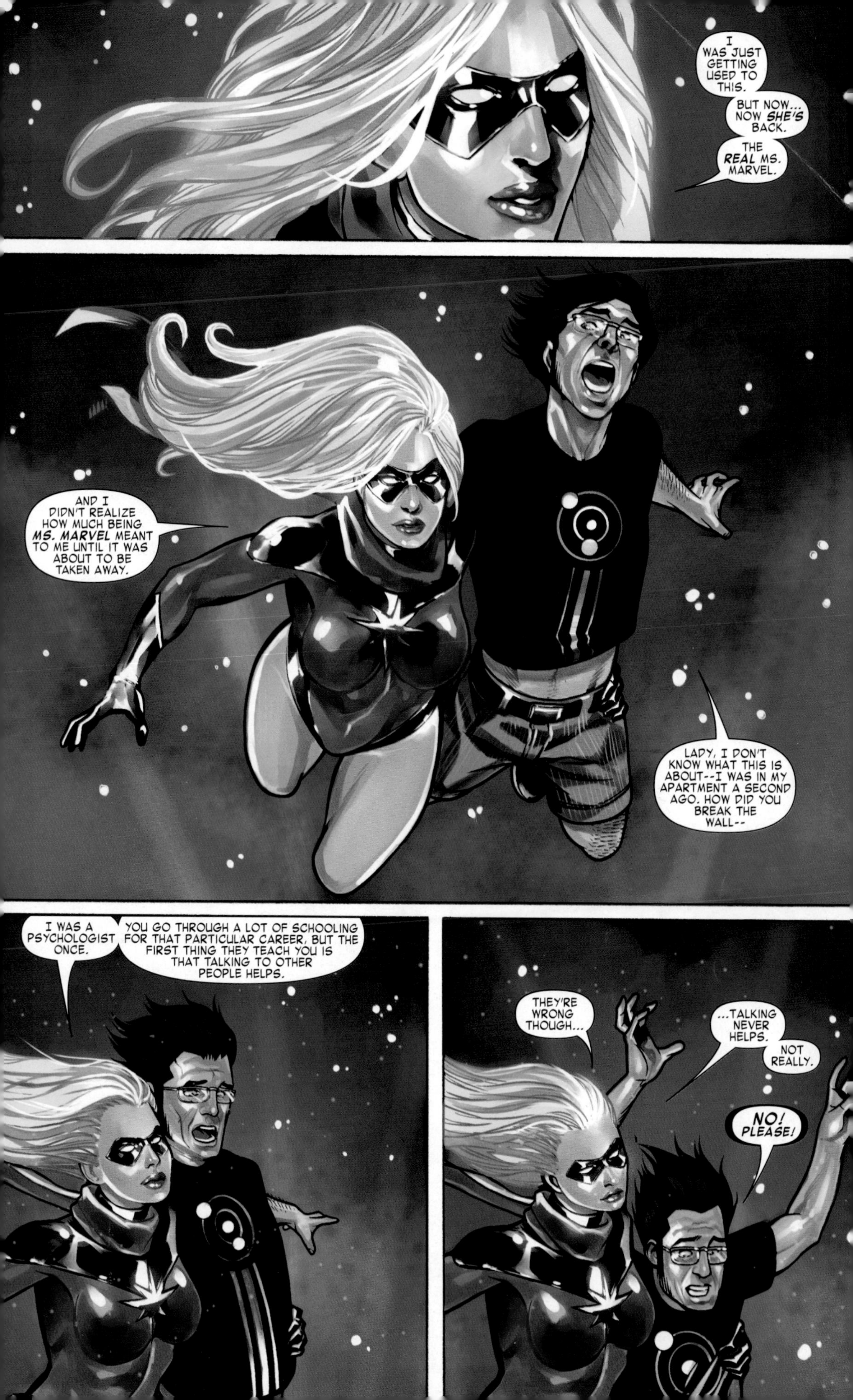
I WAS JUST GETTING USED TO THIS.
BUT NOW... NOW SHE'S BACK.
THE REAL MS. MARVEL.
AND I DIDN'T REALIZE HOW MUCH BEING MS. MARVEL MEANT TO ME UNTIL IT WAS ABOUT TO BE TAKEN AWAY.
LADY, I DON'T KNOW WHAT THIS IS ABOUT--I WAS IN MY APARTMENT A SECOND AGO. HOW DID YOU BREAK THE WALL--
I WAS A PSYCHOLOGIST ONCE.
YOU GO THROUGH A LOT OF SCHOOLING FOR THAT PARTICULAR CAREER, BUT THE FIRST THING THEY TEACH YOU IS THAT TALKING TO OTHER PEOPLE HELPS.
THEY'RE WRONG THOUGH...
...TALKING NEVER HELPS.
NOT REALLY.
NO! PLEASE!

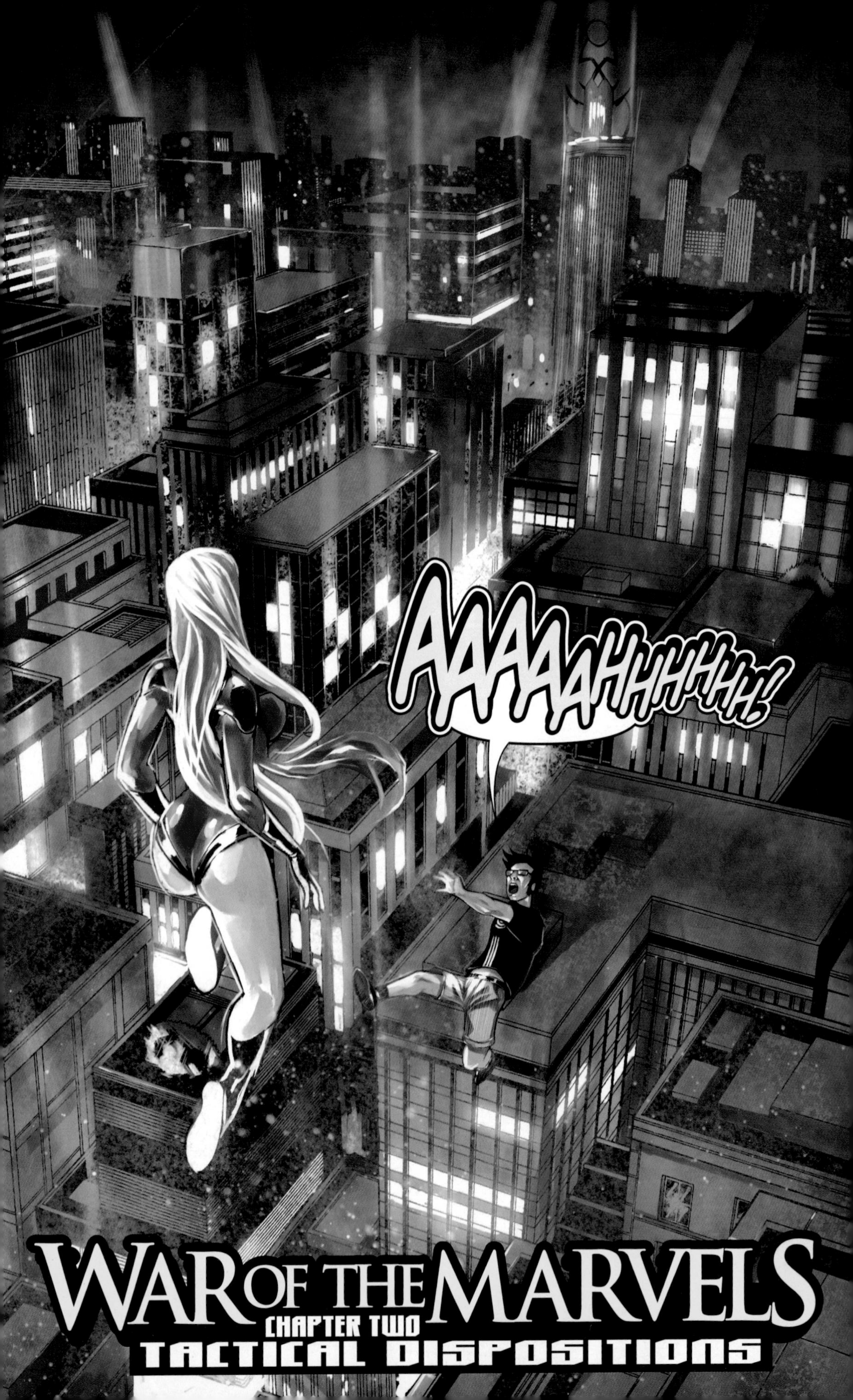
AAAAHHHHHHH!
WAR OF THE MARVELS
CHAPTER TWO
TACTICAL DISPOSITIONS

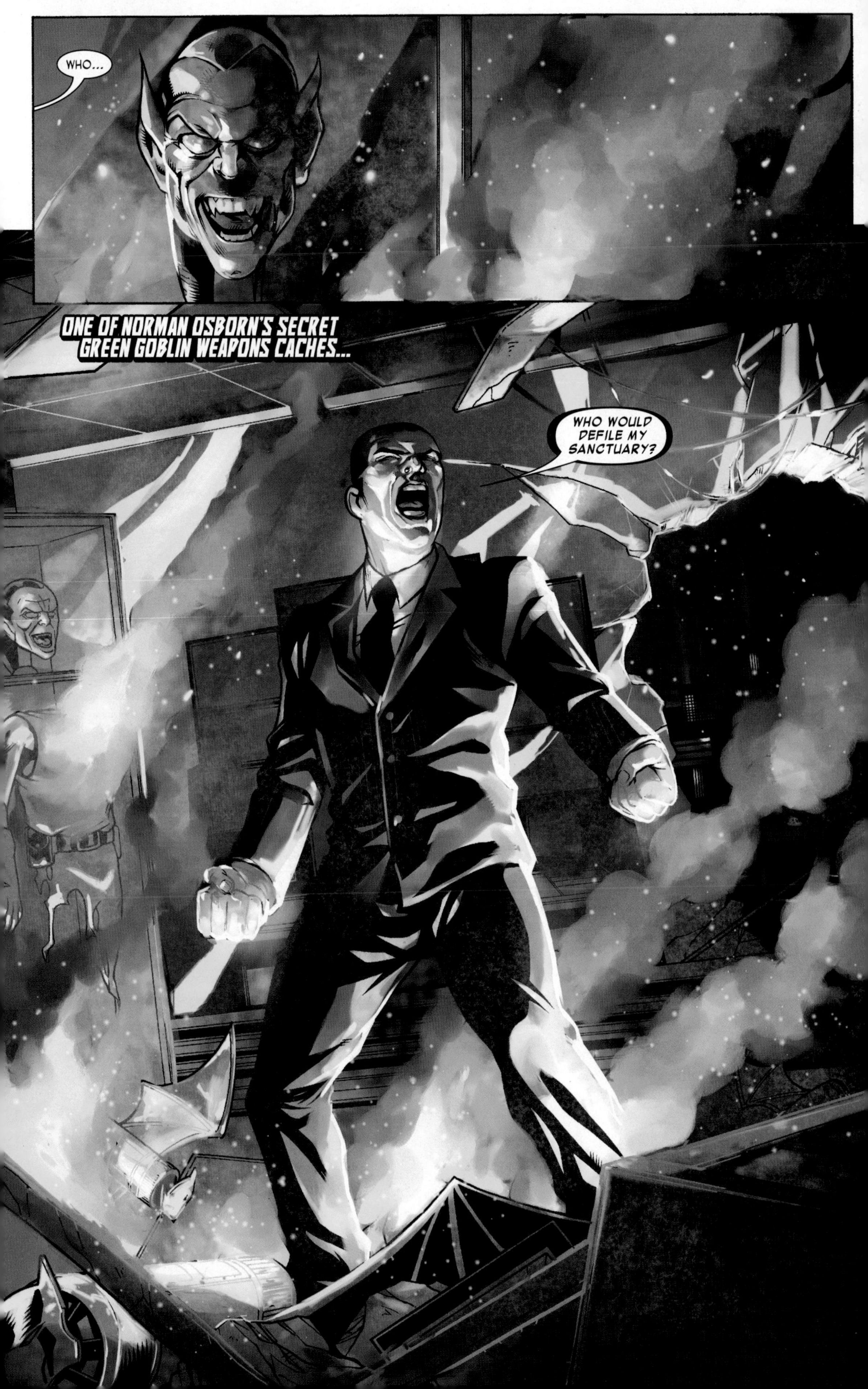
WHO...
ONE OF NORMAN OSBORN'S SECRET GREEN GOBLIN WEAPONS CACHES...
WHO WOULD DEFILE MY SANCTUARY?

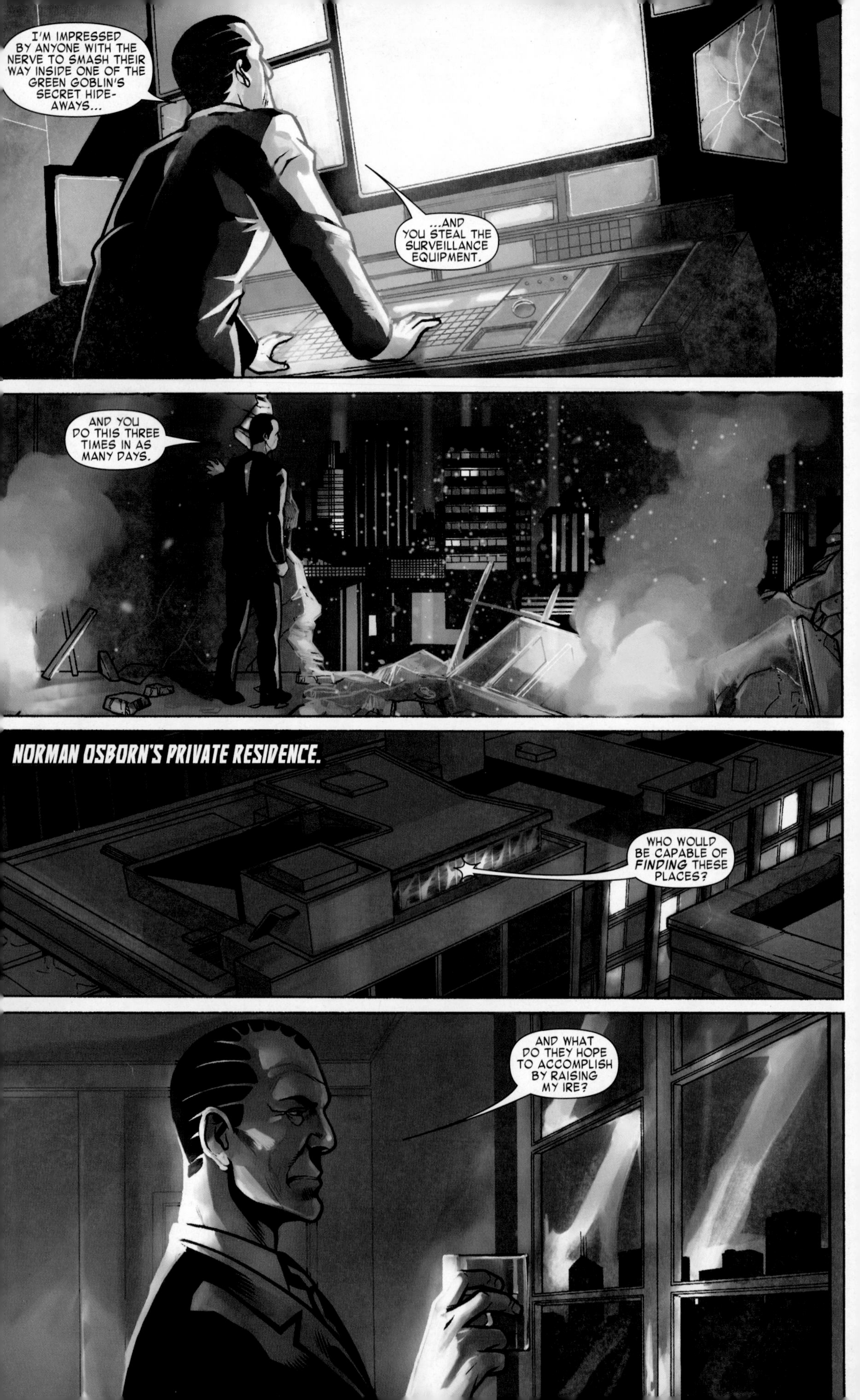
I'M IMPRESSED BY ANYONE WITH THE NERVE TO SMASH THEIR WAY INSIDE ONE OF THE GREEN GOBLIN'S SECRET HIDE-AWAYS...
...AND YOU STEAL THE SURVEILLANCE EQUIPMENT.
AND YOU DO THIS THREE TIMES IN AS MANY DAYS.
NORMAN OSBORN'S PRIVATE RESIDENCE.
WHO WOULD BE CAPABLE OF *FINDING* THESE PLACES?
AND WHAT DO THEY HOPE TO ACCOMPLISH BY RAISING MY IRE?

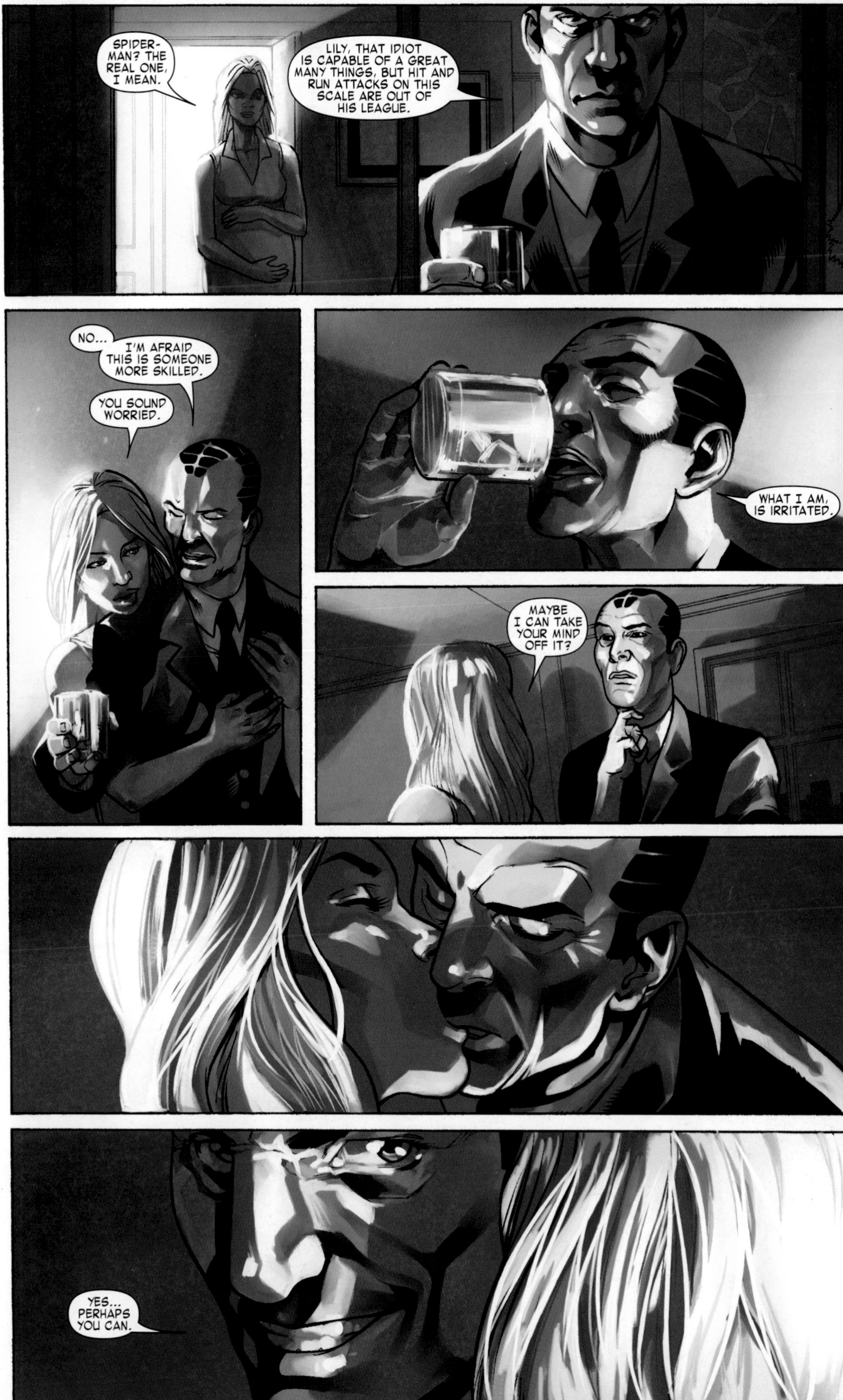

SPIDER-MAN? THE REAL ONE, I MEAN.
LILY, THAT IDIOT IS CAPABLE OF A GREAT MANY THINGS, BUT HIT AND RUN ATTACKS ON THIS SCALE ARE OUT OF HIS LEAGUE.
NO... I'M AFRAID THIS IS SOMEONE MORE SKILLED.
YOU SOUND WORRIED.
WHAT I AM, IS IRRITATED.
MAYBE I CAN TAKE YOUR MIND OFF IT?
YES... PERHAPS YOU CAN.

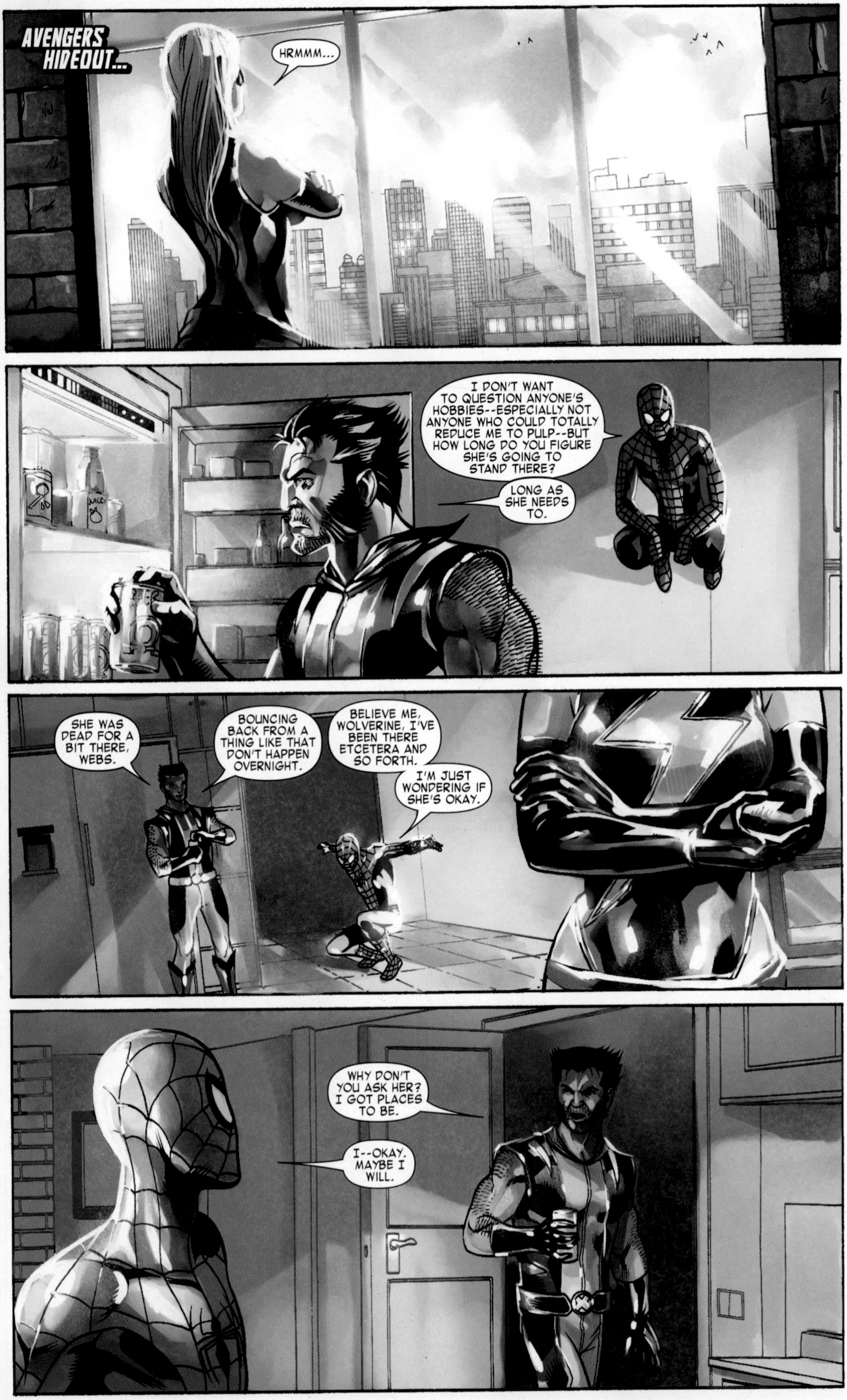
AVENGERS HIDEOUT...
HRMMM...
I DON'T WANT TO QUESTION ANYONE'S HOBBIES--ESPECIALLY NOT ANYONE WHO COULD TOTALLY REDUCE ME TO PULP--BUT HOW LONG DO YOU FIGURE SHE'S GOING TO STAND THERE?
LONG AS SHE NEEDS TO.
SHE WAS DEAD FOR A BIT THERE, WEBS.
BOUNCING BACK FROM A THING LIKE THAT DON'T HAPPEN OVERNIGHT.
BELIEVE ME, WOLVERINE, I'VE BEEN THERE ETCETERA AND SO FORTH.
I'M JUST WONDERING IF SHE'S OKAY.
WHY DON'T YOU ASK HER? I GOT PLACES TO BE.
I--OKAY. MAYBE I WILL.

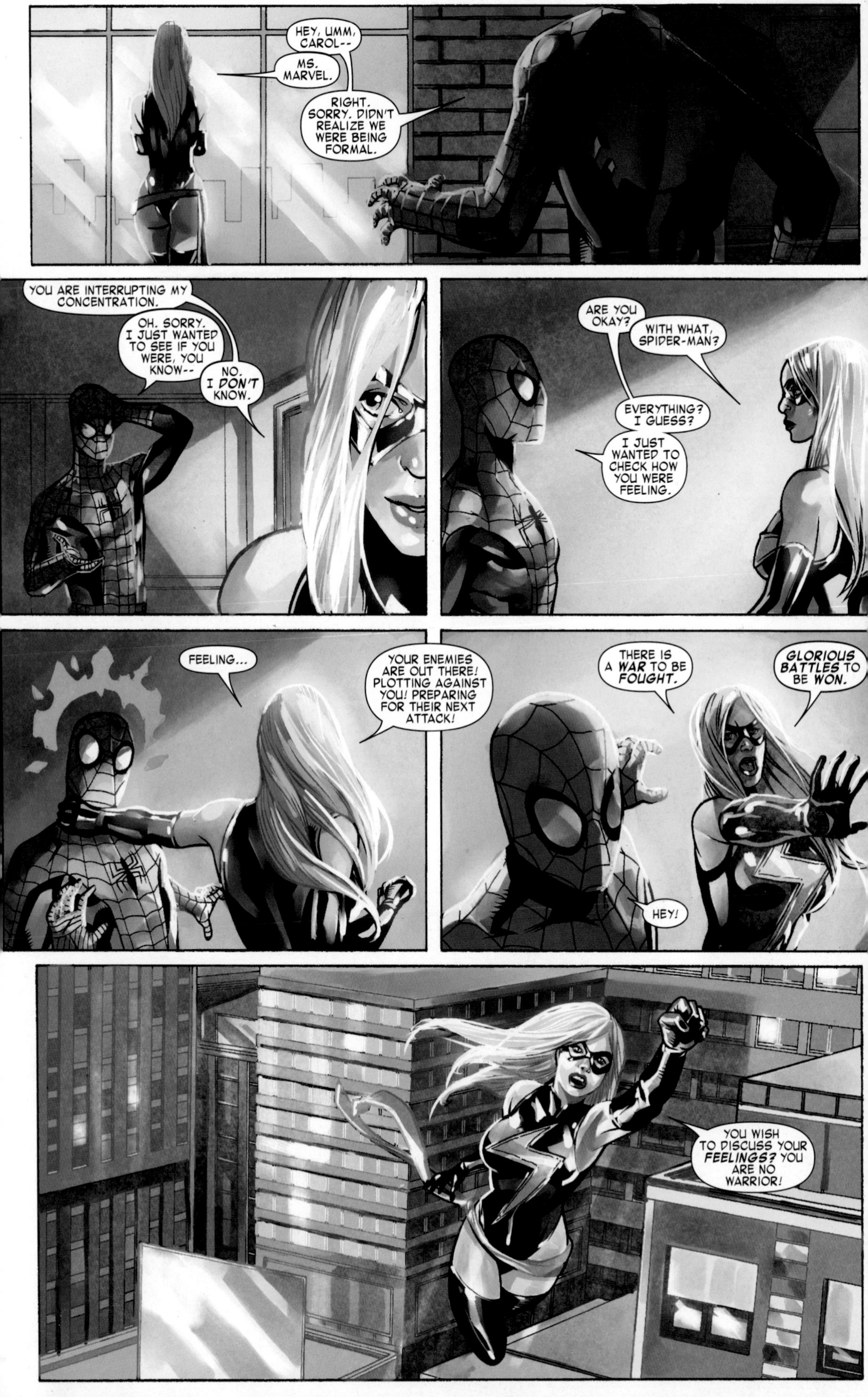
HEY, UMM, CAROL--
MS. MARVEL.
RIGHT. SORRY. DIDN'T REALIZE WE WERE BEING FORMAL.
YOU ARE INTERRUPTING MY CONCENTRATION.
OH. SORRY. I JUST WANTED TO SEE IF YOU WERE, YOU KNOW--
NO. I DON'T KNOW.
ARE YOU OKAY?
WITH WHAT, SPIDER-MAN?
EVERYTHING? I GUESS?
I JUST WANTED TO CHECK HOW YOU WERE FEELING.
FEELING...
YOUR ENEMIES ARE OUT THERE! PLOTTING AGAINST YOU! PREPARING FOR THEIR NEXT ATTACK!
THERE IS A WAR TO BE FOUGHT.
GLORIOUS BATTLES TO BE WON.
HEY!
YOU WISH TO DISCUSS YOUR FEELINGS? YOU ARE NO WARRIOR!

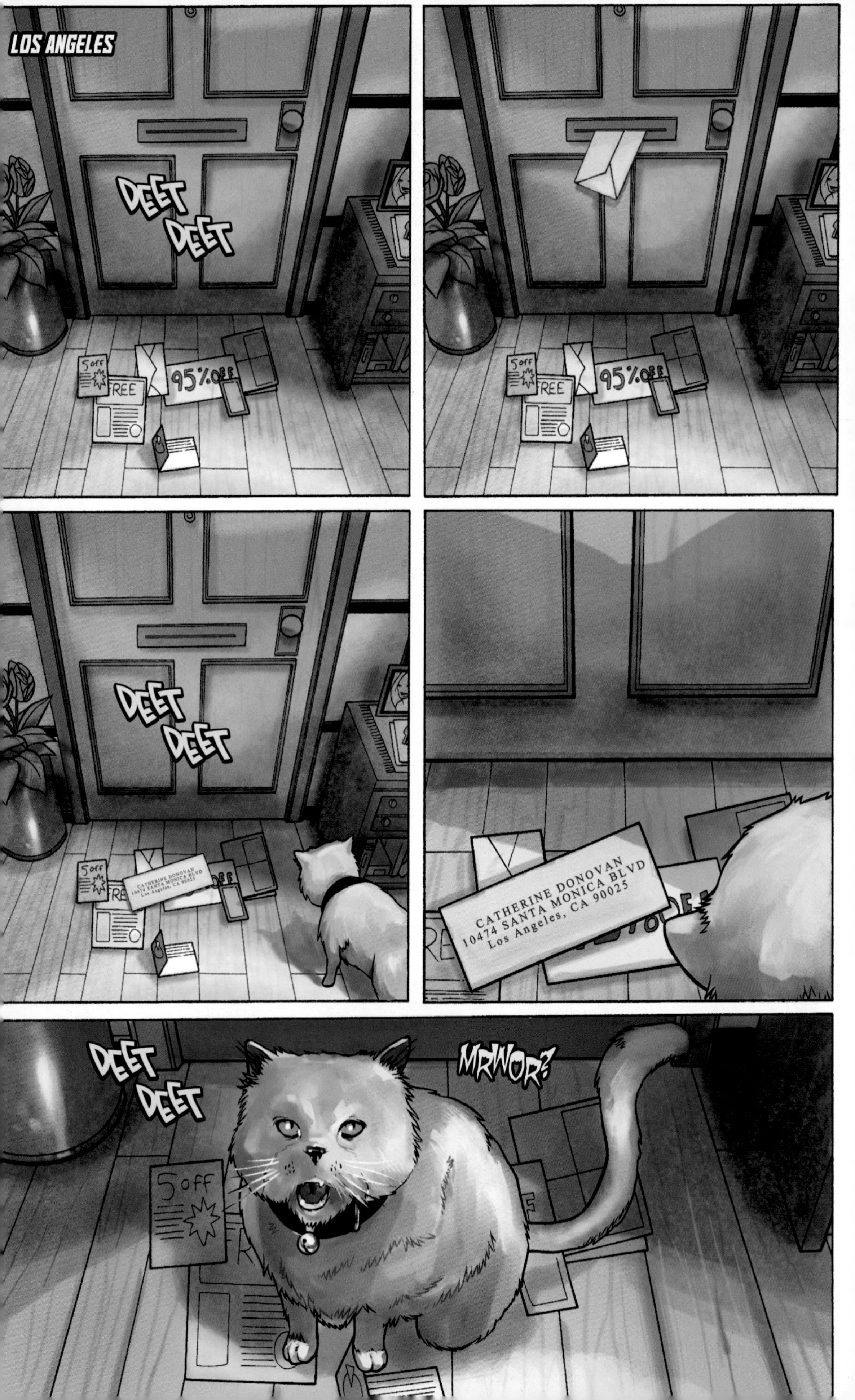
LOS ANGELES
DEET DEET
DEET DEET
CATHERINE DONOVAN
10474 SANTA MONICA BLVD
Los Angeles, CA 90025
DEET DEET
MRWOR?

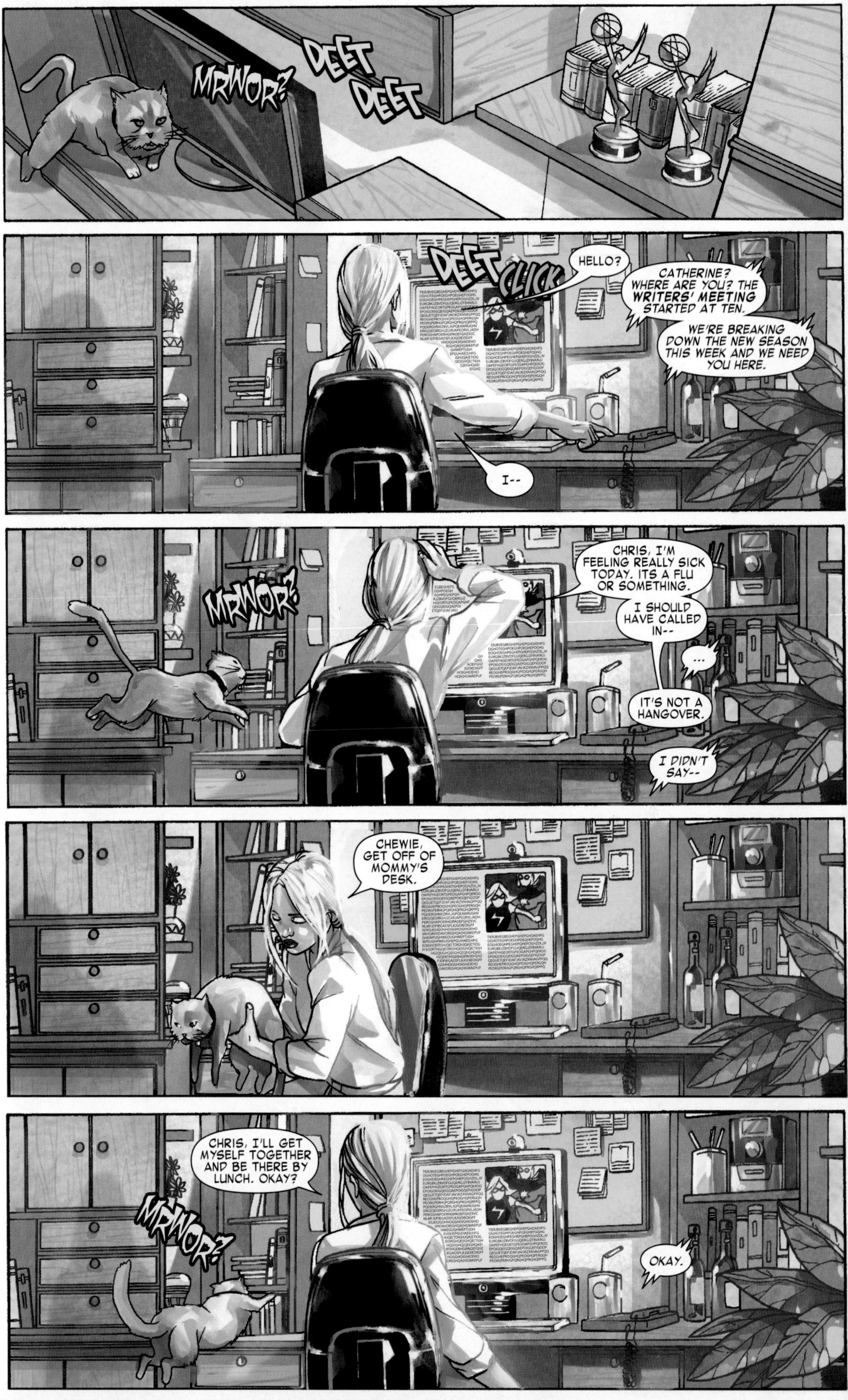
MRWOR?
DEET
DEET
DEET
CLICK
HELLO?
CATHERINE? WHERE ARE YOU? THE WRITERS' MEETING STARTED AT TEN.
WE'RE BREAKING DOWN THE NEW SEASON THIS WEEK AND WE NEED YOU HERE.
I--
MRWOR?
CHRIS, I'M FEELING REALLY SICK TODAY. ITS A FLU OR SOMETHING.
I SHOULD HAVE CALLED IN--
...
IT'S NOT A HANGOVER.
I DIDN'T SAY--
CHEWIE, GET OFF OF MOMMY'S DESK.
CHRIS, I'LL GET MYSELF TOGETHER AND BE THERE BY LUNCH. OKAY?
MRWOR?
OKAY.

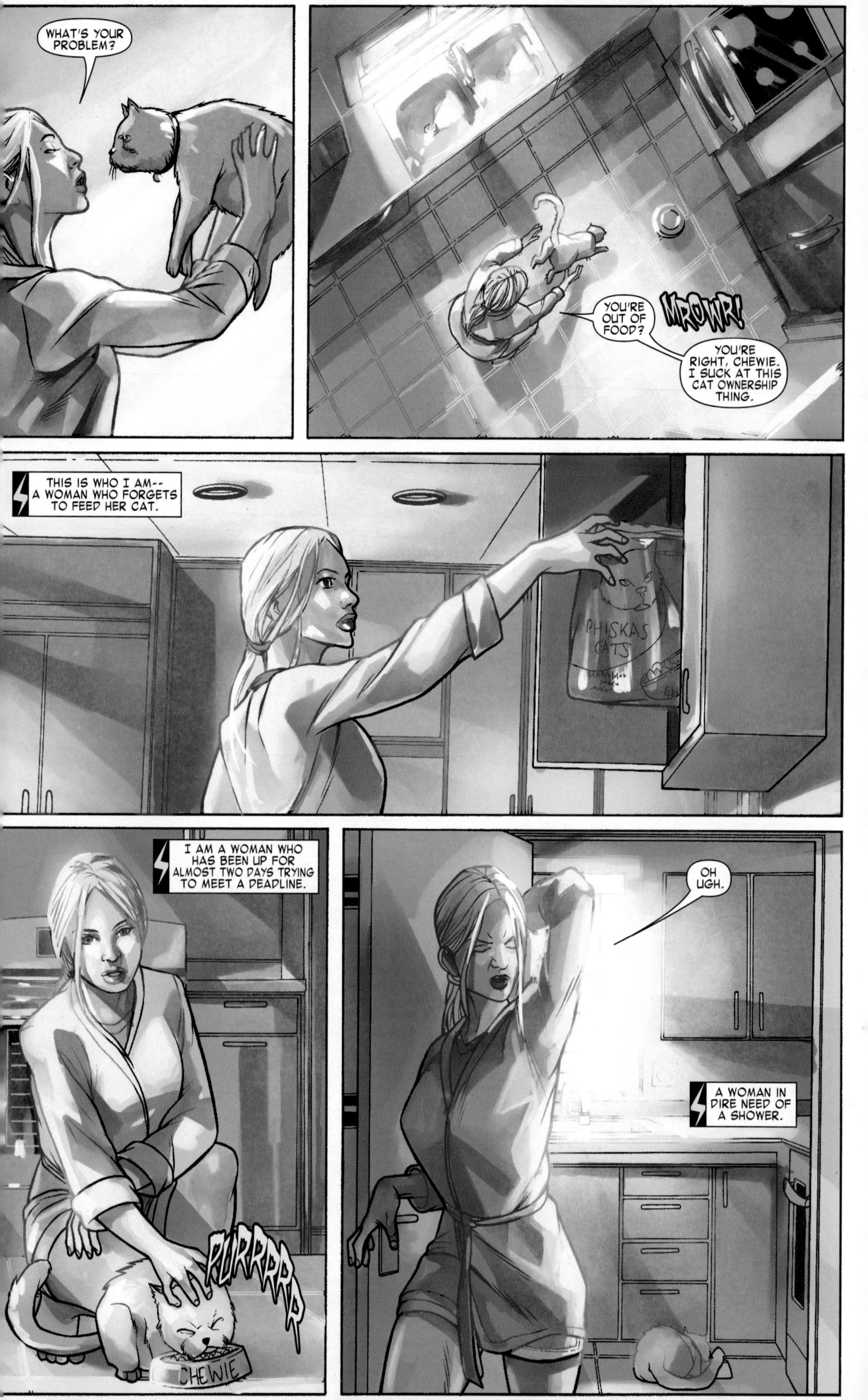
WHAT'S YOUR PROBLEM?
MROWR!
YOU'RE OUT OF FOOD?
YOU'RE RIGHT, CHEWIE. I SUCK AT THIS CAT OWNERSHIP THING.
THIS IS WHO I AM-- A WOMAN WHO FORGETS TO FEED HER CAT.
PHISKAS CATS
I AM A WOMAN WHO HAS BEEN UP FOR ALMOST TWO DAYS TRYING TO MEET A DEADLINE.
PURRRRR
CHEWIE
OH UGH.
A WOMAN IN DIRE NEED OF A SHOWER.

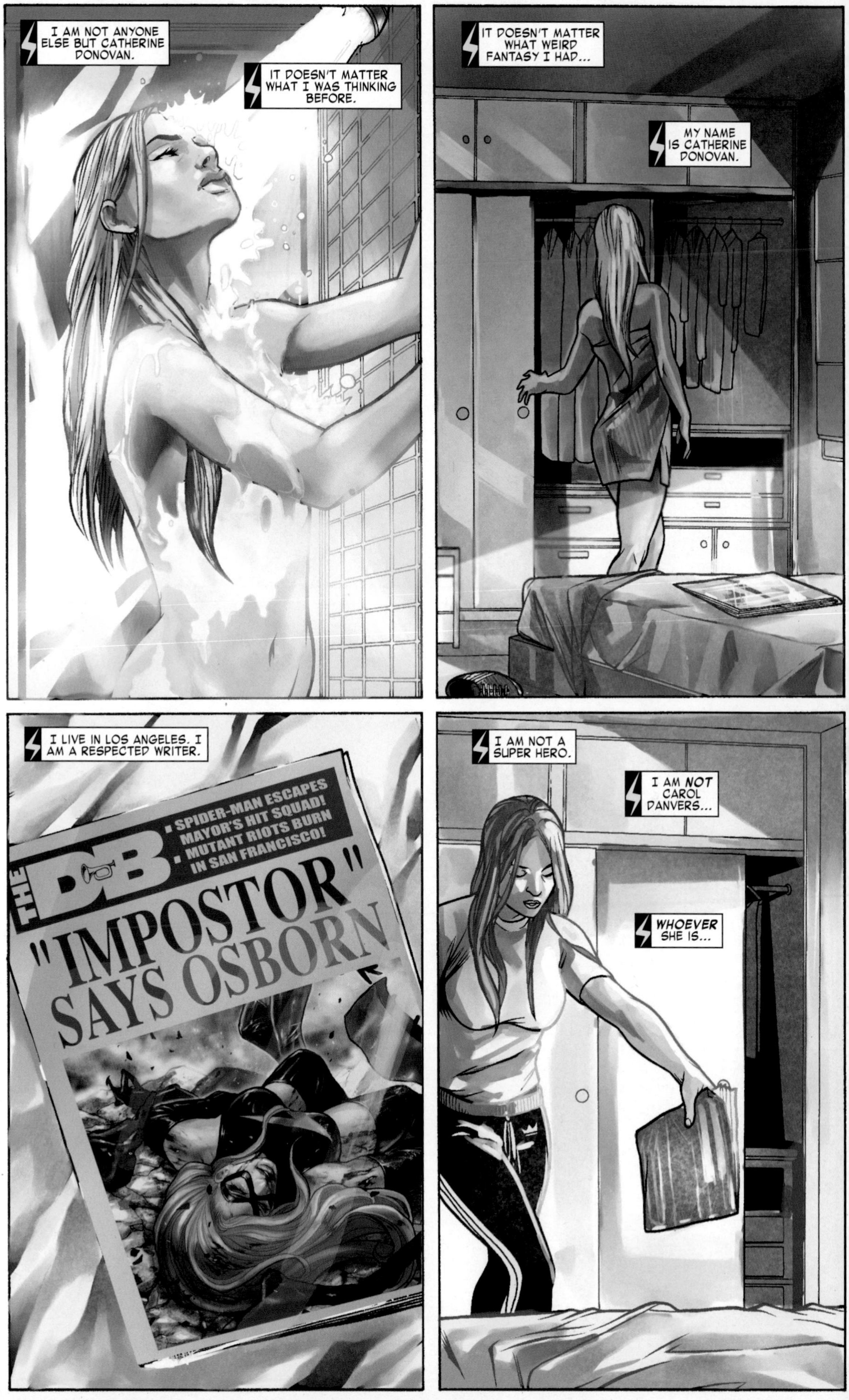
I AM NOT ANYONE ELSE BUT CATHERINE DONOVAN.
IT DOESN'T MATTER WHAT I WAS THINKING BEFORE.
IT DOESN'T MATTER WHAT WEIRD FANTASY I HAD...
MY NAME IS CATHERINE DONOVAN.
I LIVE IN LOS ANGELES. I AM A RESPECTED WRITER.
THE DB
SPIDER-MAN ESCAPES MAYOR'S HIT SQUAD!
MUTANT RIOTS BURN IN SAN FRANCISCO!
"IMPOSTOR" SAYS OSBORN
I AM NOT A SUPER HERO.
I AM *NOT* CAROL DANVERS...
WHOEVER SHE IS...

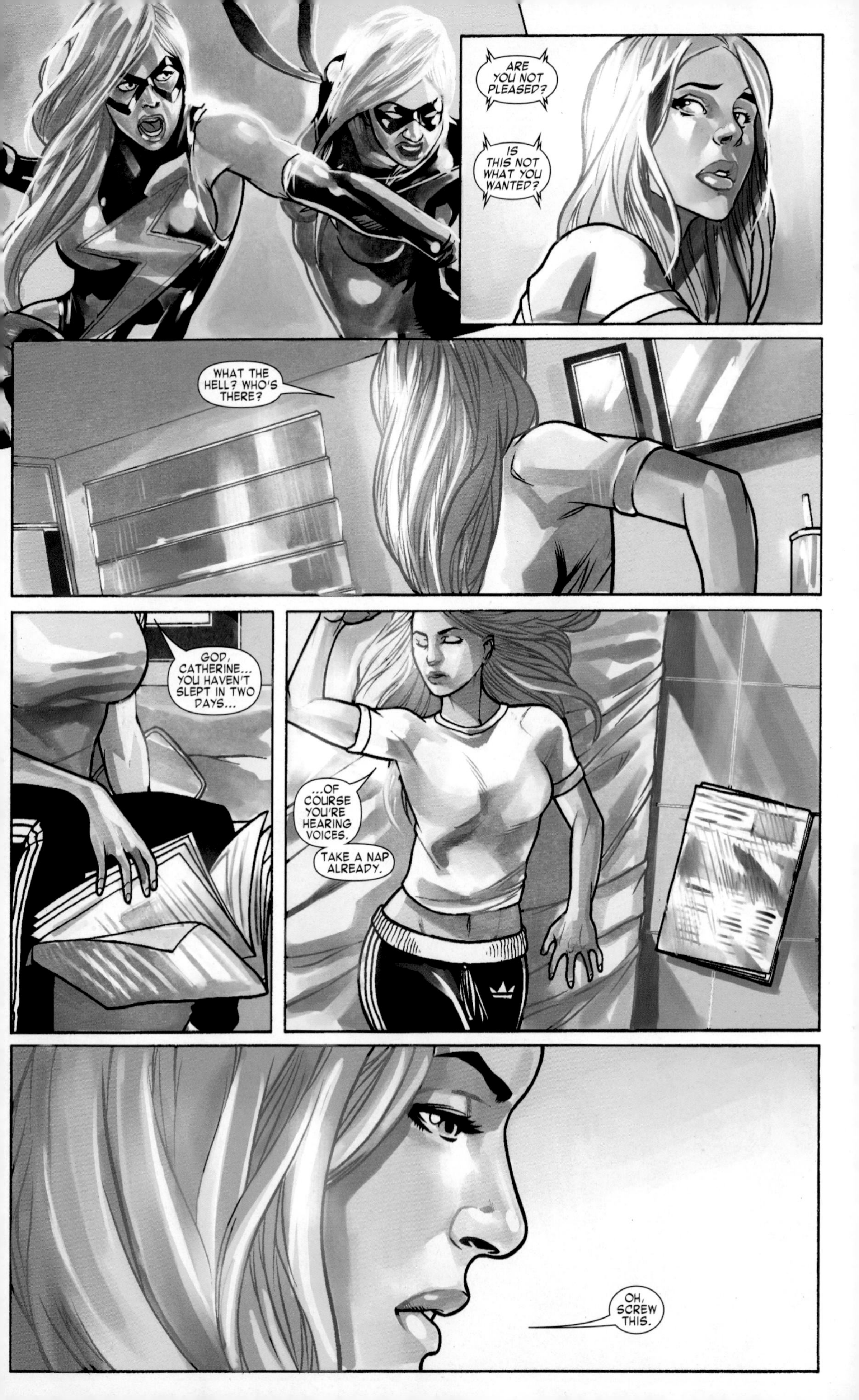
ARE YOU NOT PLEASED?
IS THIS NOT WHAT YOU WANTED?
WHAT THE HELL? WHO'S THERE?
GOD, CATHERINE... YOU HAVEN'T SLEPT IN TWO DAYS...
...OF COURSE YOU'RE HEARING VOICES.
TAKE A NAP ALREADY.
OH, SCREW THIS.

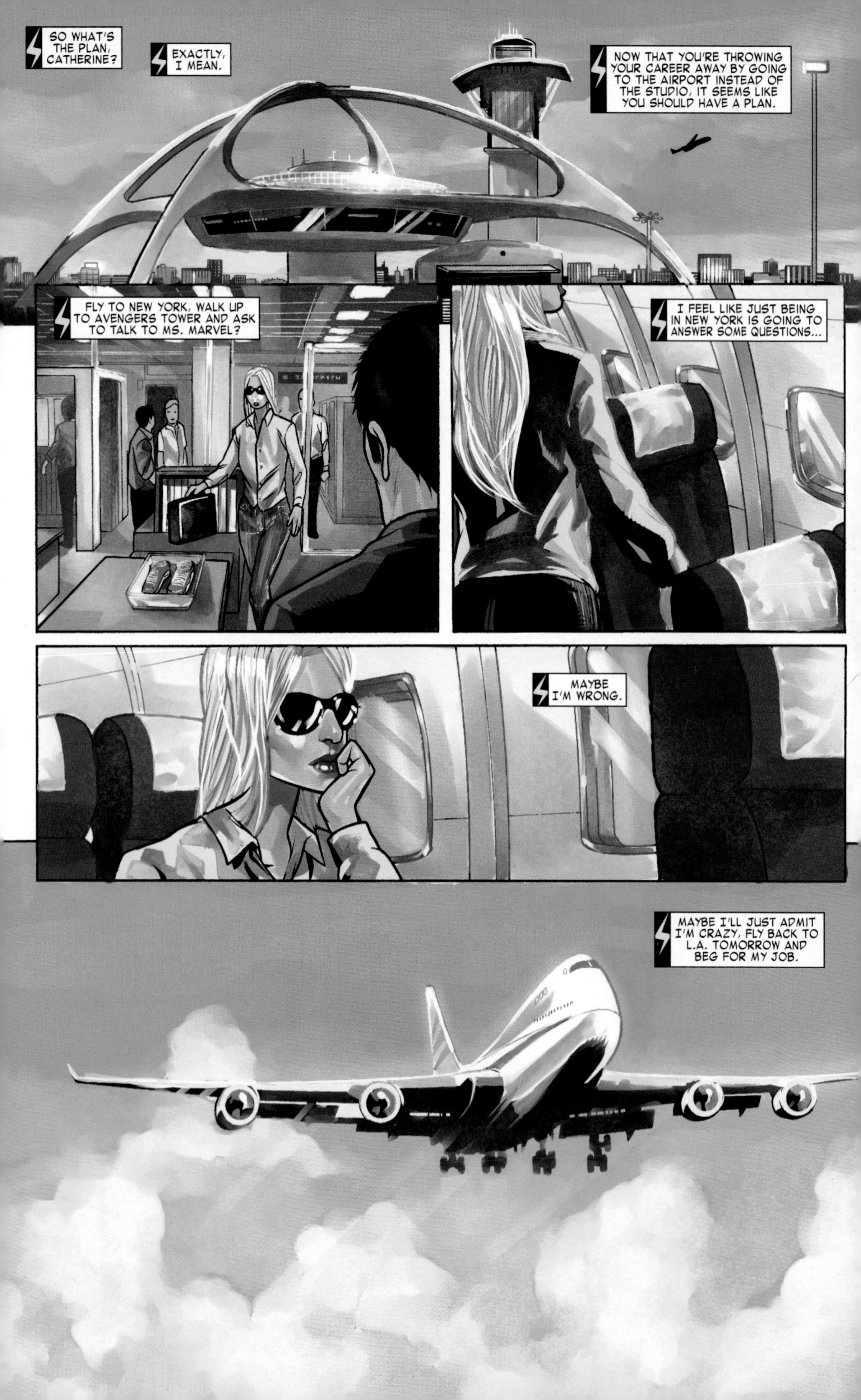
SO WHAT'S THE PLAN, CATHERINE?
EXACTLY, I MEAN.
NOW THAT YOU'RE THROWING YOUR CAREER AWAY BY GOING TO THE AIRPORT INSTEAD OF THE STUDIO, IT SEEMS LIKE YOU SHOULD HAVE A PLAN.
FLY TO NEW YORK, WALK UP TO AVENGERS TOWER AND ASK TO TALK TO MS. MARVEL?
I FEEL LIKE JUST BEING IN NEW YORK IS GOING TO ANSWER SOME QUESTIONS...
MAYBE I'M WRONG.
MAYBE I'LL JUST ADMIT I'M CRAZY, FLY BACK TO L.A. TOMORROW AND BEG FOR MY JOB.

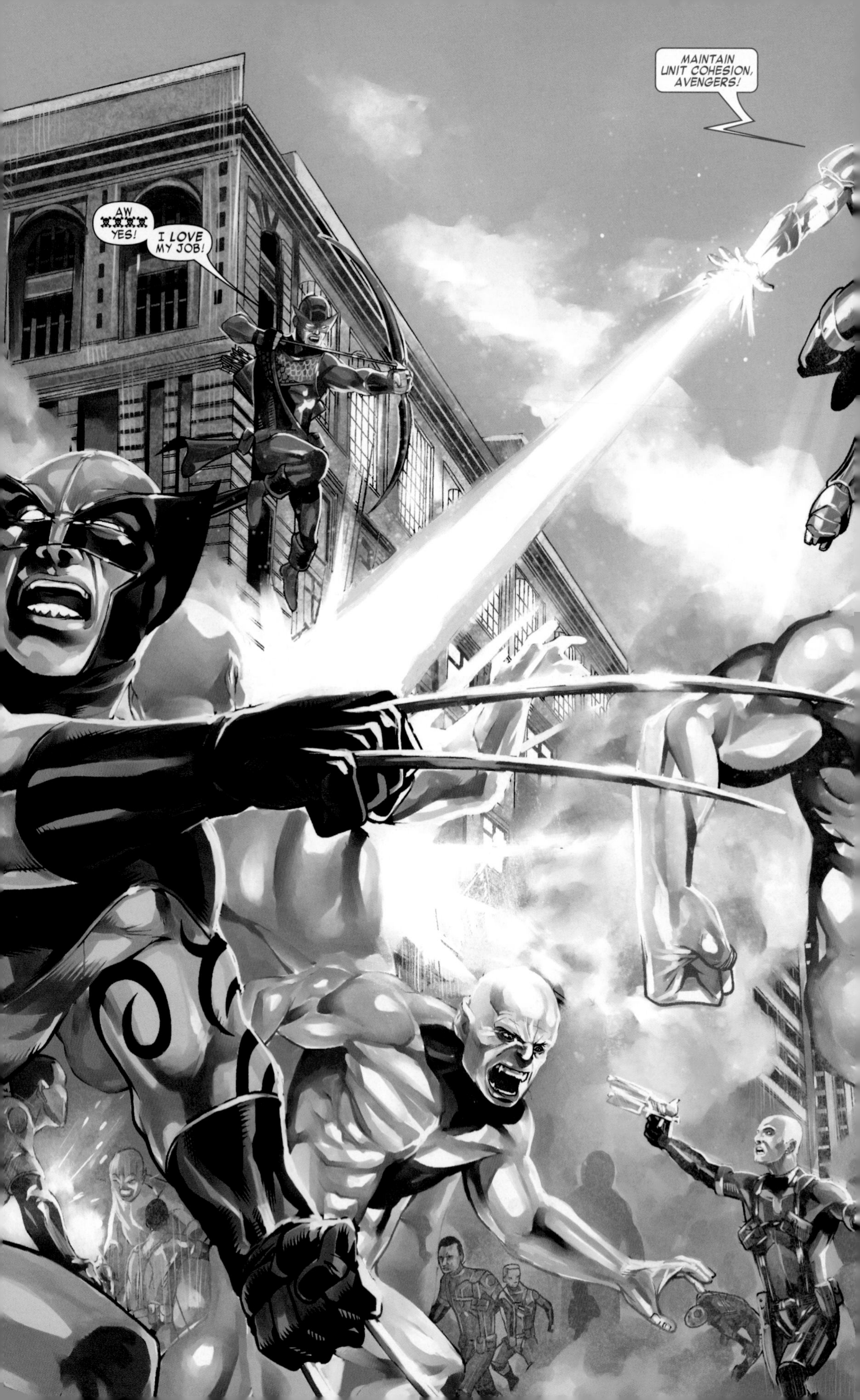
AW ☠☠☠ YES!
I LOVE MY JOB!
MAINTAIN UNIT COHESION, AVENGERS!

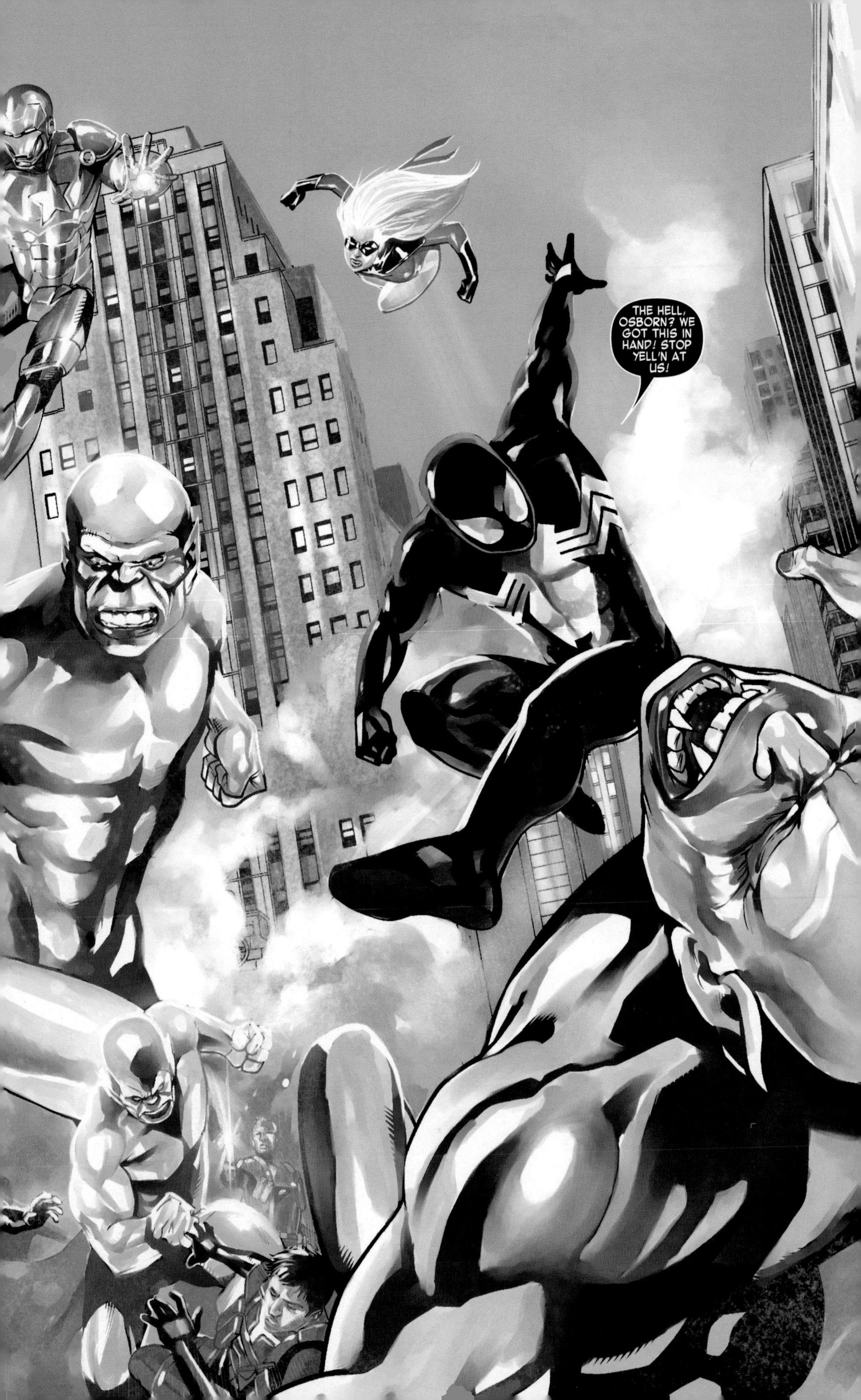
THE HELL, OSBORN? WE GOT THIS IN HAND! STOP YELL'N AT US!

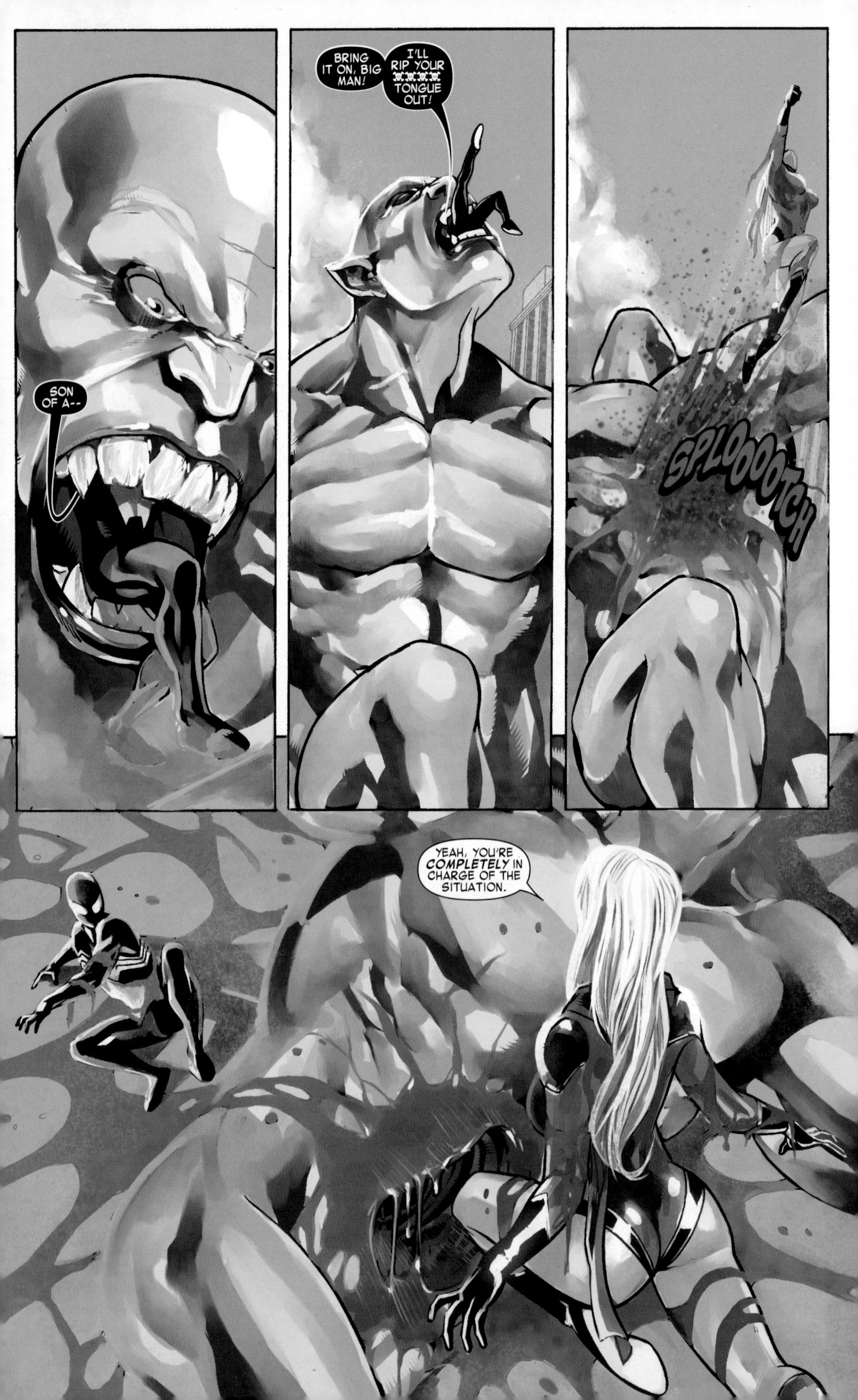
SON OF A--
BRING IT ON, BIG MAN!
I'LL RIP YOUR ☠☠☠ TONGUE OUT!
SPLOOOOTCH
YEAH, YOU'RE COMPLETELY IN CHARGE OF THE SITUATION.

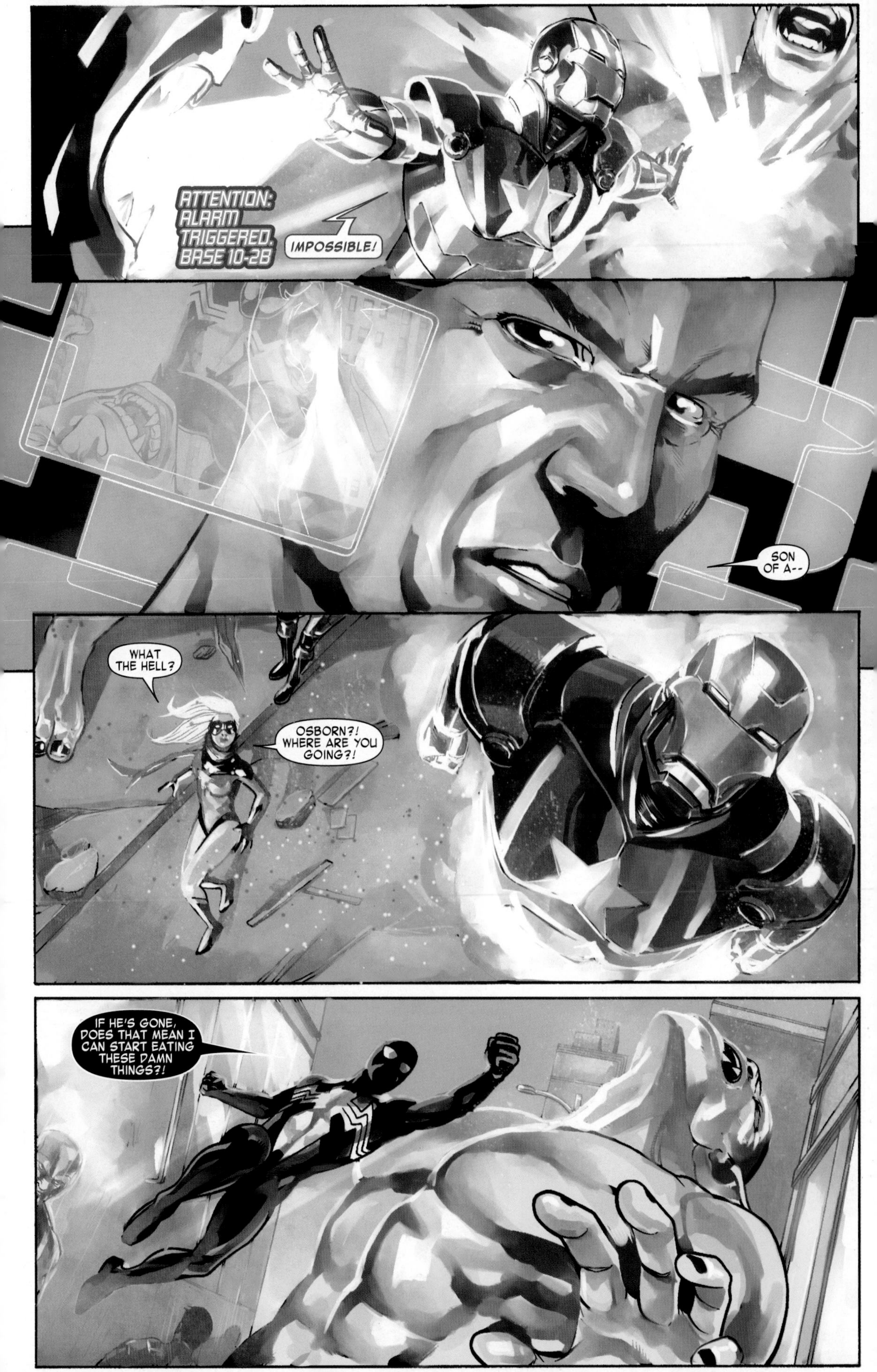
ATTENTION: ALARM TRIGGERED. BASE 10-2B
IMPOSSIBLE!
SON OF A--
WHAT THE HELL?
OSBORN?! WHERE ARE YOU GOING?!
IF HE'S GONE, DOES THAT MEAN I CAN START EATING THESE DAMN THINGS?!

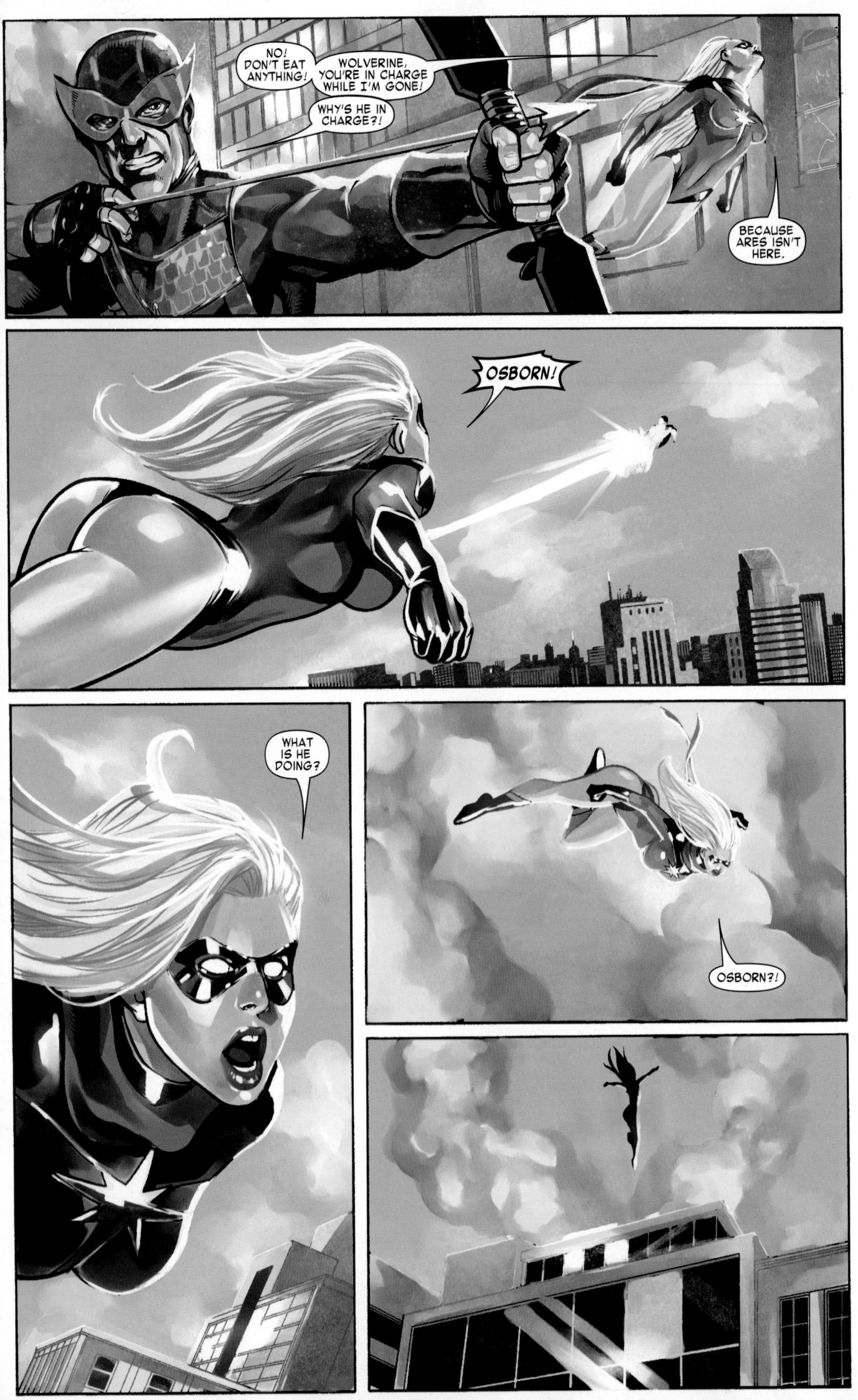
NO! DON'T EAT ANYTHING!
WOLVERINE, YOU'RE IN CHARGE WHILE I'M GONE!
WHY'S HE IN CHARGE?!
BECAUSE ARES ISN'T HERE.
OSBORN!
WHAT IS HE DOING?
OSBORN?!

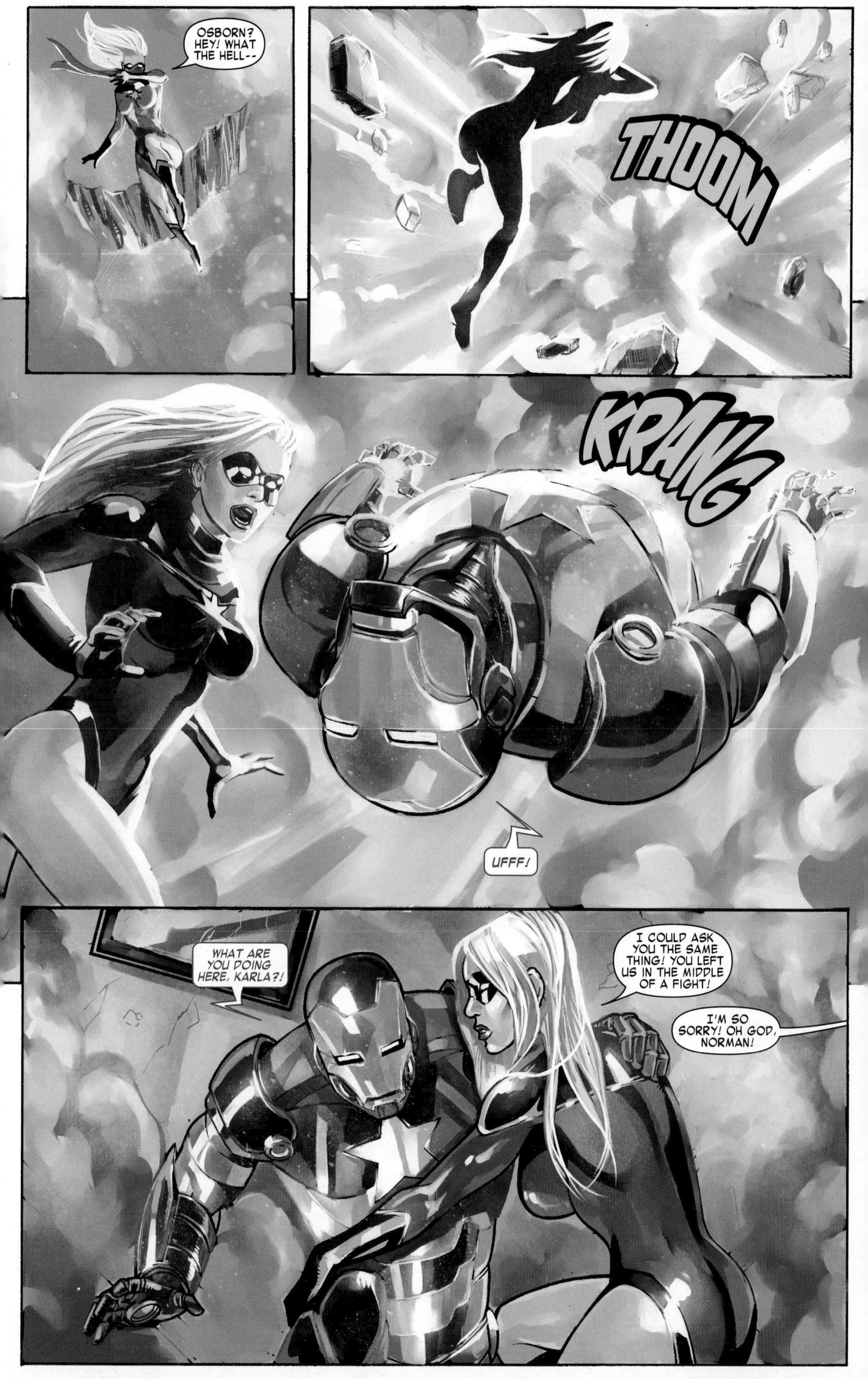
OSBORN? HEY! WHAT THE HELL--
THOOM
KRANG
UFFF!
WHAT ARE YOU DOING HERE, KARLA?!
I COULD ASK YOU THE SAME THING! YOU LEFT US IN THE MIDDLE OF A FIGHT!
I'M SO SORRY! OH GOD, NORMAN!

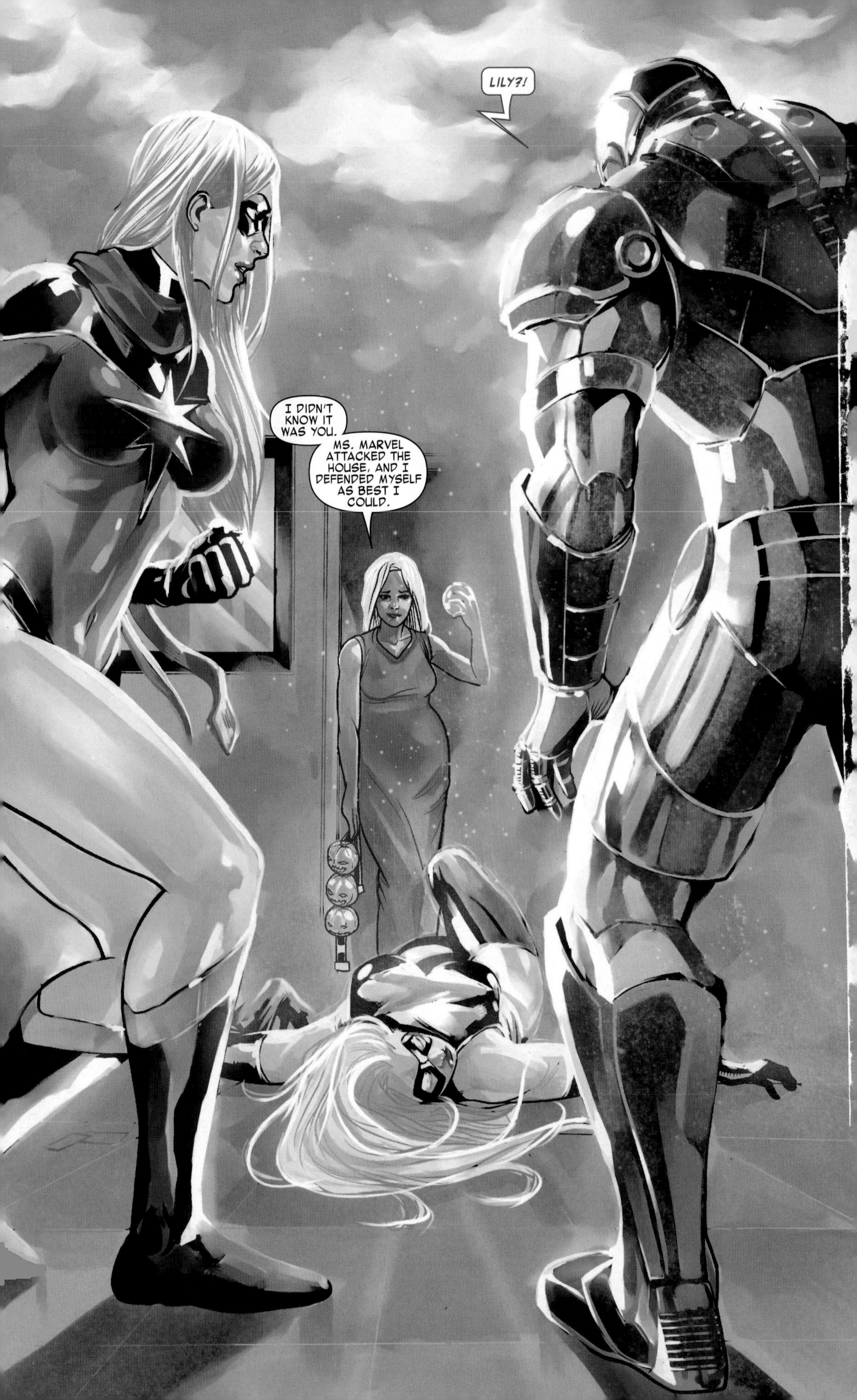
LILY?!
I DIDN'T KNOW IT WAS YOU.
MS. MARVEL ATTACKED THE HOUSE, AND I DEFENDED MYSELF AS BEST I COULD.

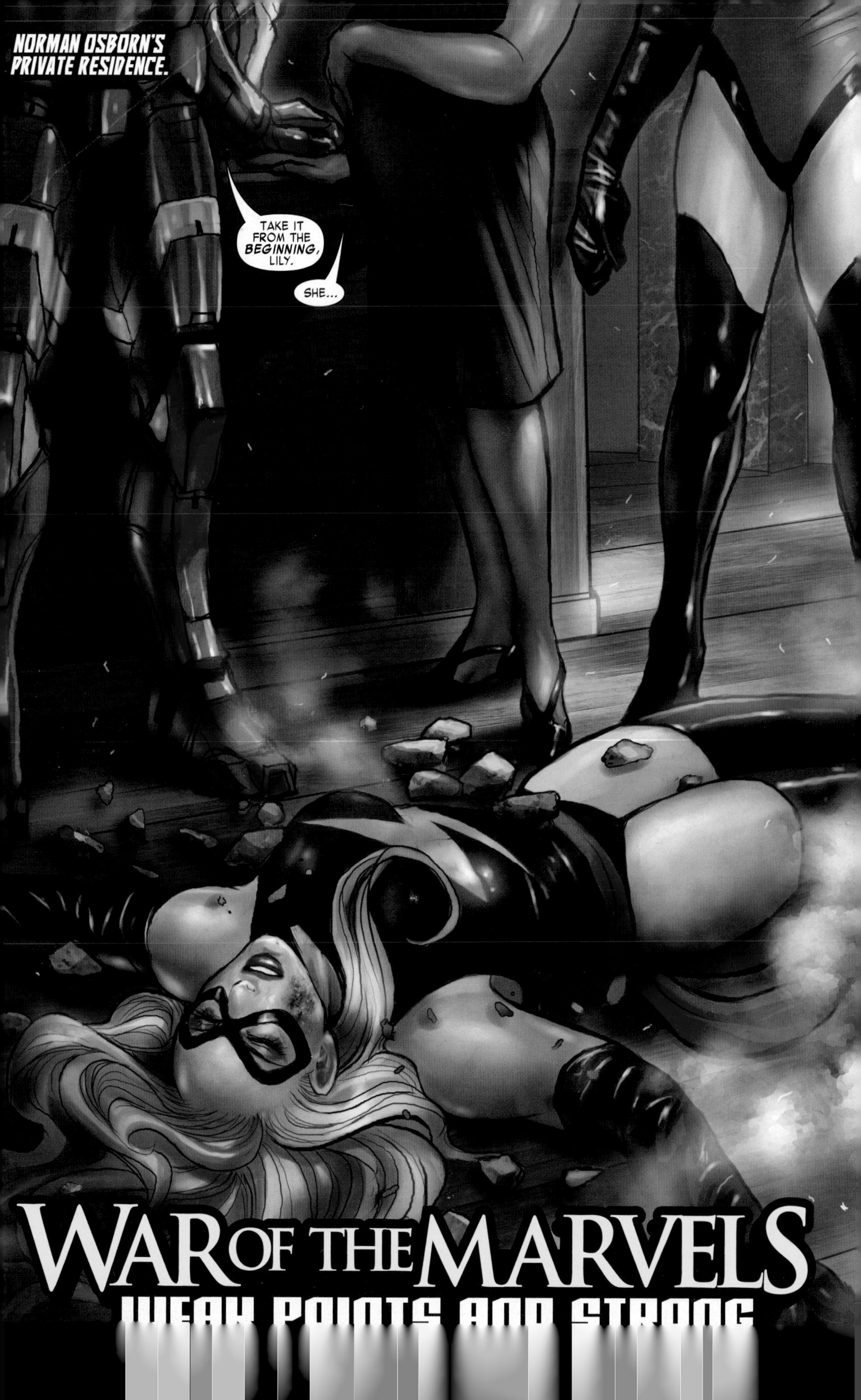
NORMAN OSBORN'S PRIVATE RESIDENCE.
TAKE IT FROM THE *BEGINNING*, LILY.
SHE...
WAR OF THE MARVELS

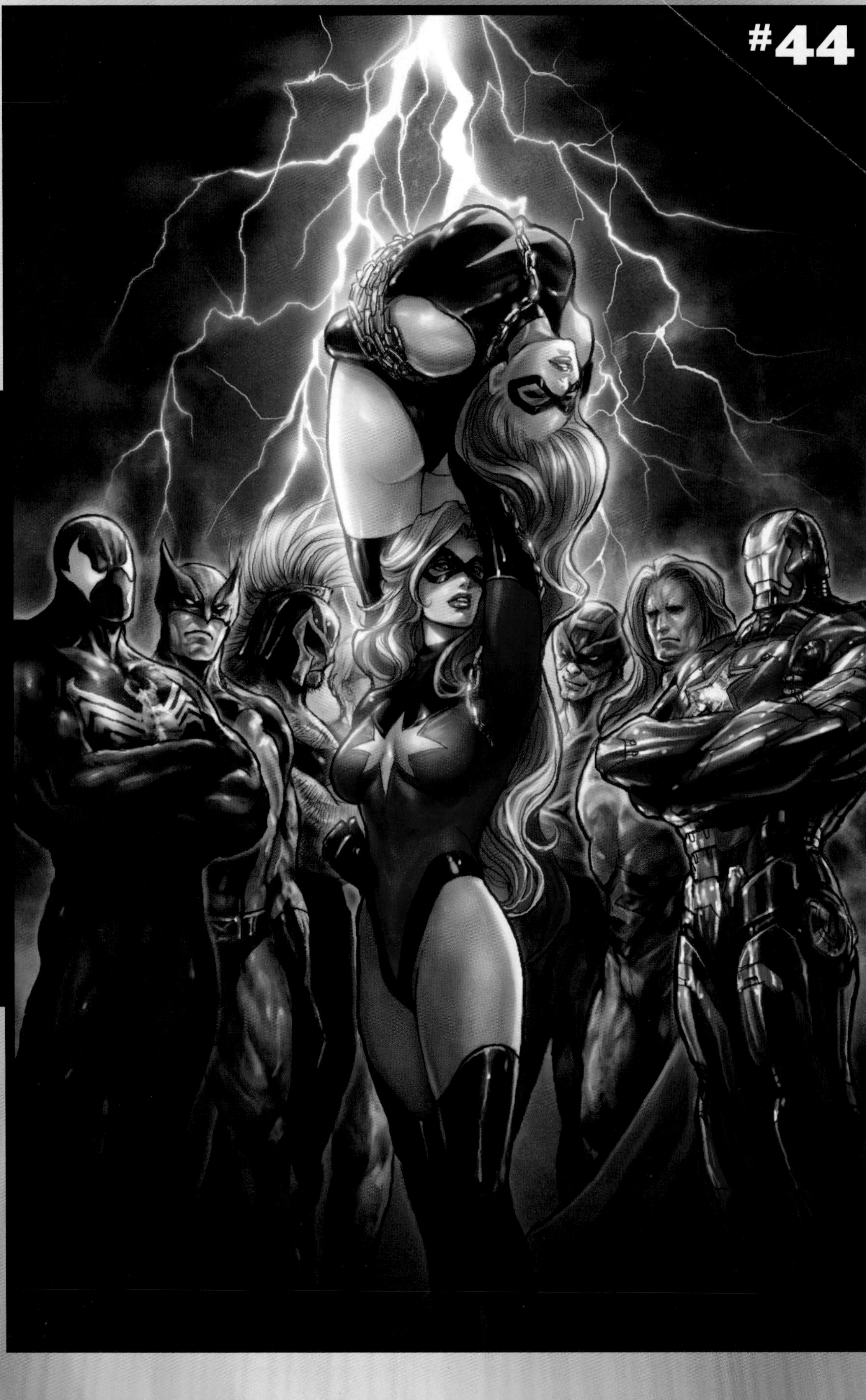
#44

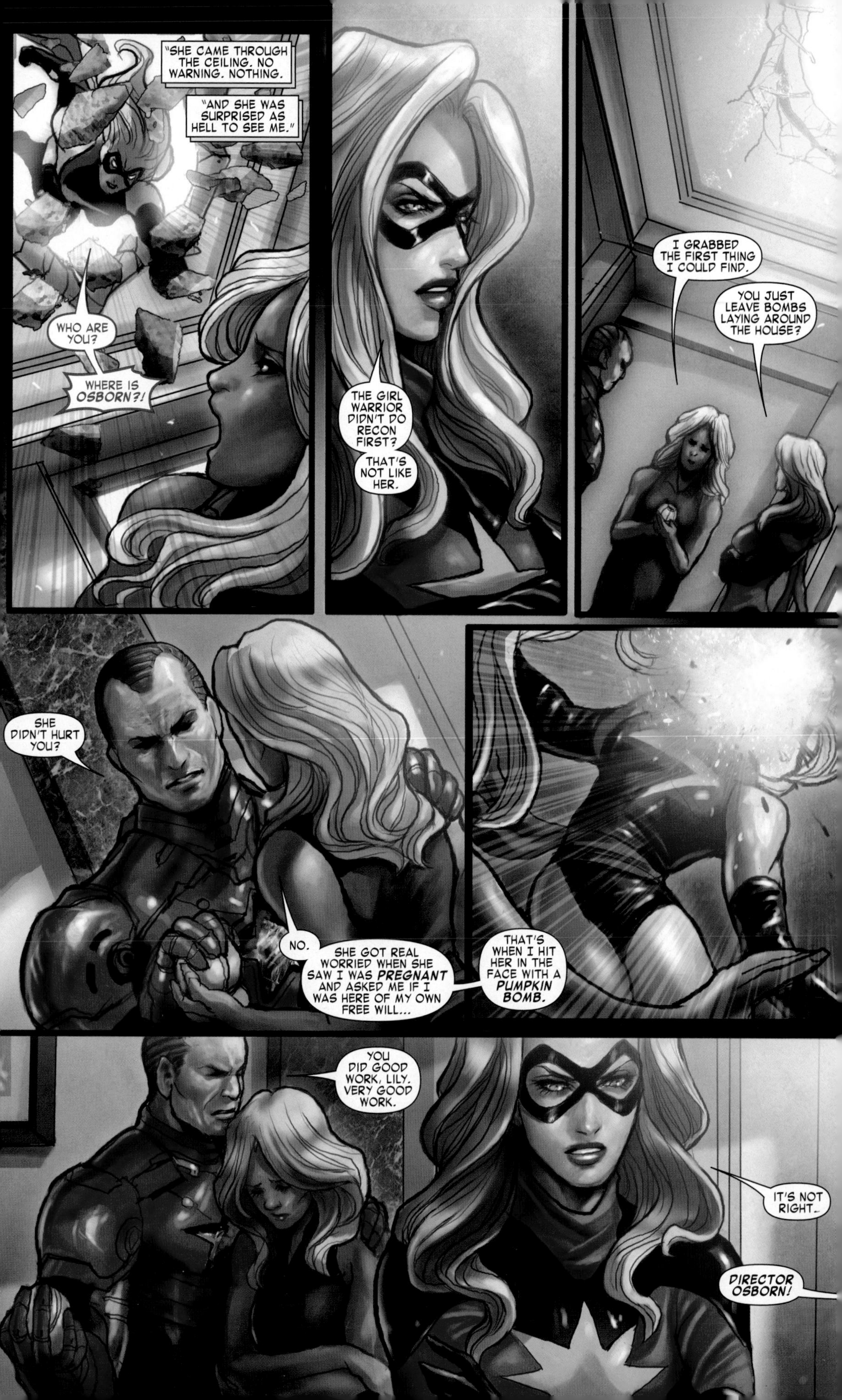
"SHE CAME THROUGH THE CEILING. NO WARNING. NOTHING.
"AND SHE WAS SURPRISED AS HELL TO SEE ME."
WHO ARE YOU?
WHERE IS OSBORN?!
THE GIRL WARRIOR DIDN'T DO RECON FIRST?
THAT'S NOT LIKE HER.
I GRABBED THE FIRST THING I COULD FIND.
YOU JUST LEAVE BOMBS LAYING AROUND THE HOUSE?
SHE DIDN'T HURT YOU?
NO.
SHE GOT REAL WORRIED WHEN SHE SAW I WAS PREGNANT AND ASKED ME IF I WAS HERE OF MY OWN FREE WILL...
THAT'S WHEN I HIT HER IN THE FACE WITH A PUMPKIN BOMB.
YOU DID GOOD WORK, LILY. VERY GOOD WORK.
IT'S NOT RIGHT.
DIRECTOR OSBORN!

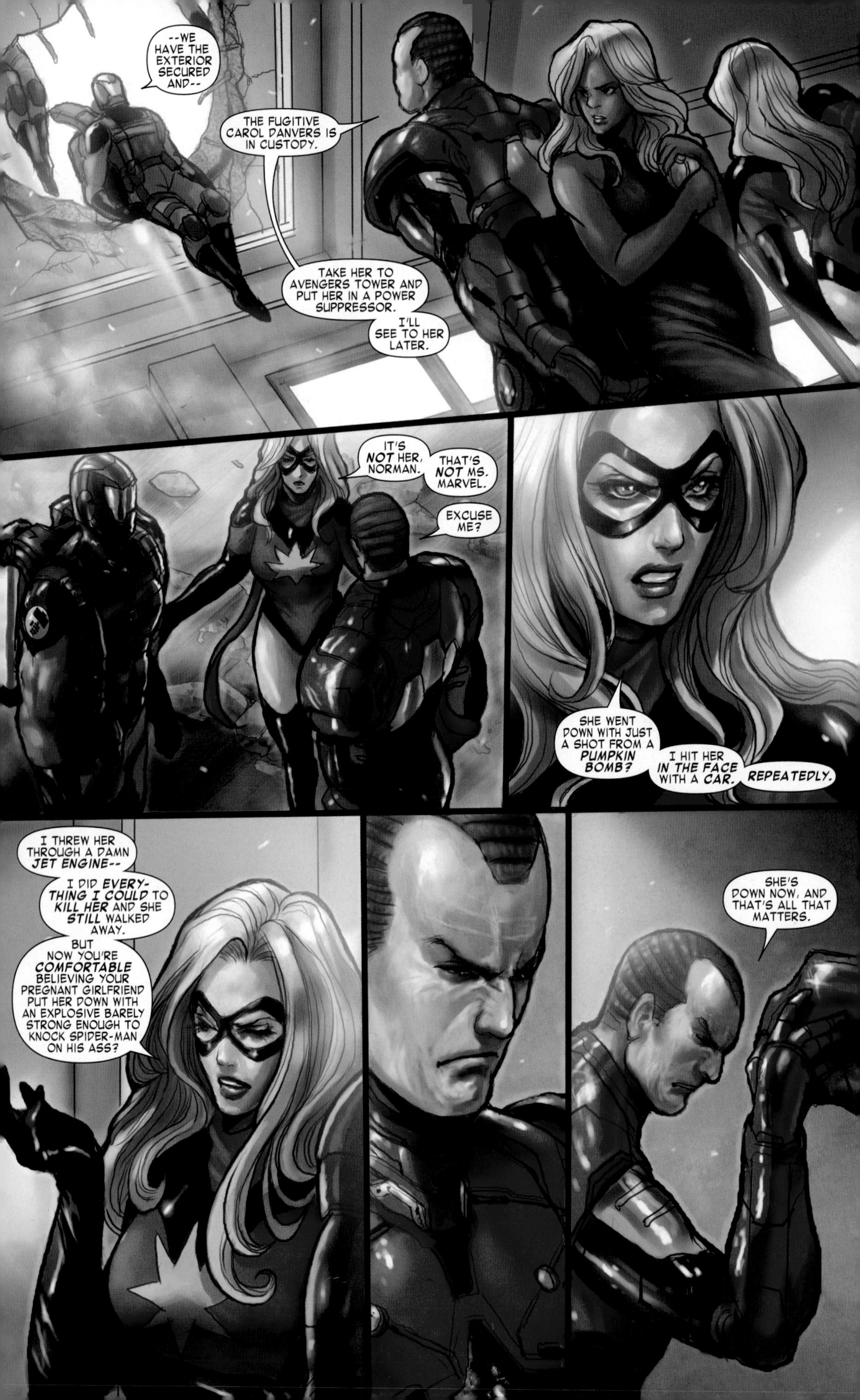
--WE HAVE THE EXTERIOR SECURED AND--
THE FUGITIVE CAROL DANVERS IS IN CUSTODY.
TAKE HER TO AVENGERS TOWER AND PUT HER IN A POWER SUPPRESSOR.
I'LL SEE TO HER LATER.
IT'S NOT HER, NORMAN.
THAT'S NOT MS. MARVEL.
EXCUSE ME?
SHE WENT DOWN WITH JUST A SHOT FROM A PUMPKIN BOMB?
I HIT HER IN THE FACE WITH A CAR.
REPEATEDLY.
I THREW HER THROUGH A DAMN JET ENGINE--
I DID EVERY-THING I COULD TO KILL HER AND SHE STILL WALKED AWAY.
BUT NOW YOU'RE COMFORTABLE BELIEVING YOUR PREGNANT GIRLFRIEND PUT HER DOWN WITH AN EXPLOSIVE BARELY STRONG ENOUGH TO KNOCK SPIDER-MAN ON HIS ASS?
SHE'S DOWN NOW, AND THAT'S ALL THAT MATTERS.

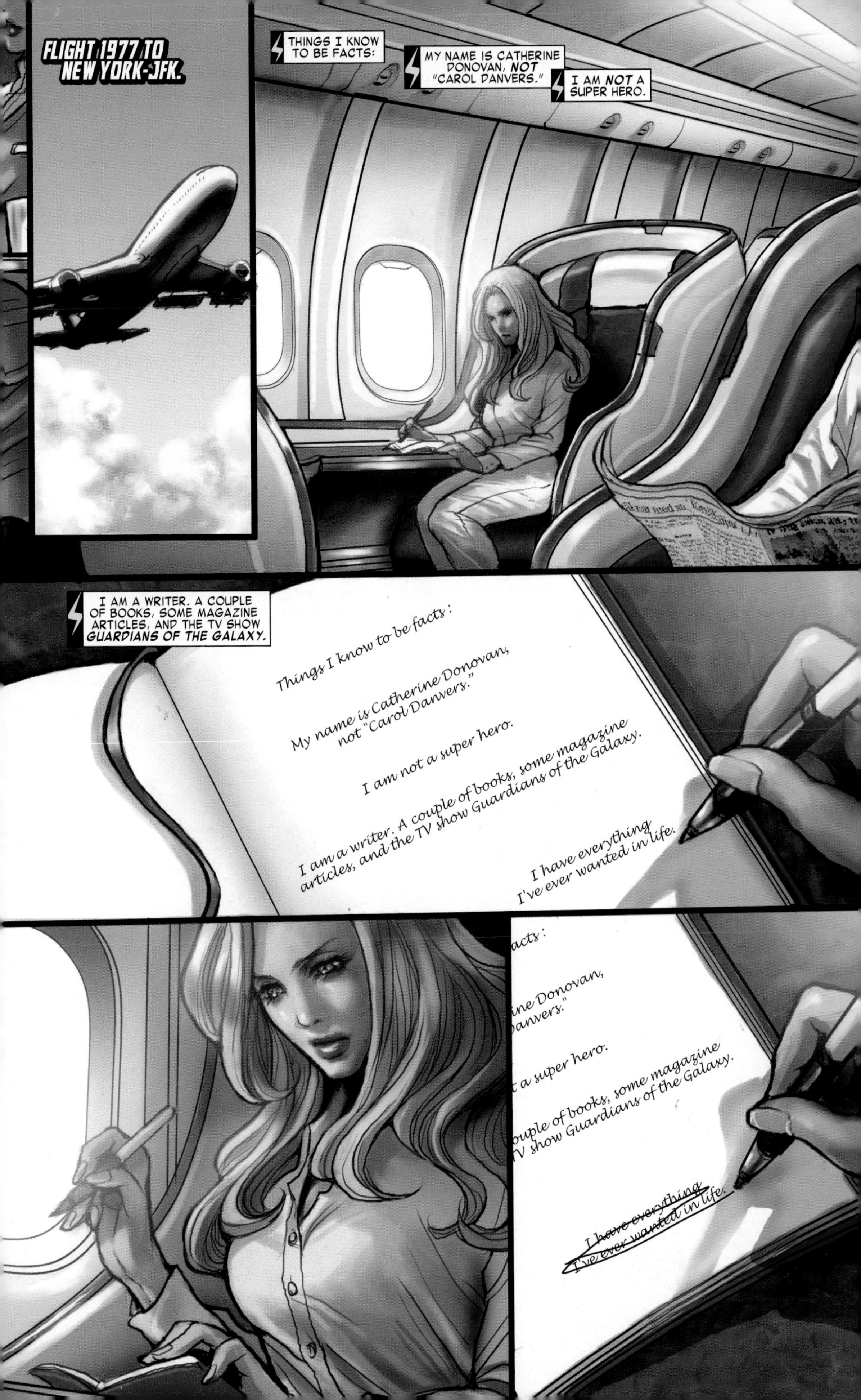

FLIGHT 1977 TO NEW YORK-JFK.
THINGS I KNOW TO BE FACTS:
MY NAME IS CATHERINE DONOVAN, *NOT* "CAROL DANVERS."
I AM *NOT* A SUPER HERO.
I AM A WRITER. A COUPLE OF BOOKS, SOME MAGAZINE ARTICLES, AND THE TV SHOW *GUARDIANS OF THE GALAXY.*
Things I know to be facts:
My name is Catherine Donovan, not "Carol Danvers."
I am not a super hero.
I am a writer. A couple of books, some magazine articles, and the TV show Guardians of the Galaxy.
I have everything I've ever wanted in life.
~~I have everything I've ever wanted in life.~~

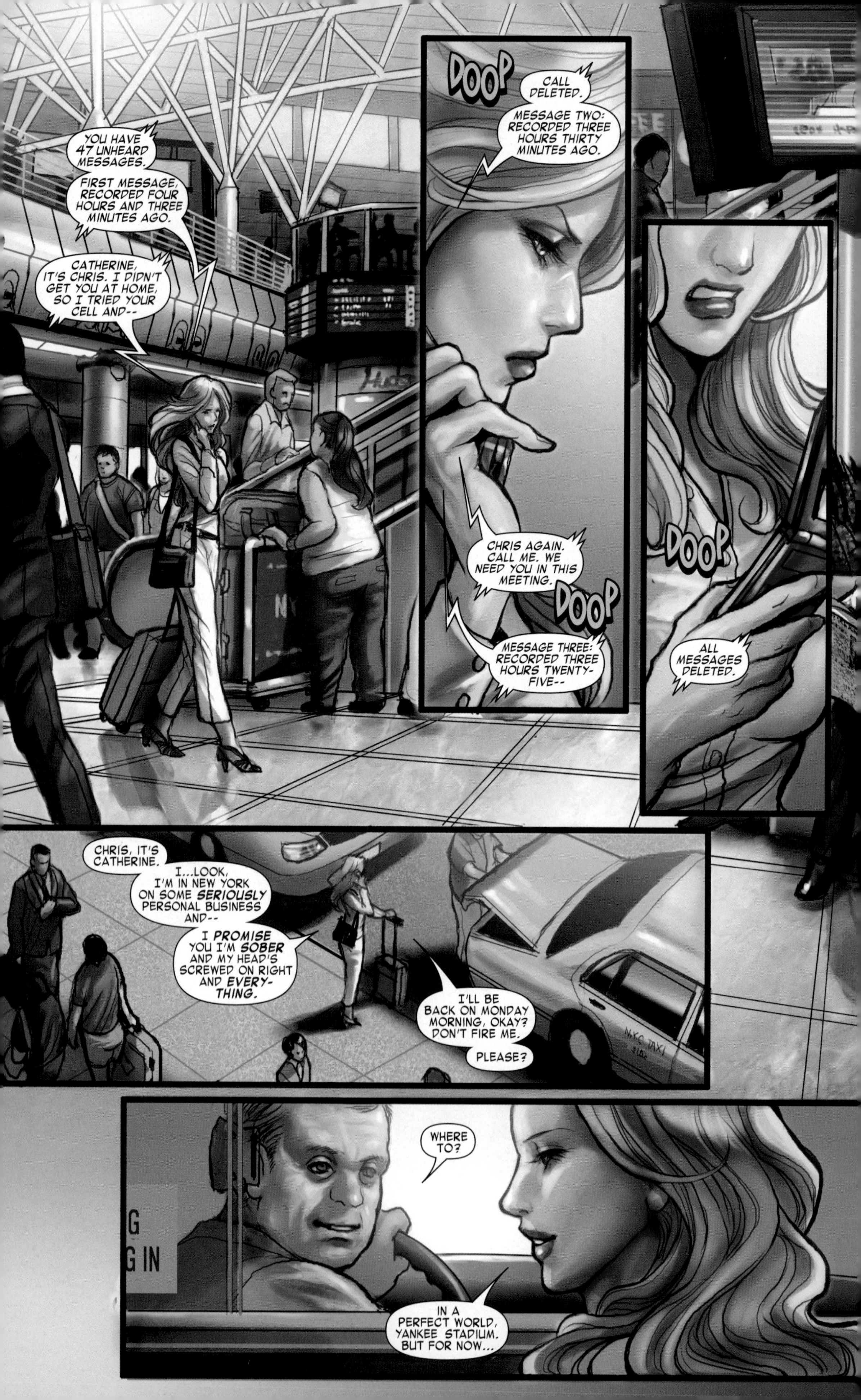
YOU HAVE 47 UNHEARD MESSAGES.
FIRST MESSAGE, RECORDED FOUR HOURS AND THREE MINUTES AGO.
CATHERINE, IT'S CHRIS. I DIDN'T GET YOU AT HOME, SO I TRIED YOUR CELL AND--
DOOP
CALL DELETED.
MESSAGE TWO: RECORDED THREE HOURS THIRTY MINUTES AGO.
CHRIS AGAIN. CALL ME. WE NEED YOU IN THIS MEETING.
DOOP
MESSAGE THREE: RECORDED THREE HOURS TWENTY-FIVE--
DOOP
ALL MESSAGES DELETED.
CHRIS, IT'S CATHERINE.
I...LOOK, I'M IN NEW YORK ON SOME SERIOUSLY PERSONAL BUSINESS AND--
I PROMISE YOU I'M SOBER AND MY HEAD'S SCREWED ON RIGHT AND EVERYTHING.
I'LL BE BACK ON MONDAY MORNING, OKAY? DON'T FIRE ME.
PLEASE?
N.Y.C. TAXI
WHERE TO?
G
G IN
IN A PERFECT WORLD, YANKEE STADIUM. BUT FOR NOW...

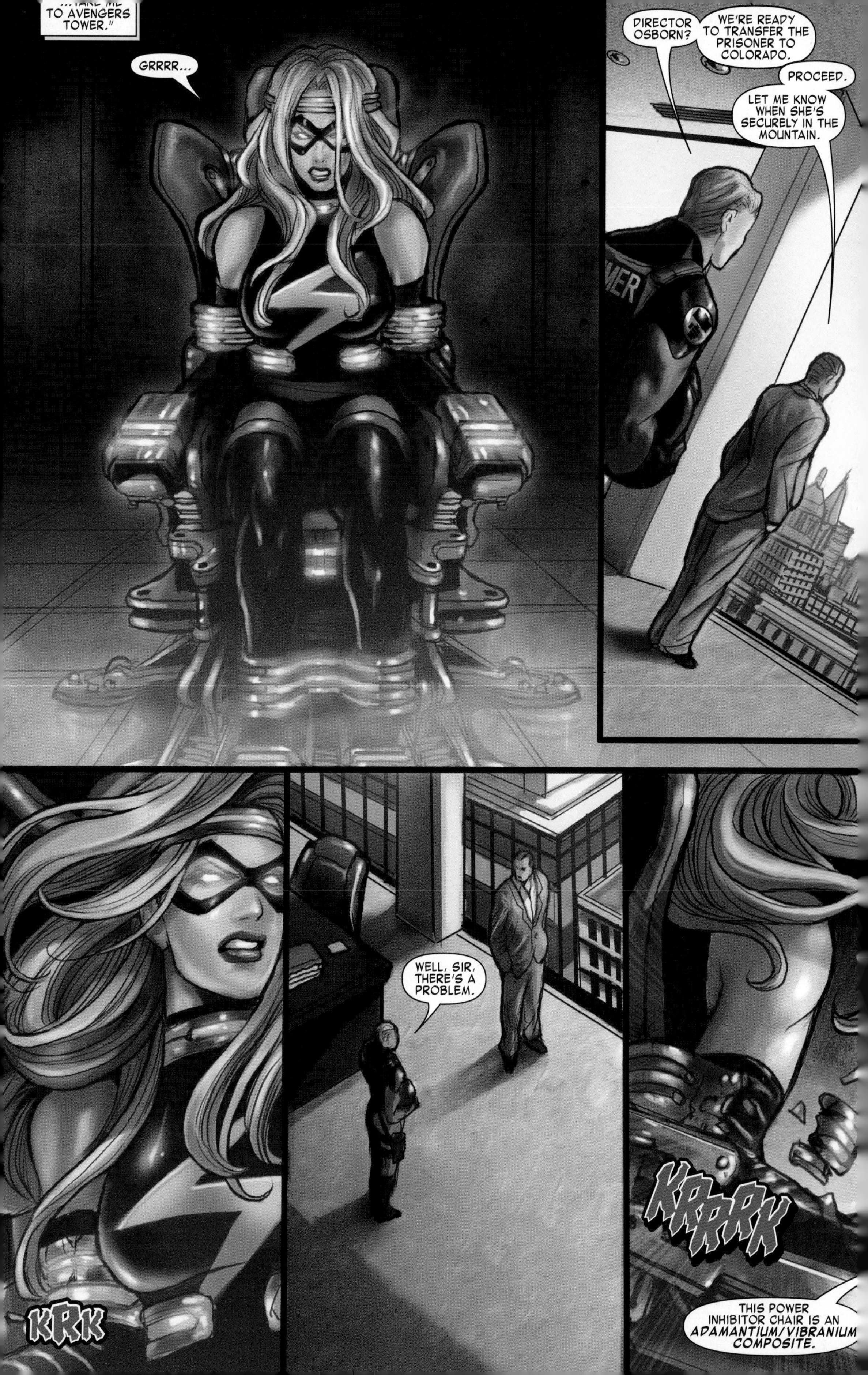
TO AVENGERS TOWER."
GRRRR...
DIRECTOR OSBORN?
WE'RE READY TO TRANSFER THE PRISONER TO COLORADO.
PROCEED.
LET ME KNOW WHEN SHE'S SECURELY IN THE MOUNTAIN.
KRK
WELL, SIR, THERE'S A PROBLEM.
KRRRK
THIS POWER INHIBITOR CHAIR IS AN ADAMANTIUM/VIBRANIUM COMPOSITE.

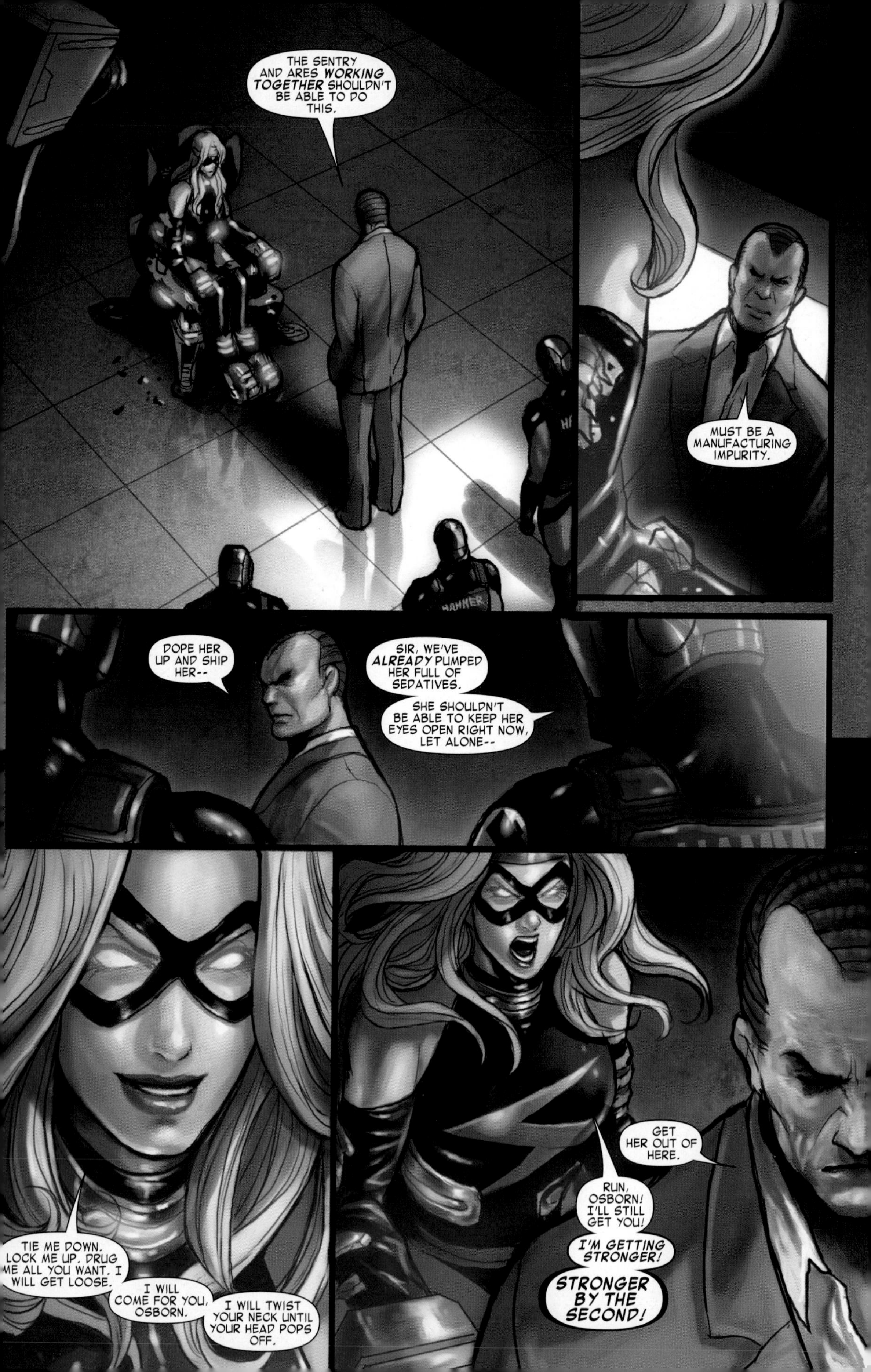

THE SENTRY AND ARES WORKING TOGETHER SHOULDN'T BE ABLE TO DO THIS.
MUST BE A MANUFACTURING IMPURITY.
DOPE HER UP AND SHIP HER--
SIR, WE'VE ALREADY PUMPED HER FULL OF SEDATIVES.
SHE SHOULDN'T BE ABLE TO KEEP HER EYES OPEN RIGHT NOW, LET ALONE--
TIE ME DOWN. LOCK ME UP. DRUG ME ALL YOU WANT. I WILL GET LOOSE.
I WILL COME FOR YOU, OSBORN.
I WILL TWIST YOUR NECK UNTIL YOUR HEAD POPS OFF.
GET HER OUT OF HERE.
RUN, OSBORN! I'LL STILL GET YOU!
I'M GETTING STRONGER!
STRONGER BY THE SECOND!

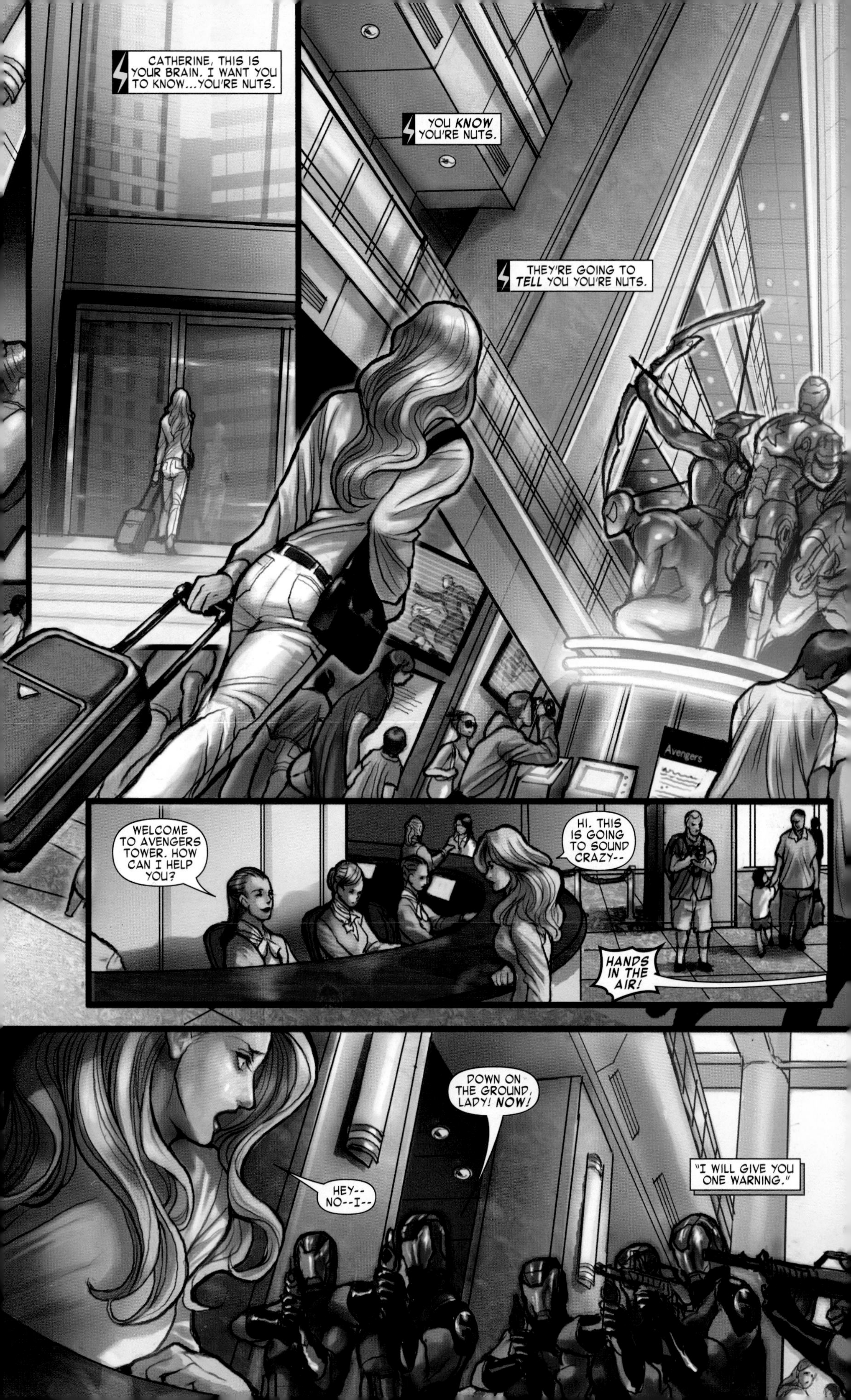
CATHERINE, THIS IS YOUR BRAIN. I WANT YOU TO KNOW...YOU'RE NUTS.
YOU KNOW YOU'RE NUTS.
THEY'RE GOING TO TELL YOU YOU'RE NUTS.
Avengers
WELCOME TO AVENGERS TOWER. HOW CAN I HELP YOU?
HI. THIS IS GOING TO SOUND CRAZY--
HANDS IN THE AIR!
DOWN ON THE GROUND, LADY! NOW!
HEY-- NO--I--
"I WILL GIVE YOU ONE WARNING."

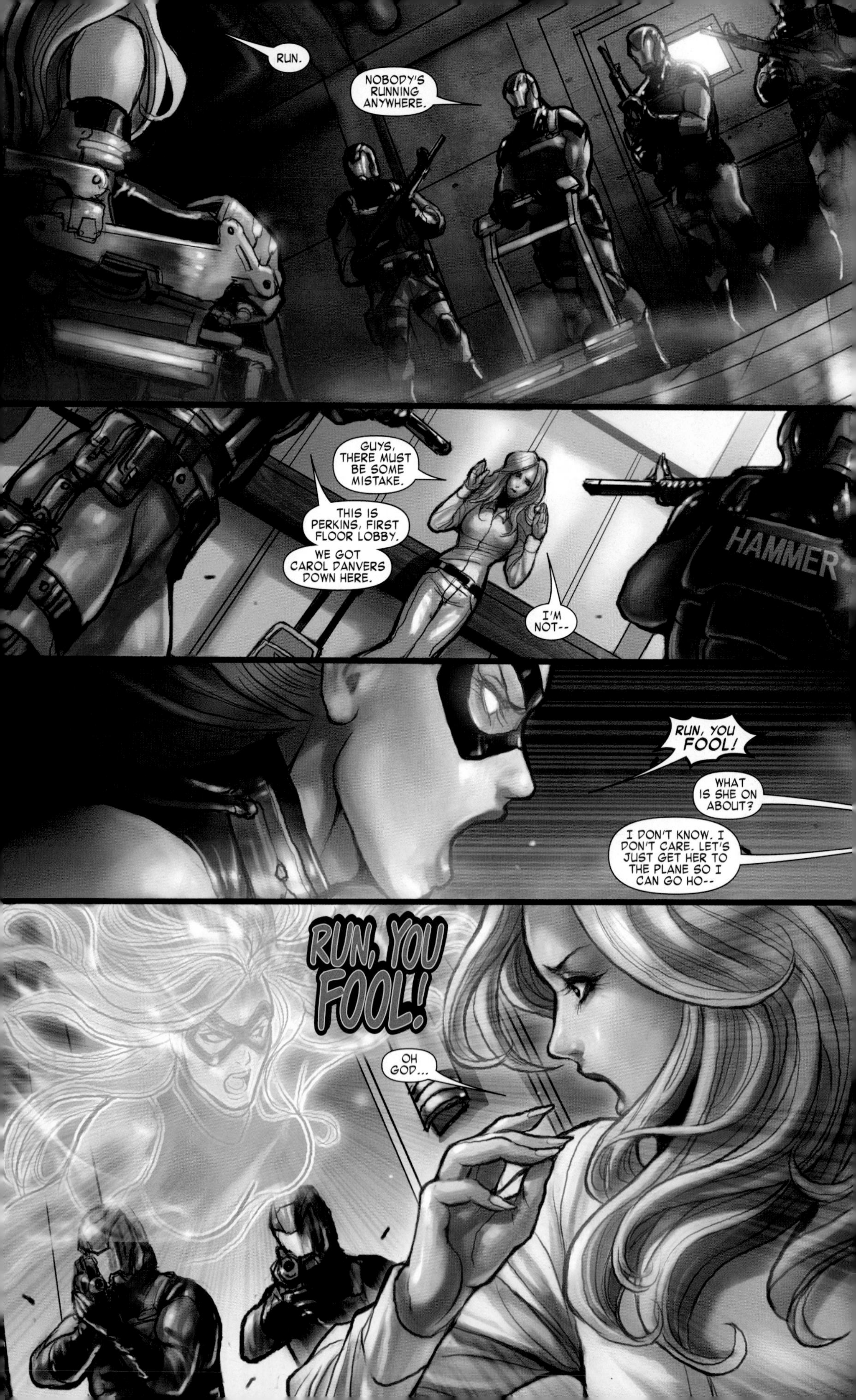
RUN.
NOBODY'S RUNNING ANYWHERE.
GUYS, THERE MUST BE SOME MISTAKE.
THIS IS PERKINS, FIRST FLOOR LOBBY.
WE GOT CAROL DANVERS DOWN HERE.
HAMMER
I'M NOT--
RUN, YOU FOOL!
WHAT IS SHE ON ABOUT?
I DON'T KNOW. I DON'T CARE. LET'S JUST GET HER TO THE PLANE SO I CAN GO HO--
RUN, YOU FOOL!
OH GOD...

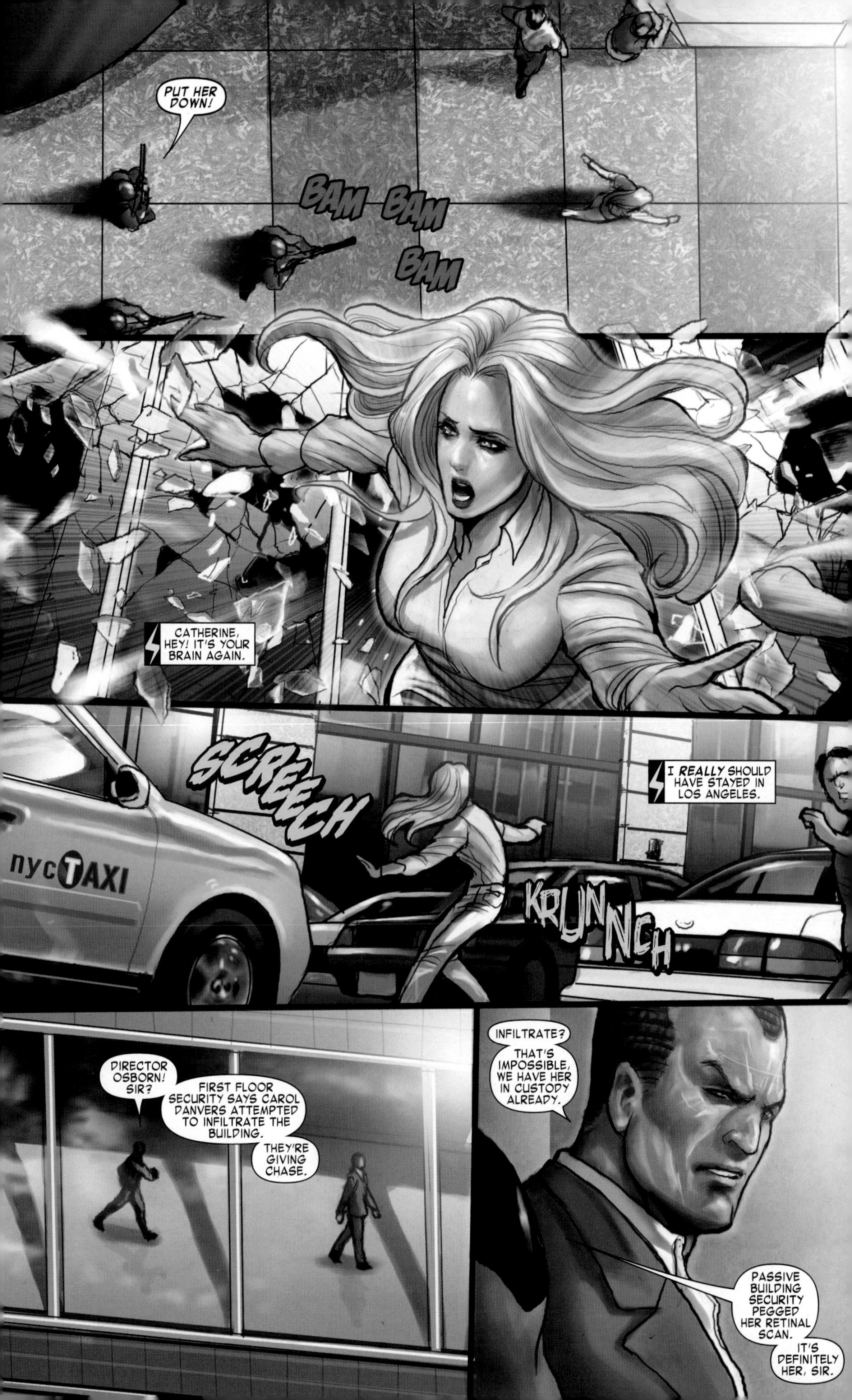
PUT HER DOWN!
BAM BAM
BAM
CATHERINE, HEY! IT'S YOUR BRAIN AGAIN.
SCREEECH
I REALLY SHOULD HAVE STAYED IN LOS ANGELES.
nycTAXI
KRUNNCH
DIRECTOR OSBORN! SIR?
FIRST FLOOR SECURITY SAYS CAROL DANVERS ATTEMPTED TO INFILTRATE THE BUILDING.
THEY'RE GIVING CHASE.
INFILTRATE?
THAT'S IMPOSSIBLE, WE HAVE HER IN CUSTODY ALREADY.
PASSIVE BUILDING SECURITY PEGGED HER RETINAL SCAN.
IT'S DEFINITELY HER, SIR.

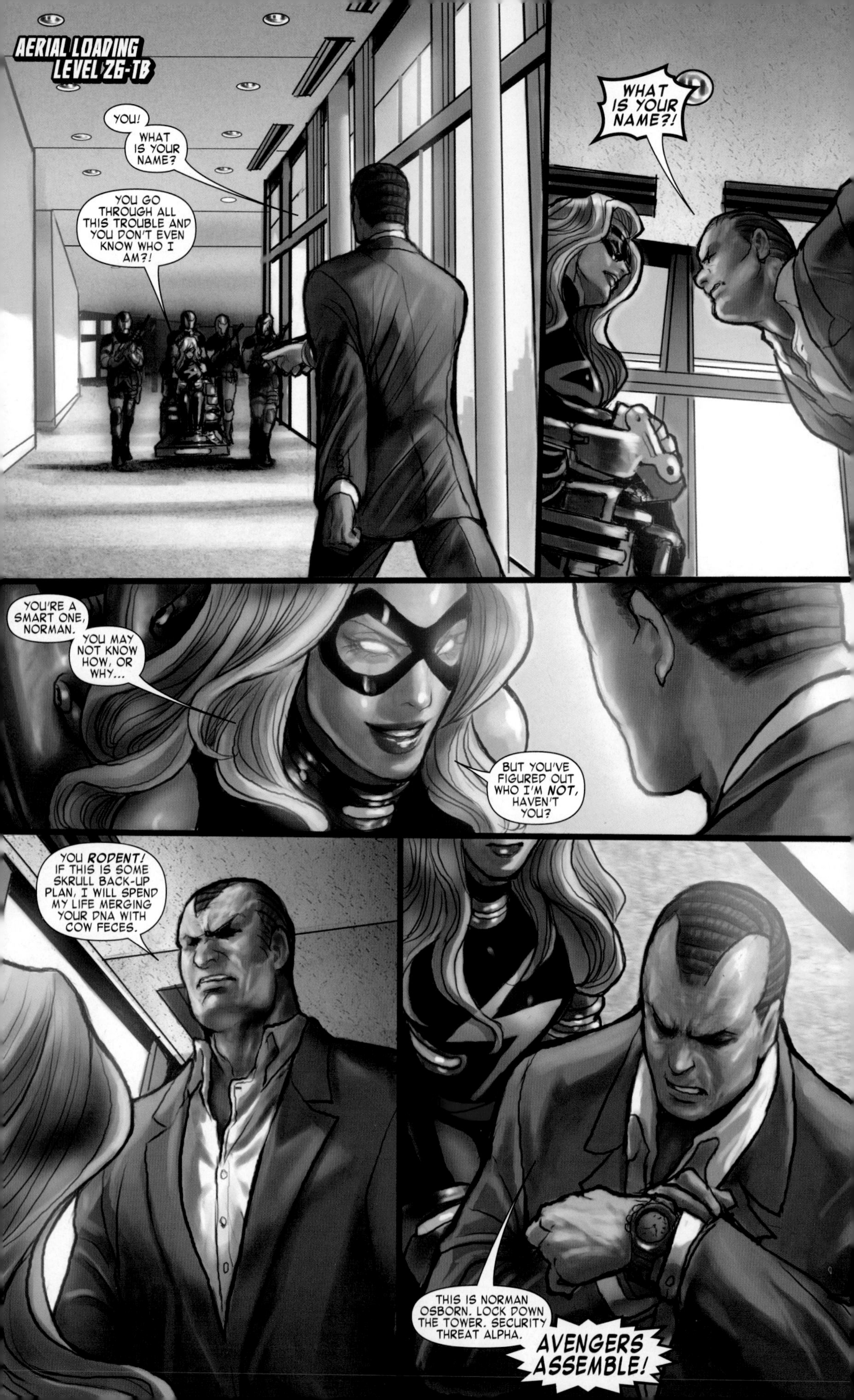
AERIAL LOADING LEVEL 26-TB
YOU! WHAT IS YOUR NAME?
YOU GO THROUGH ALL THIS TROUBLE AND YOU DON'T EVEN KNOW WHO I AM?!
WHAT IS YOUR NAME?!
YOU'RE A SMART ONE, NORMAN.
YOU MAY NOT KNOW HOW, OR WHY...
BUT YOU'VE FIGURED OUT WHO I'M NOT, HAVEN'T YOU?
YOU RODENT! IF THIS IS SOME SKRULL BACK-UP PLAN, I WILL SPEND MY LIFE MERGING YOUR DNA WITH COW FECES.
THIS IS NORMAN OSBORN. LOCK DOWN THE TOWER. SECURITY THREAT ALPHA.
AVENGERS ASSEMBLE!

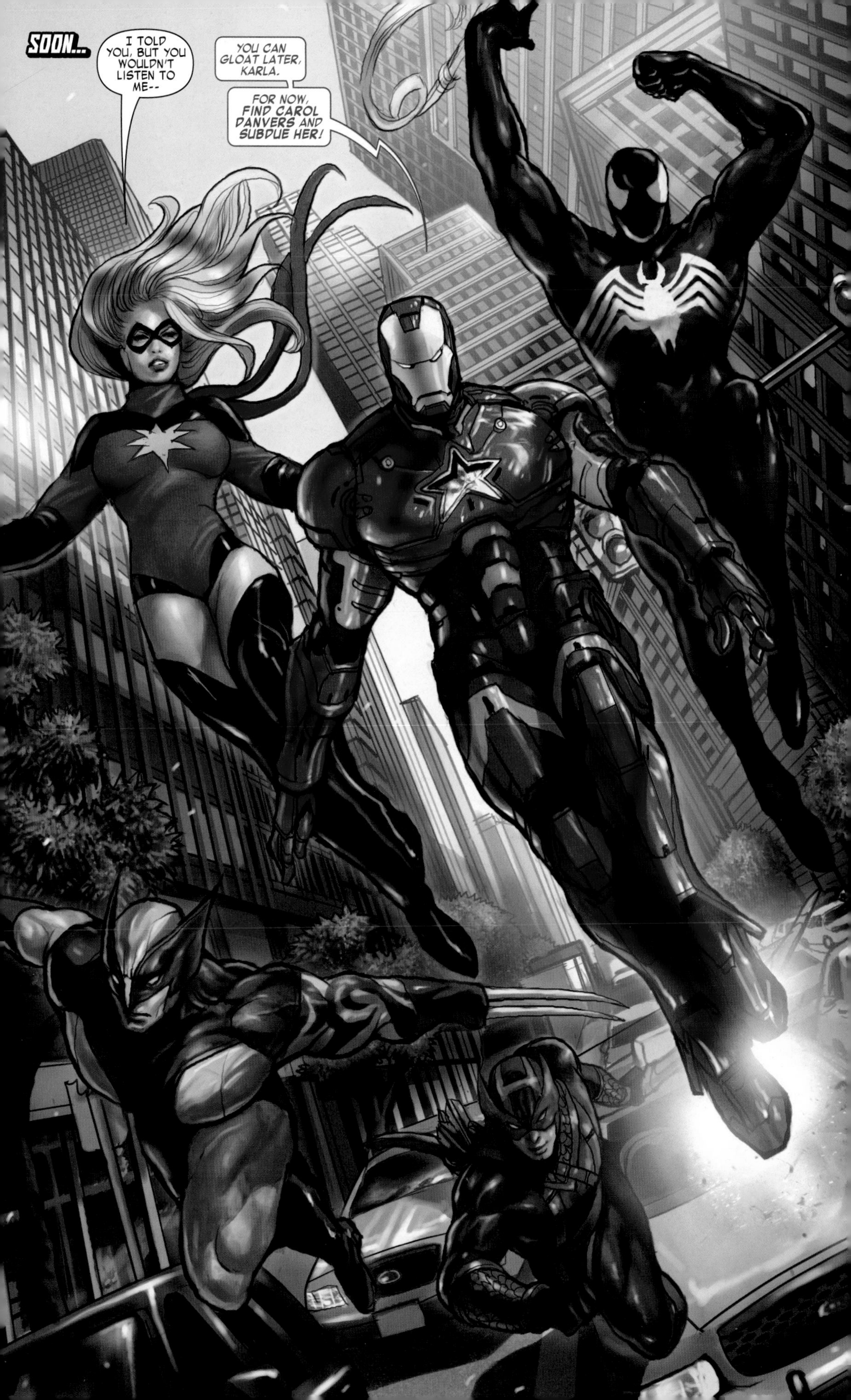
SOON...
I TOLD YOU, BUT YOU WOULDN'T LISTEN TO ME--
YOU CAN GLOAT LATER, KARLA.
FOR NOW, FIND CAROL DANVERS AND SUBDUE HER!

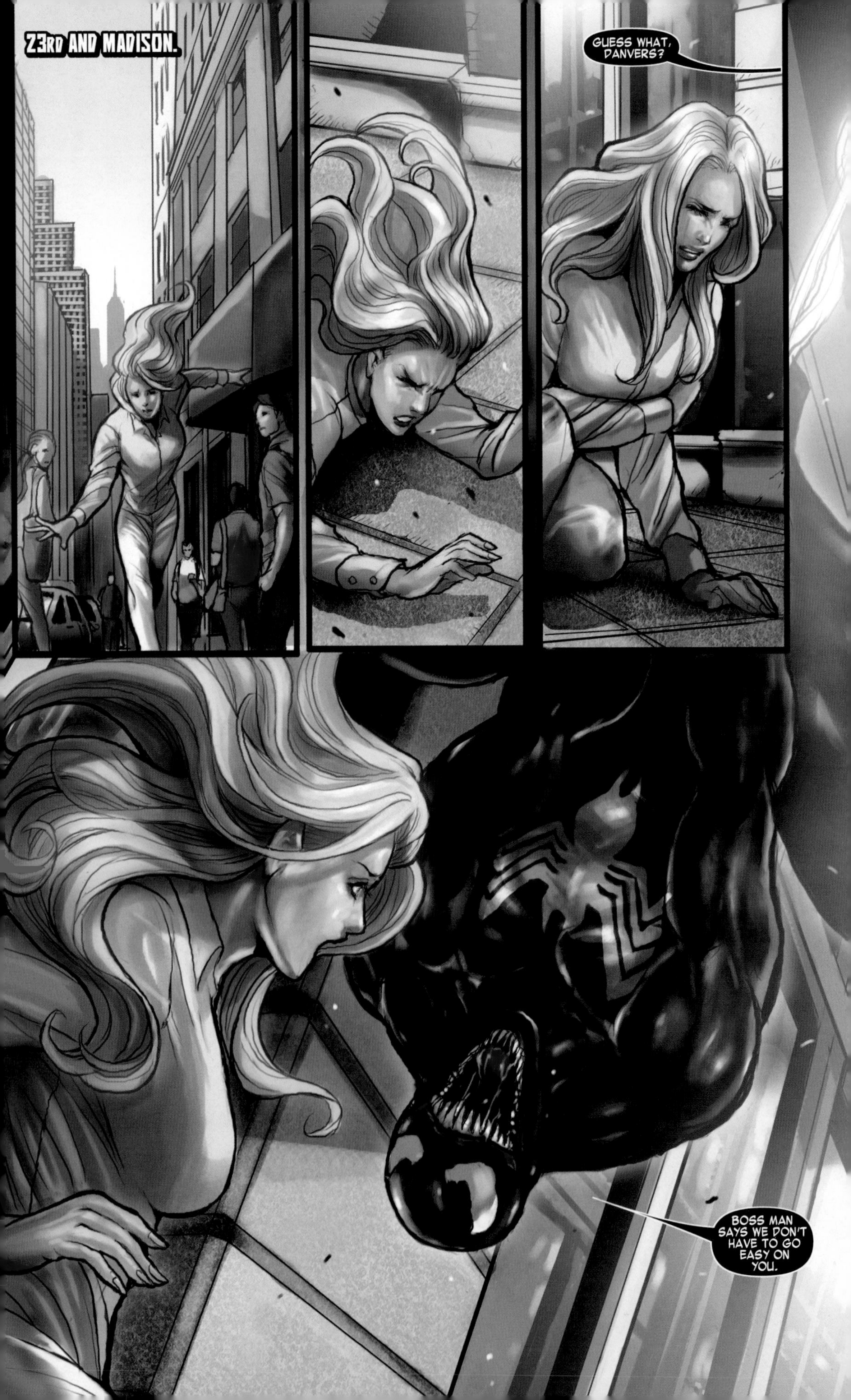
23rd AND MADISON.
GUESS WHAT, DANVERS?
BOSS MAN SAYS WE DON'T HAVE TO GO EASY ON YOU.

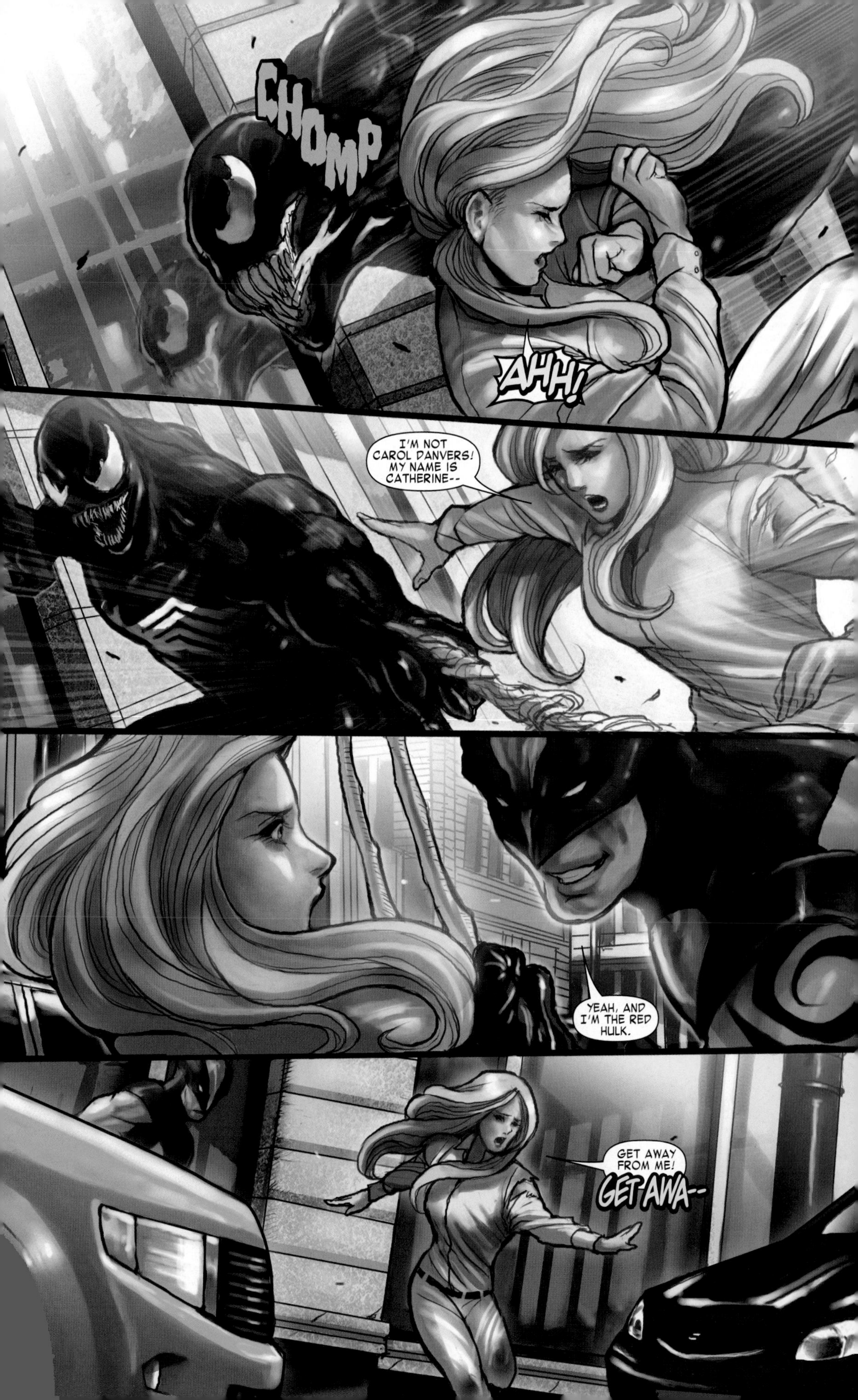
CHOMP
AHH!
I'M NOT CAROL DANVERS! MY NAME IS CATHERINE--
YEAH, AND I'M THE RED HULK.
GET AWAY FROM ME!
GET AWA--

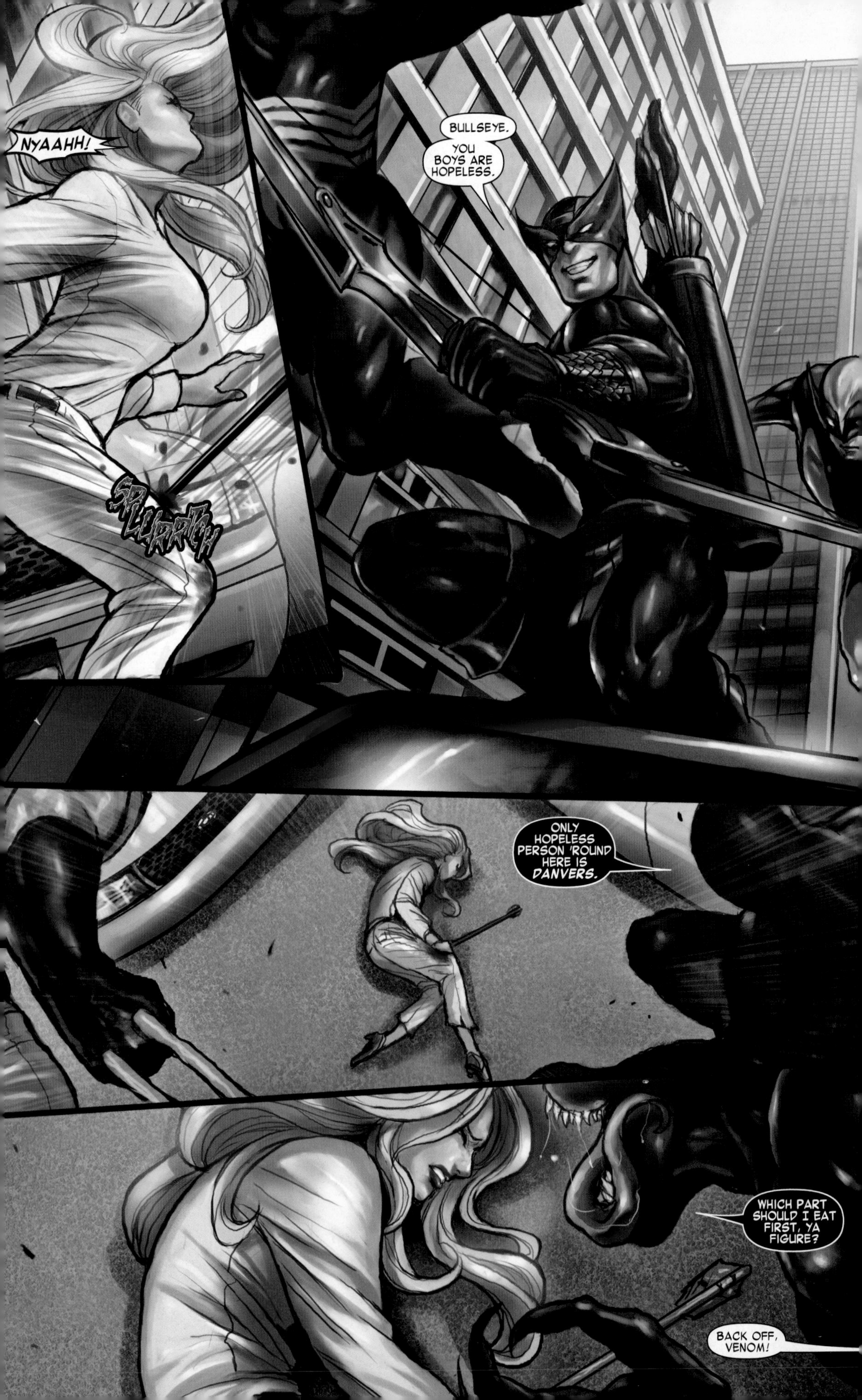
NYAAHH!
SPLURRTCH
BULLSEYE.
YOU BOYS ARE HOPELESS.
ONLY HOPELESS PERSON 'ROUND HERE IS DANVERS.
WHICH PART SHOULD I EAT FIRST, YA FIGURE?
BACK OFF, VENOM!

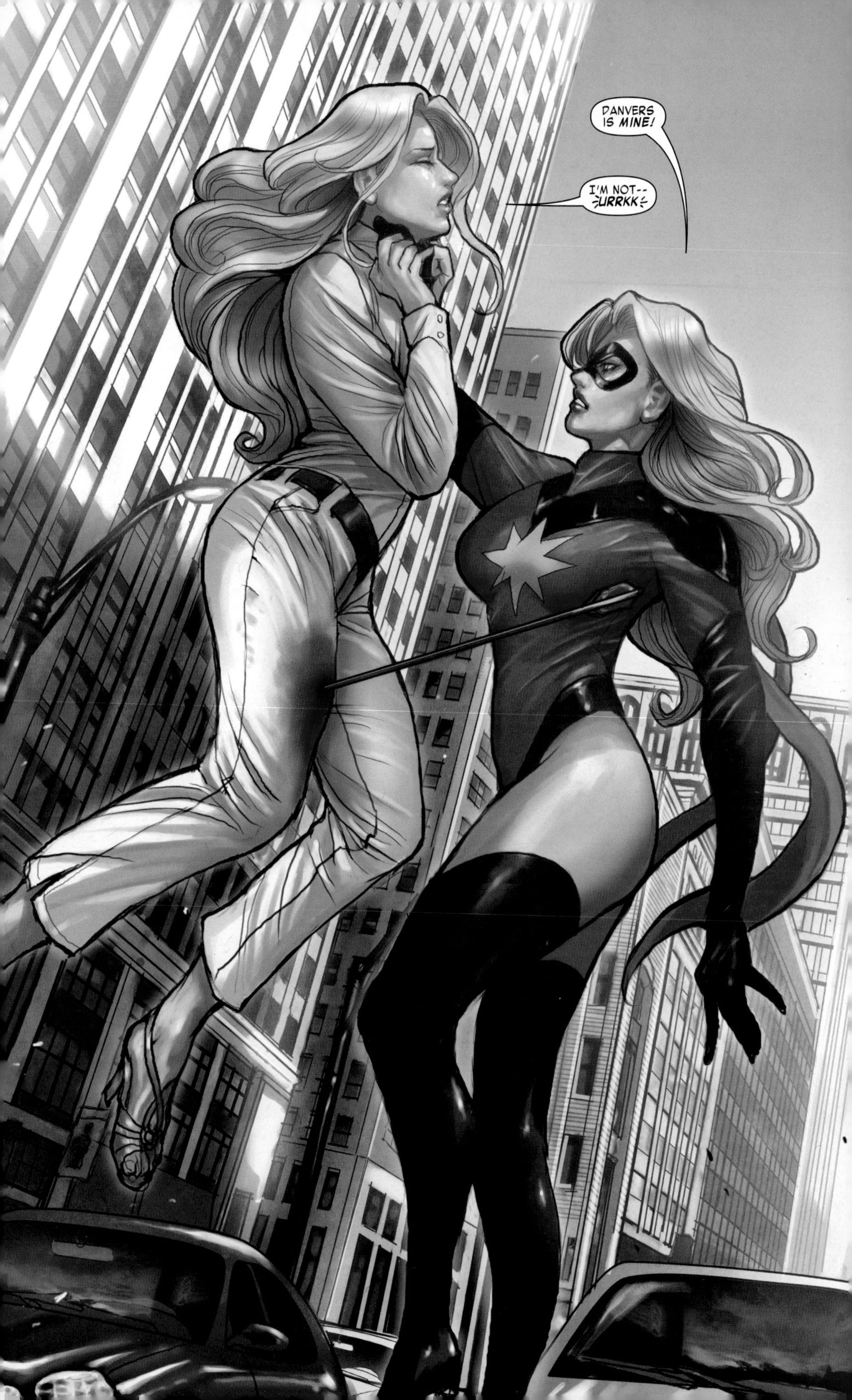
DANVERS IS MINE!
I'M NOT-- URRKK

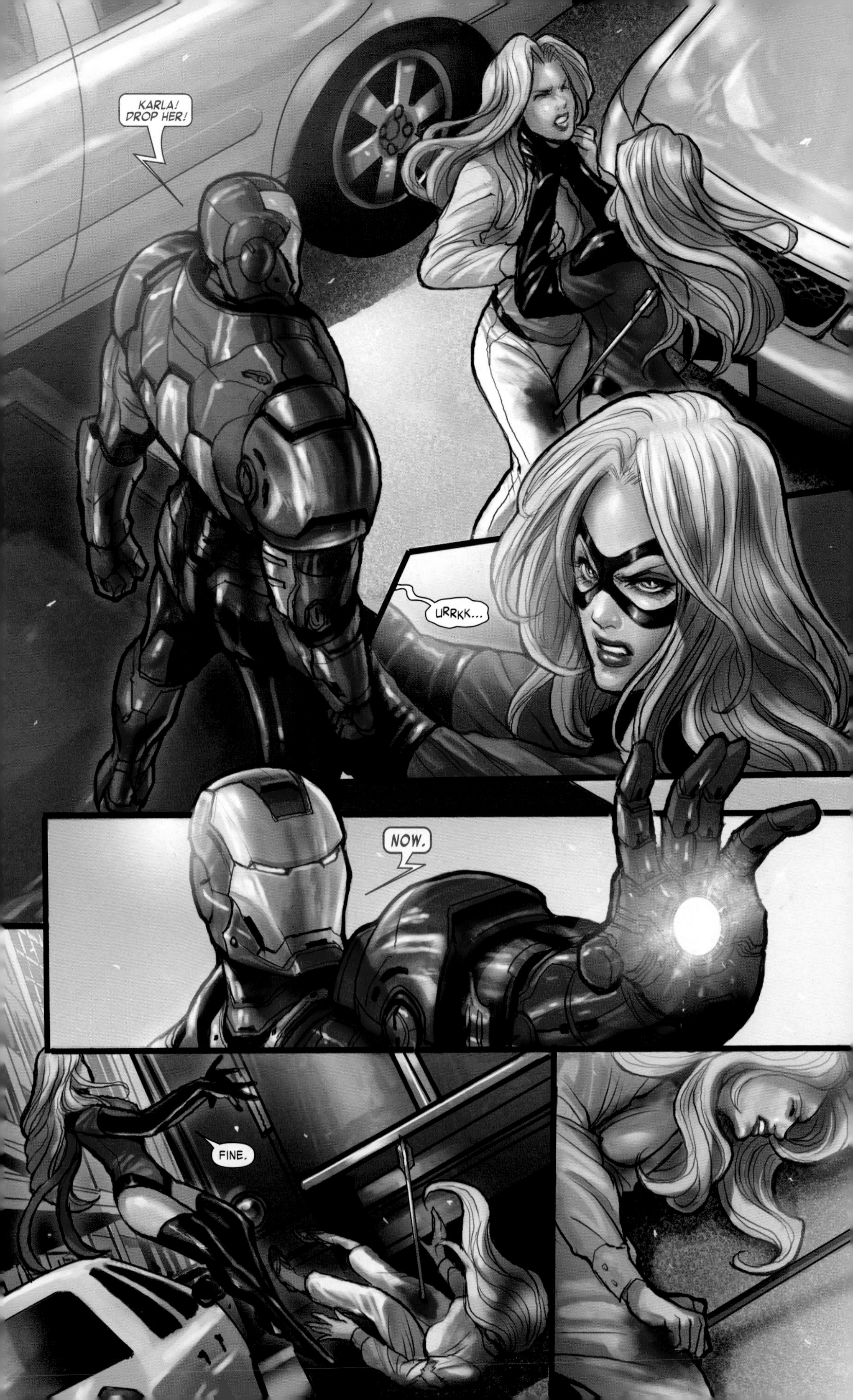
KARLA! DROP HER!
URRKK...
NOW.
FINE.

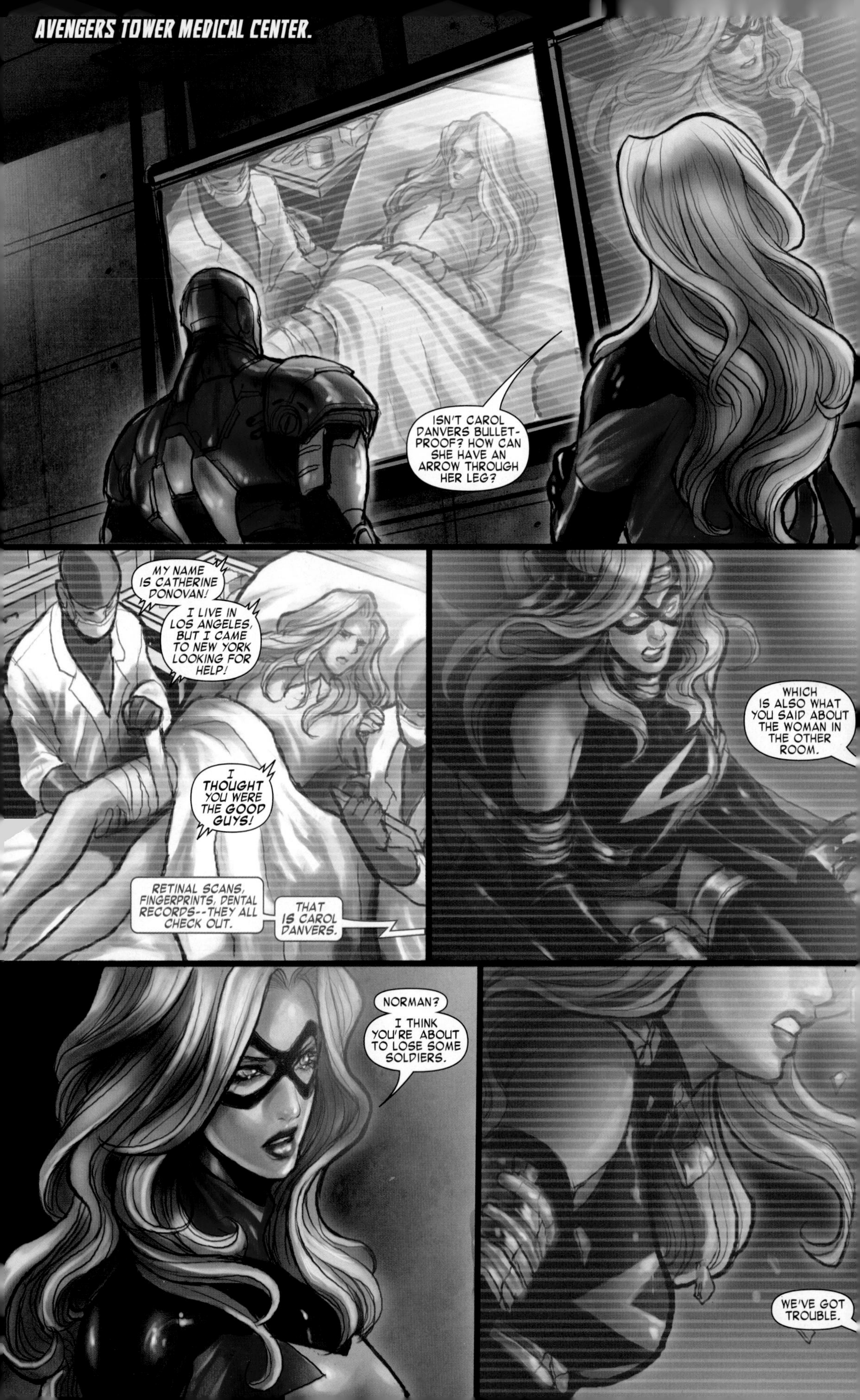

AVENGERS TOWER MEDICAL CENTER.
ISN'T CAROL DANVERS BULLET-PROOF? HOW CAN SHE HAVE AN ARROW THROUGH HER LEG?
MY NAME IS CATHERINE DONOVAN!
I LIVE IN LOS ANGELES, BUT I CAME TO NEW YORK LOOKING FOR HELP!
I THOUGHT YOU WERE THE GOOD GUYS!
RETINAL SCANS, FINGERPRINTS, DENTAL RECORDS--THEY ALL CHECK OUT.
THAT IS CAROL DANVERS.
WHICH IS ALSO WHAT YOU SAID ABOUT THE WOMAN IN THE OTHER ROOM.
NORMAN?
I THINK YOU'RE ABOUT TO LOSE SOME SOLDIERS.
WE'VE GOT TROUBLE.

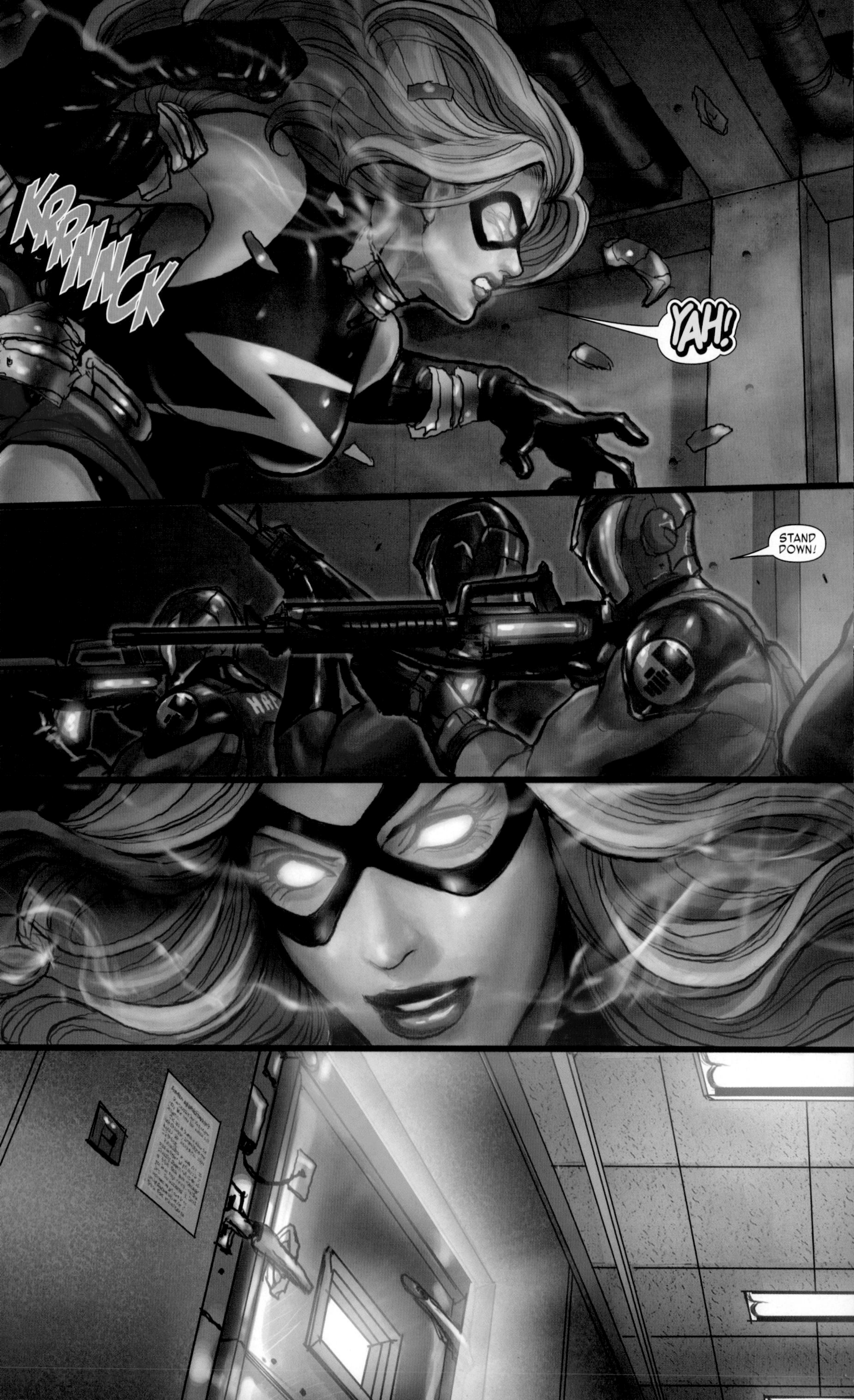
KRRNNCK
YAH!
STAND DOWN!

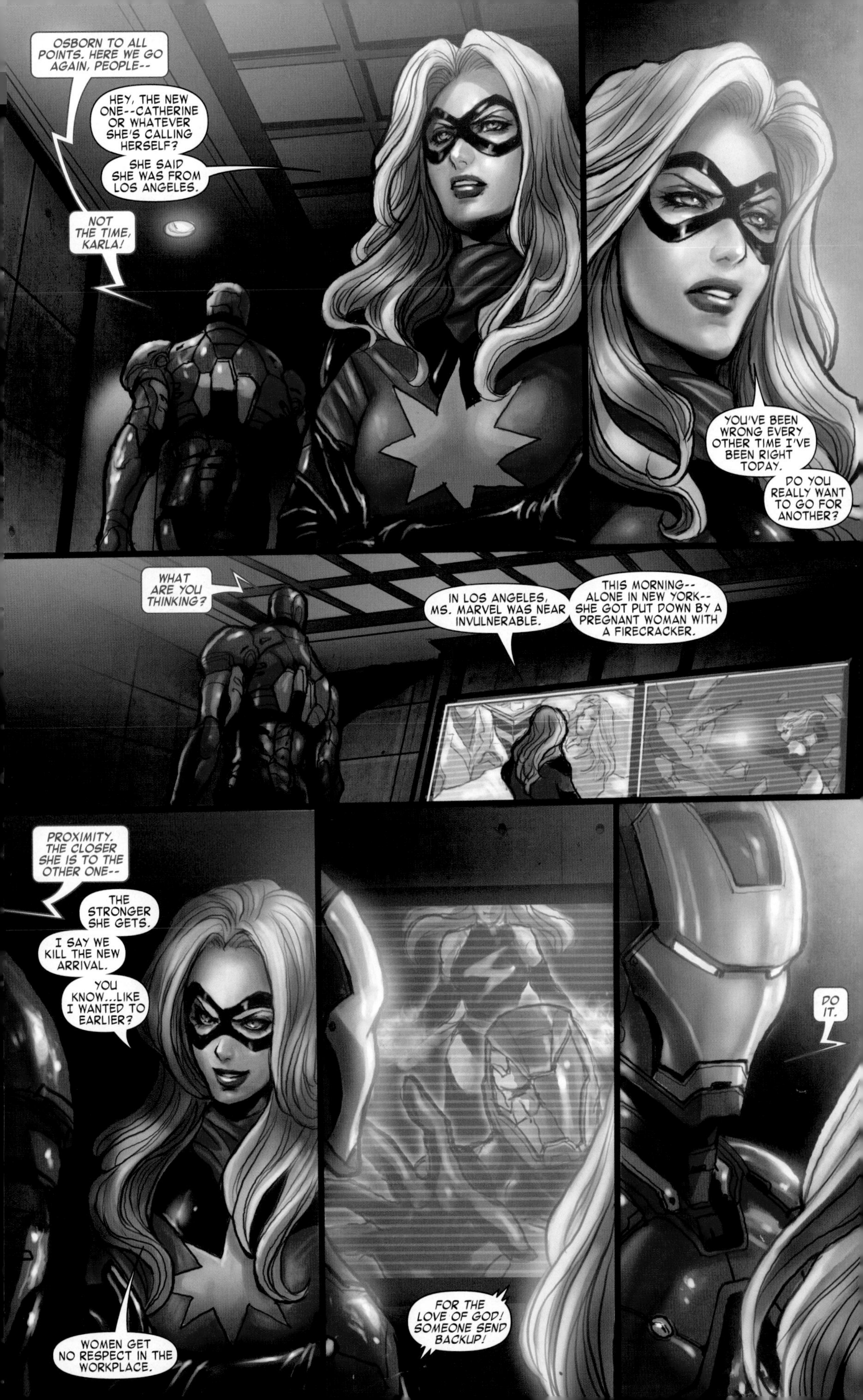
OSBORN TO ALL POINTS. HERE WE GO AGAIN, PEOPLE--
HEY, THE NEW ONE--CATHERINE OR WHATEVER SHE'S CALLING HERSELF?
SHE SAID SHE WAS FROM LOS ANGELES.
NOT THE TIME, KARLA!
YOU'VE BEEN WRONG EVERY OTHER TIME I'VE BEEN RIGHT TODAY.
DO YOU REALLY WANT TO GO FOR ANOTHER?
WHAT ARE YOU THINKING?
IN LOS ANGELES, MS. MARVEL WAS NEAR INVULNERABLE.
THIS MORNING--ALONE IN NEW YORK--SHE GOT PUT DOWN BY A PREGNANT WOMAN WITH A FIRECRACKER.
PROXIMITY. THE CLOSER SHE IS TO THE OTHER ONE--
THE STRONGER SHE GETS.
I SAY WE KILL THE NEW ARRIVAL.
YOU KNOW...LIKE I WANTED TO EARLIER?
WOMEN GET NO RESPECT IN THE WORKPLACE.
FOR THE LOVE OF GOD! SOMEONE SEND BACKUP!
DO IT.

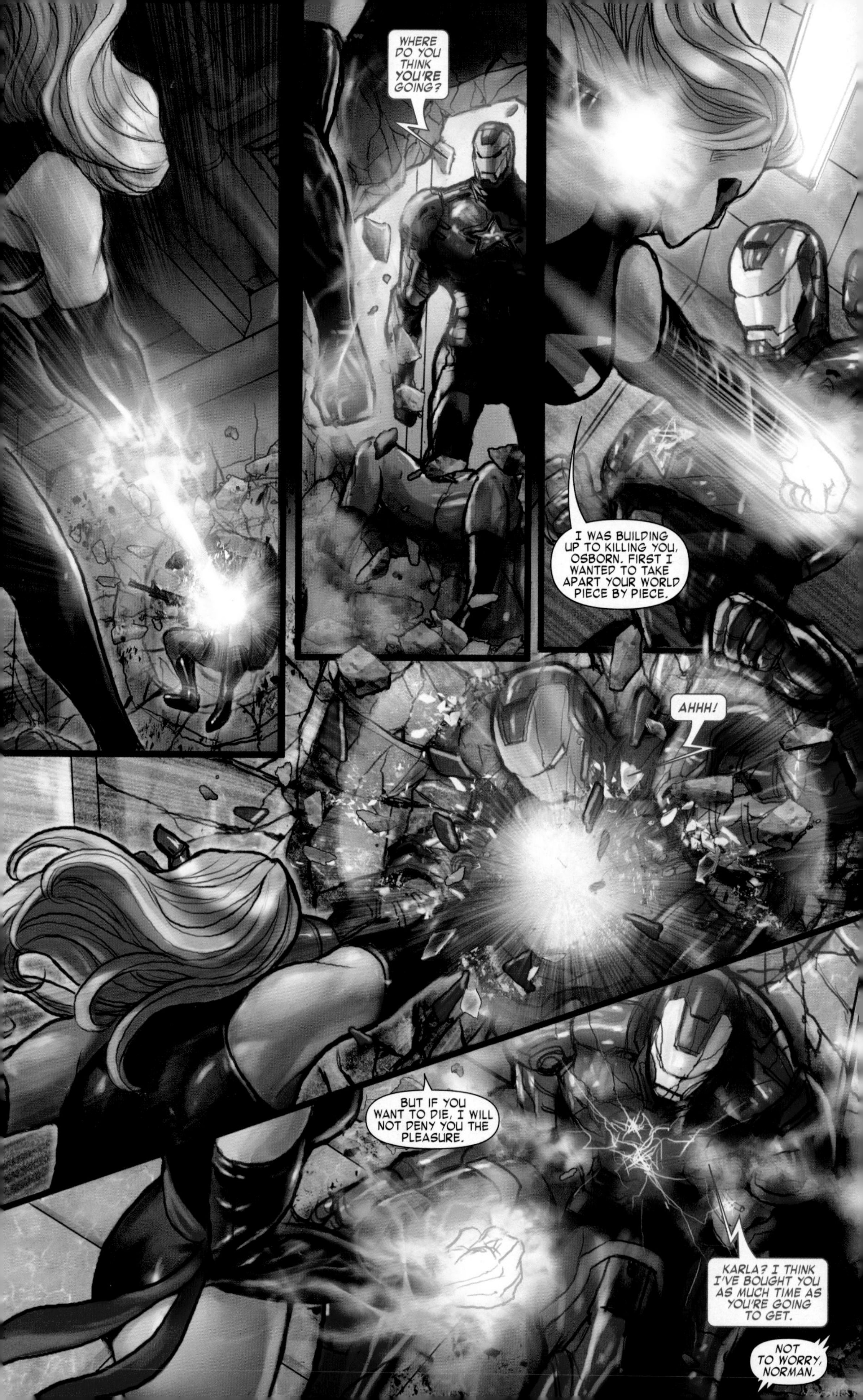
WHERE DO YOU THINK YOU'RE GOING?
I WAS BUILDING UP TO KILLING YOU, OSBORN. FIRST I WANTED TO TAKE APART YOUR WORLD PIECE BY PIECE.
AHHH!
BUT IF YOU WANT TO DIE, I WILL NOT DENY YOU THE PLEASURE.
KARLA? I THINK I'VE BOUGHT YOU AS MUCH TIME AS YOU'RE GOING TO GET.
NOT TO WORRY, NORMAN.

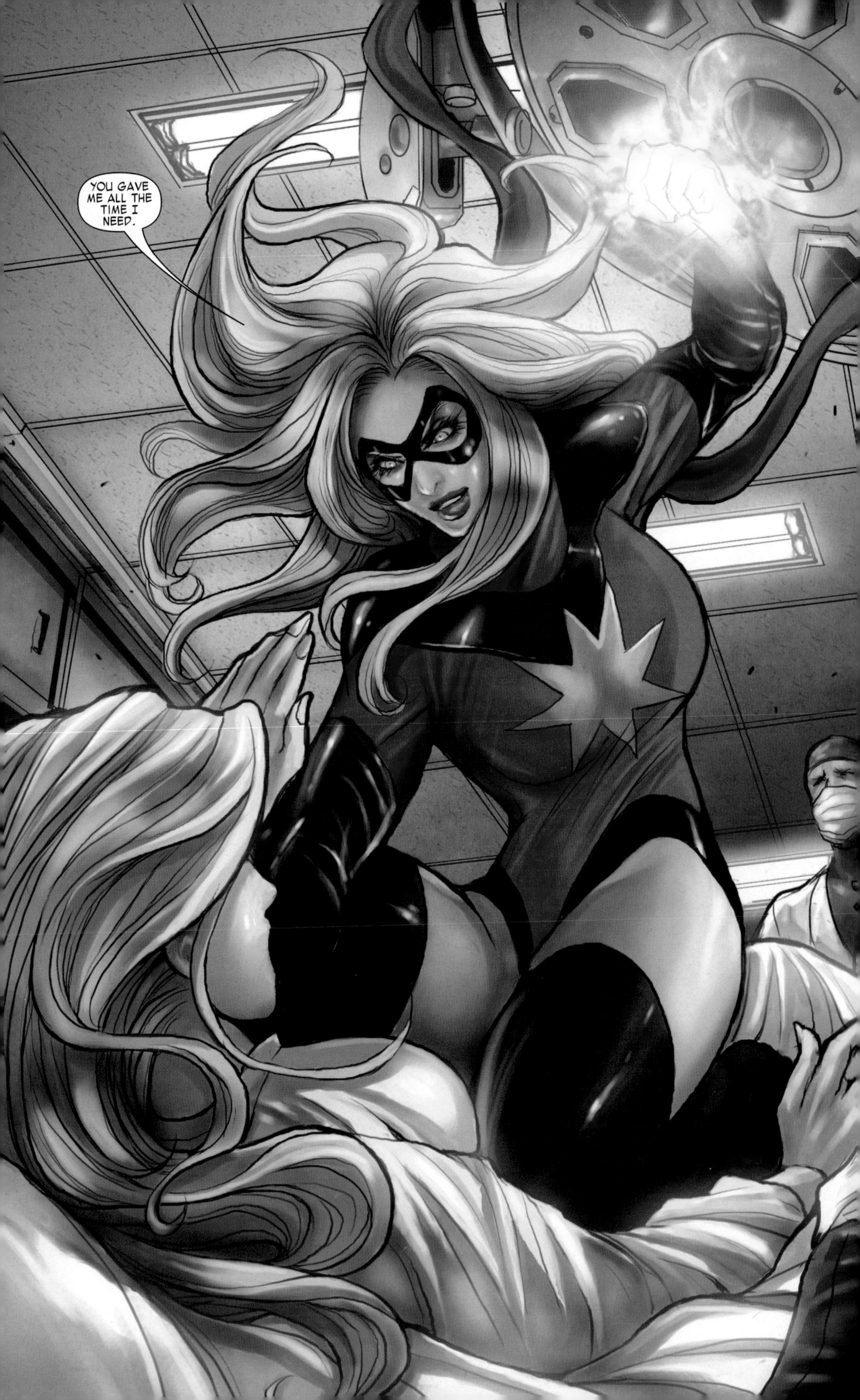
YOU GAVE ME ALL THE TIME I NEED.

#45

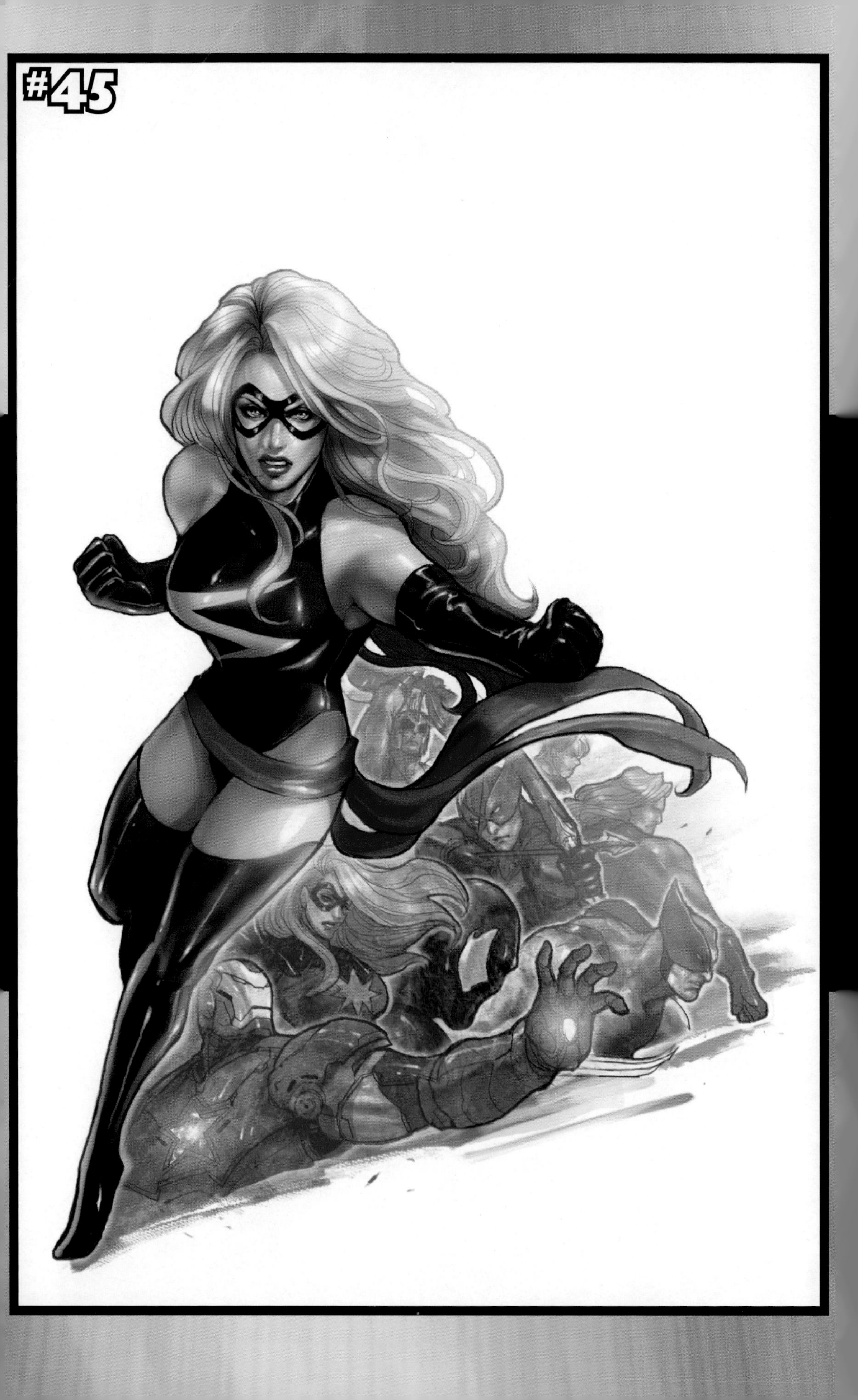

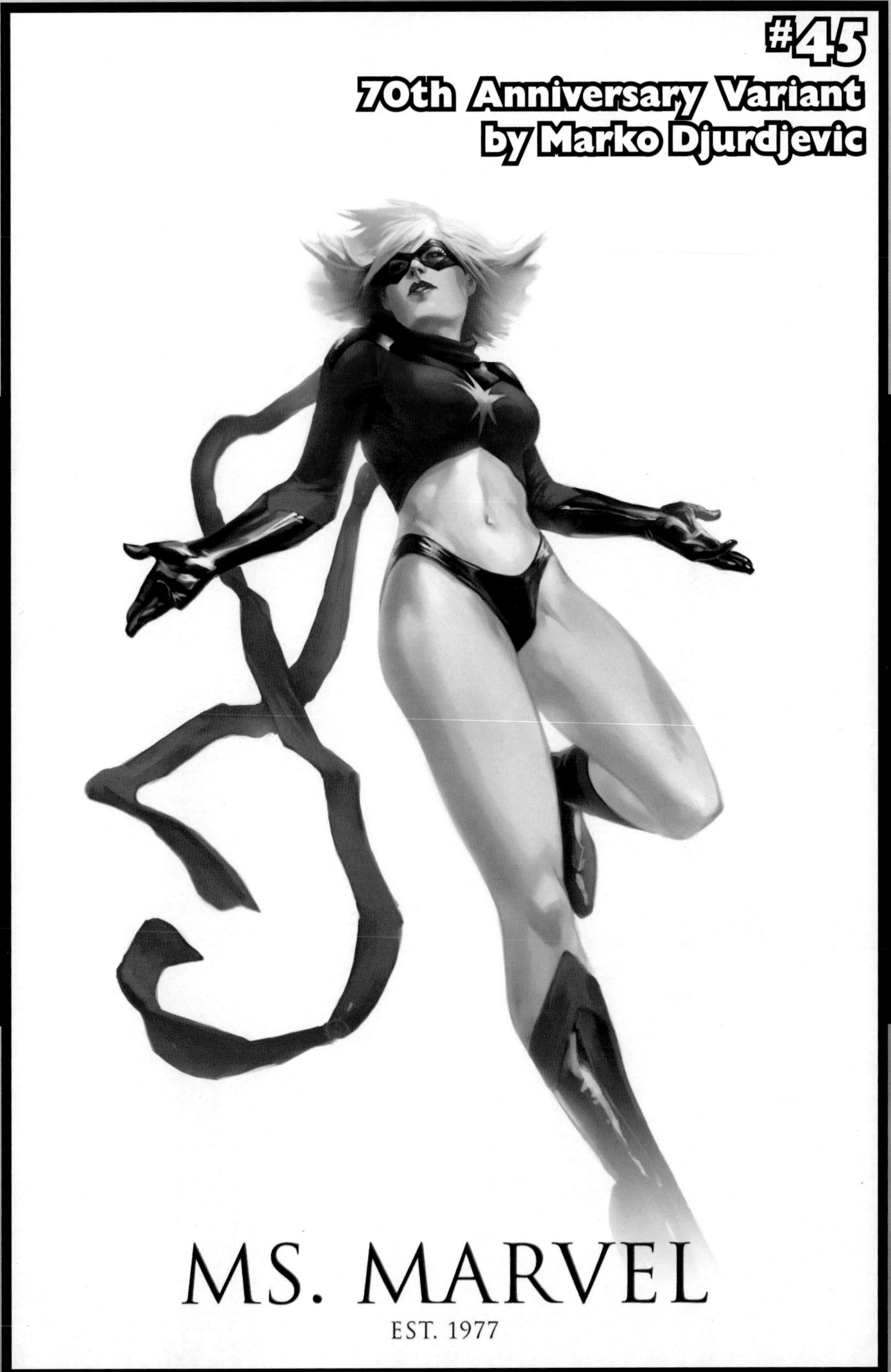
#45
70th Anniversary Variant
by Marko Djurdjevic
MS. MARVEL
EST. 1977

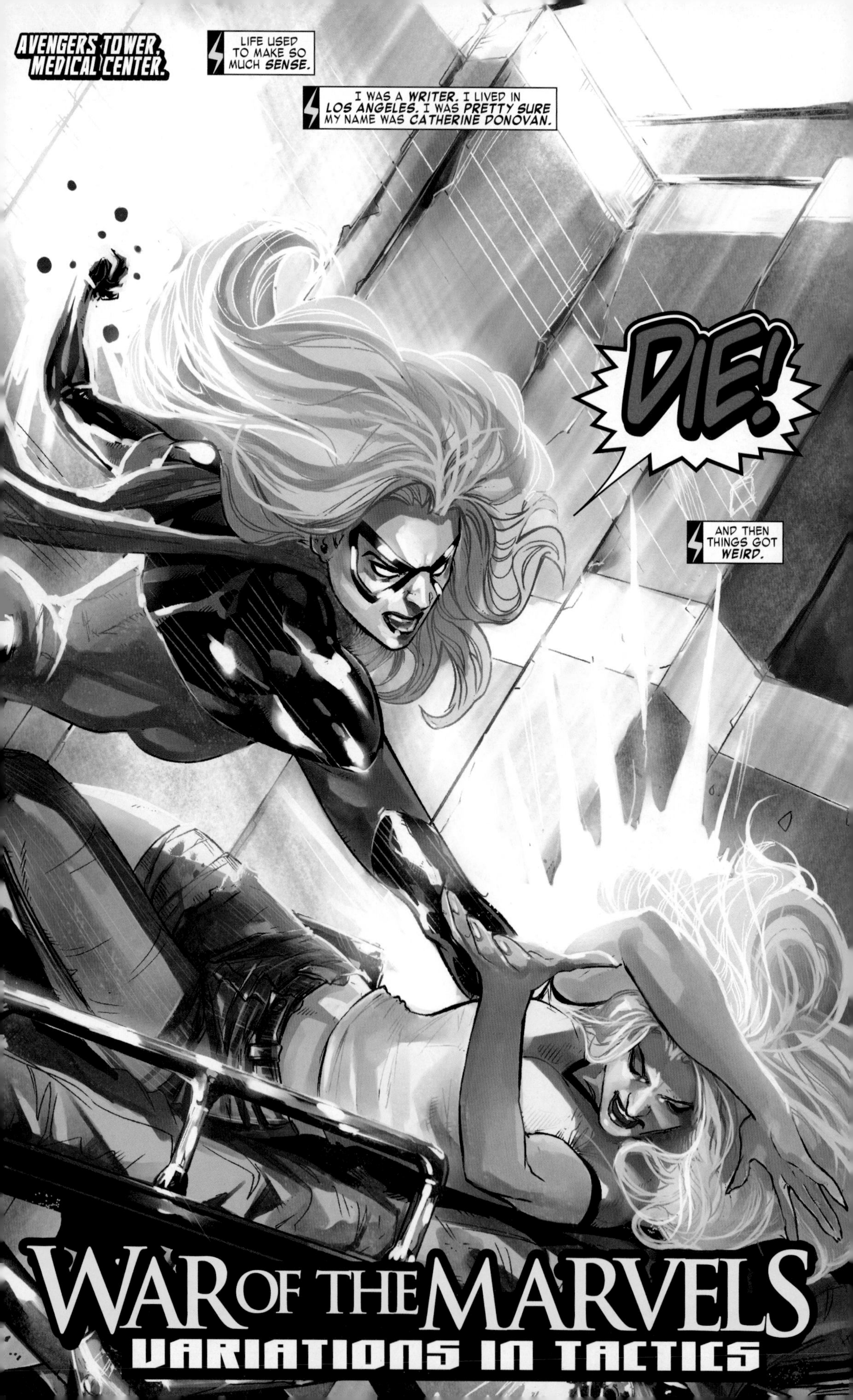
AVENGERS TOWER, MEDICAL CENTER.
LIFE USED TO MAKE SO MUCH SENSE.
I WAS A WRITER. I LIVED IN LOS ANGELES. I WAS PRETTY SURE MY NAME WAS CATHERINE DONOVAN.
DIE!
AND THEN THINGS GOT WEIRD.
WAR OF THE MARVELS
VARIATIONS IN TACTICS

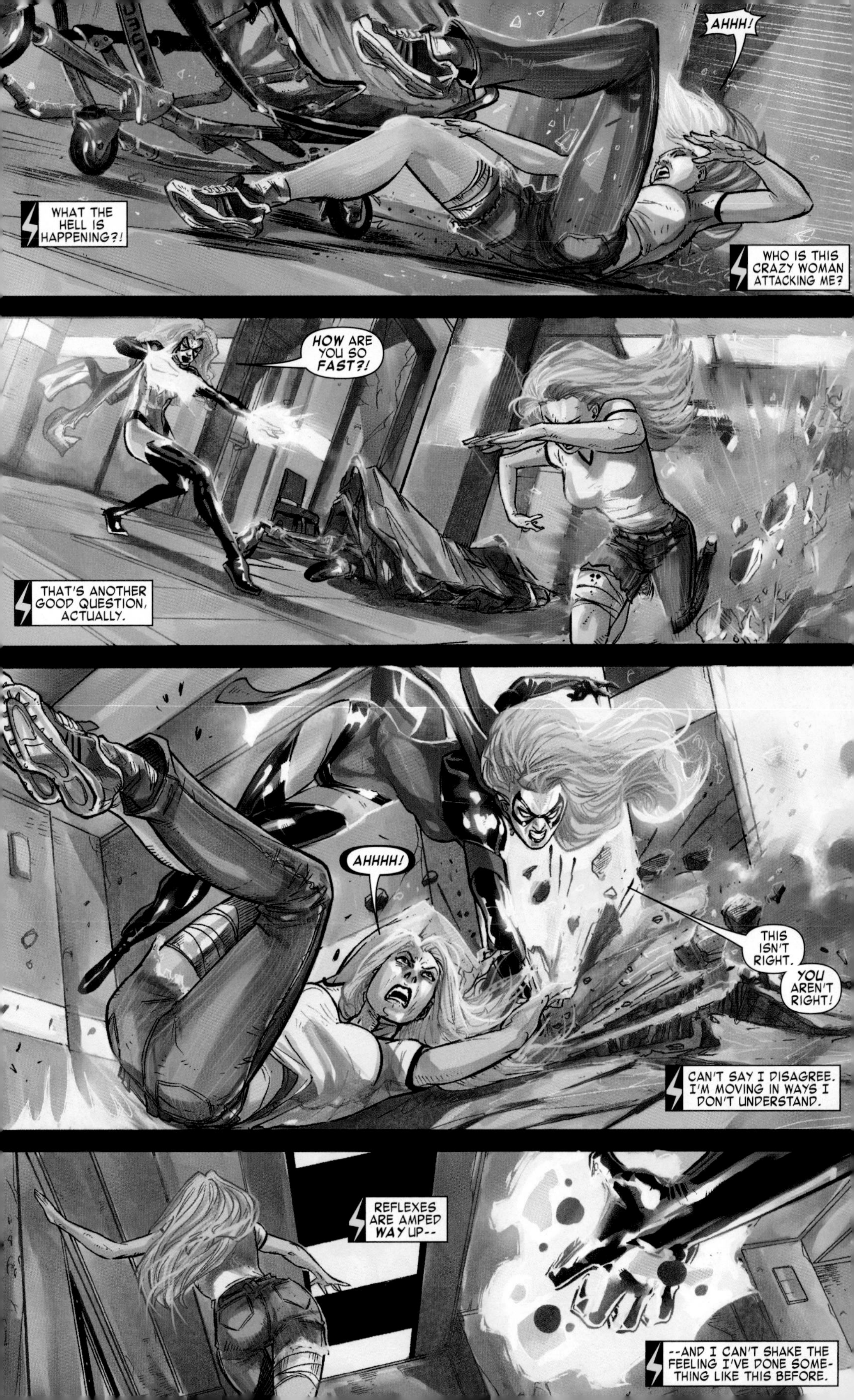
AHHH!
WHAT THE HELL IS HAPPENING?!
WHO IS THIS CRAZY WOMAN ATTACKING ME?
HOW ARE YOU SO FAST?!
THAT'S ANOTHER GOOD QUESTION, ACTUALLY.
AHHHH!
THIS ISN'T RIGHT.
YOU AREN'T RIGHT!
CAN'T SAY I DISAGREE. I'M MOVING IN WAYS I DON'T UNDERSTAND.
REFLEXES ARE AMPED WAY UP--
--AND I CAN'T SHAKE THE FEELING I'VE DONE SOMETHING LIKE THIS BEFORE.

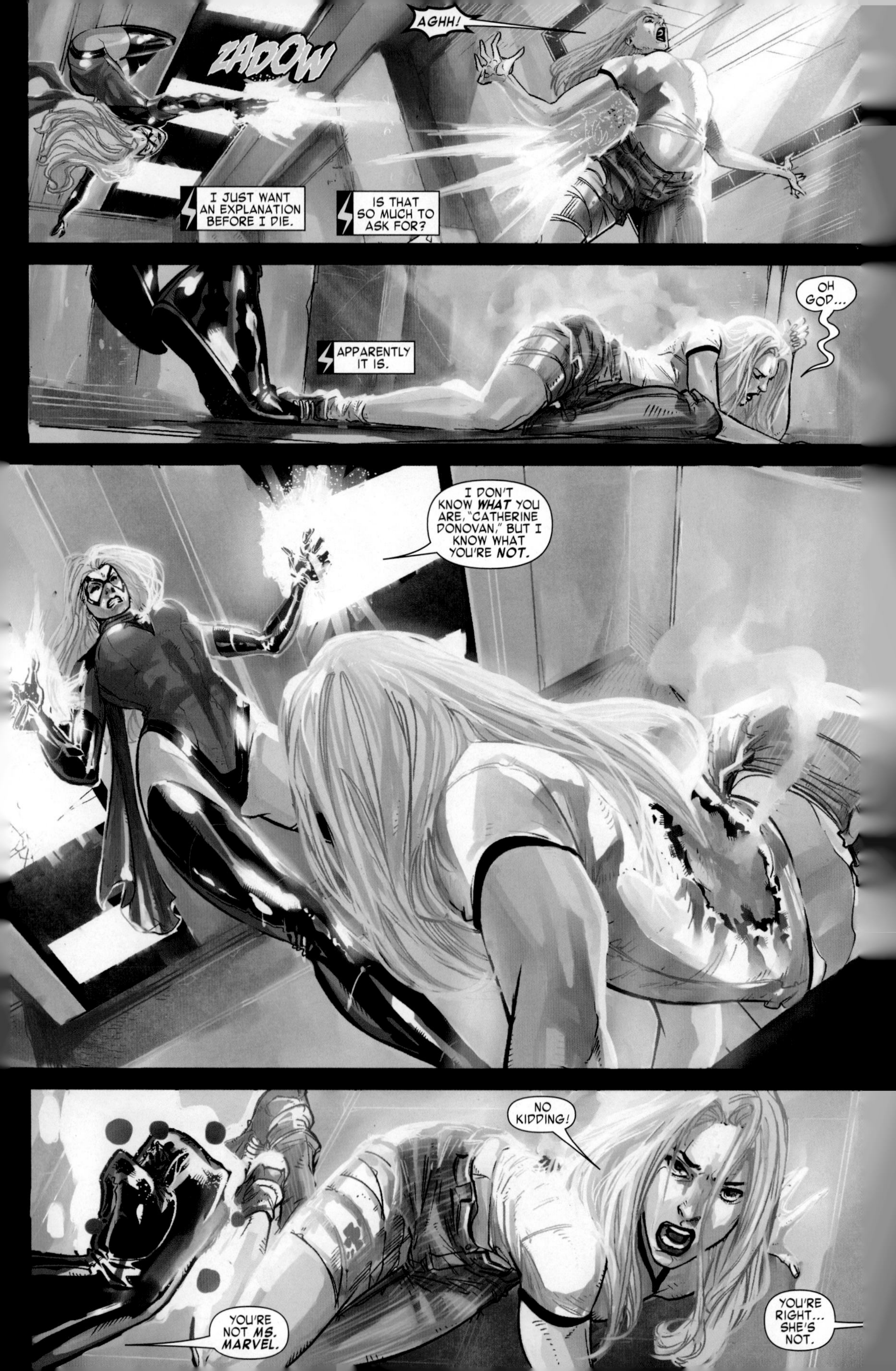
ZADOW
AGHH!
I JUST WANT AN EXPLANATION BEFORE I DIE.
IS THAT SO MUCH TO ASK FOR?
APPARENTLY IT IS.
OH GOD...
I DON'T KNOW WHAT YOU ARE, "CATHERINE DONOVAN," BUT I KNOW WHAT YOU'RE NOT.
YOU'RE NOT MS. MARVEL.
NO KIDDING!
YOU'RE RIGHT... SHE'S NOT.

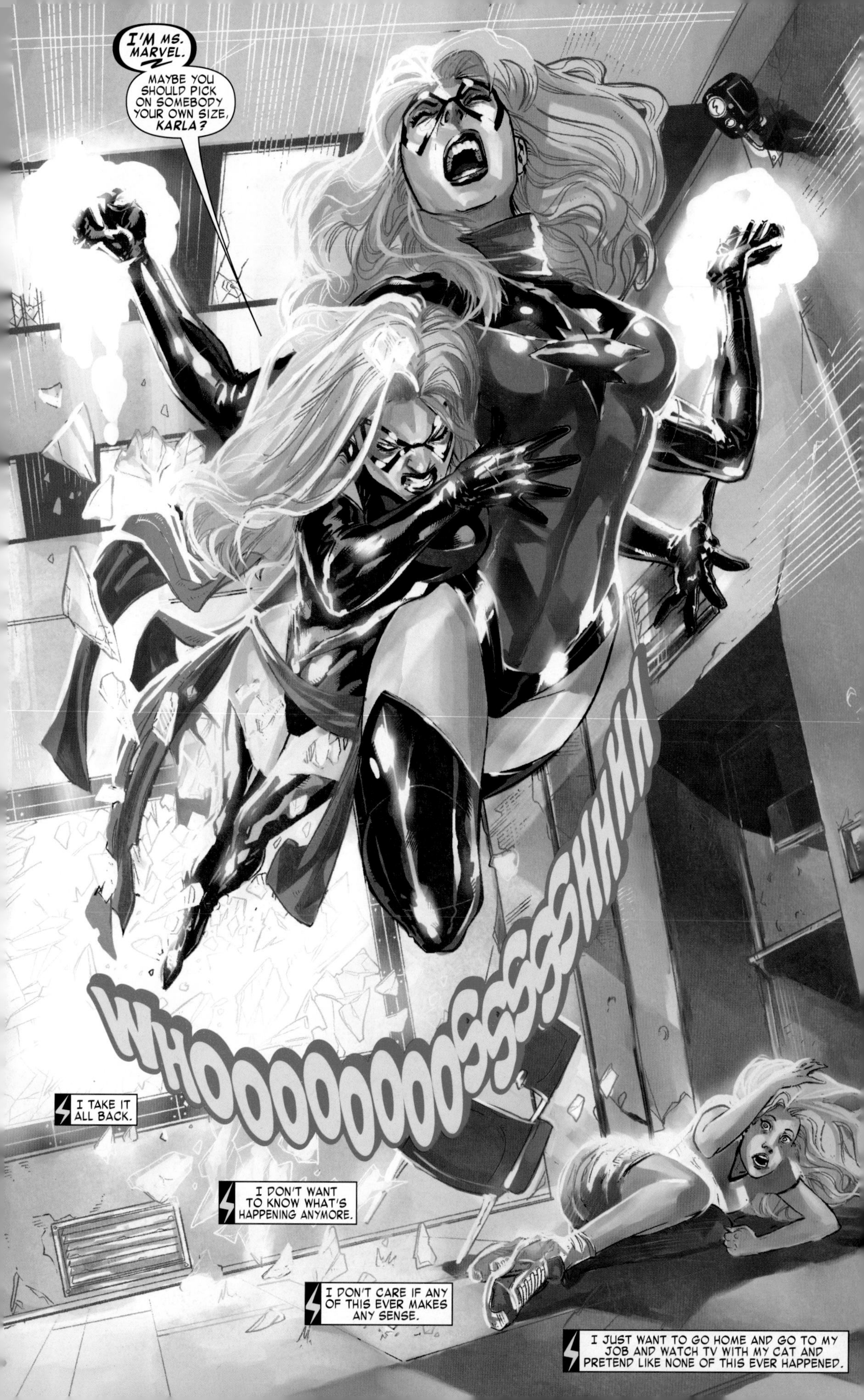
I'M MS. MARVEL.
MAYBE YOU SHOULD PICK ON SOMEBODY YOUR OWN SIZE, KARLA?
WHOOOOOOOOOSSSSHHHH
I TAKE IT ALL BACK.
I DON'T WANT TO KNOW WHAT'S HAPPENING ANYMORE.
I DON'T CARE IF ANY OF THIS EVER MAKES ANY SENSE.
I JUST WANT TO GO HOME AND GO TO MY JOB AND WATCH TV WITH MY CAT AND PRETEND LIKE NONE OF THIS EVER HAPPENED.

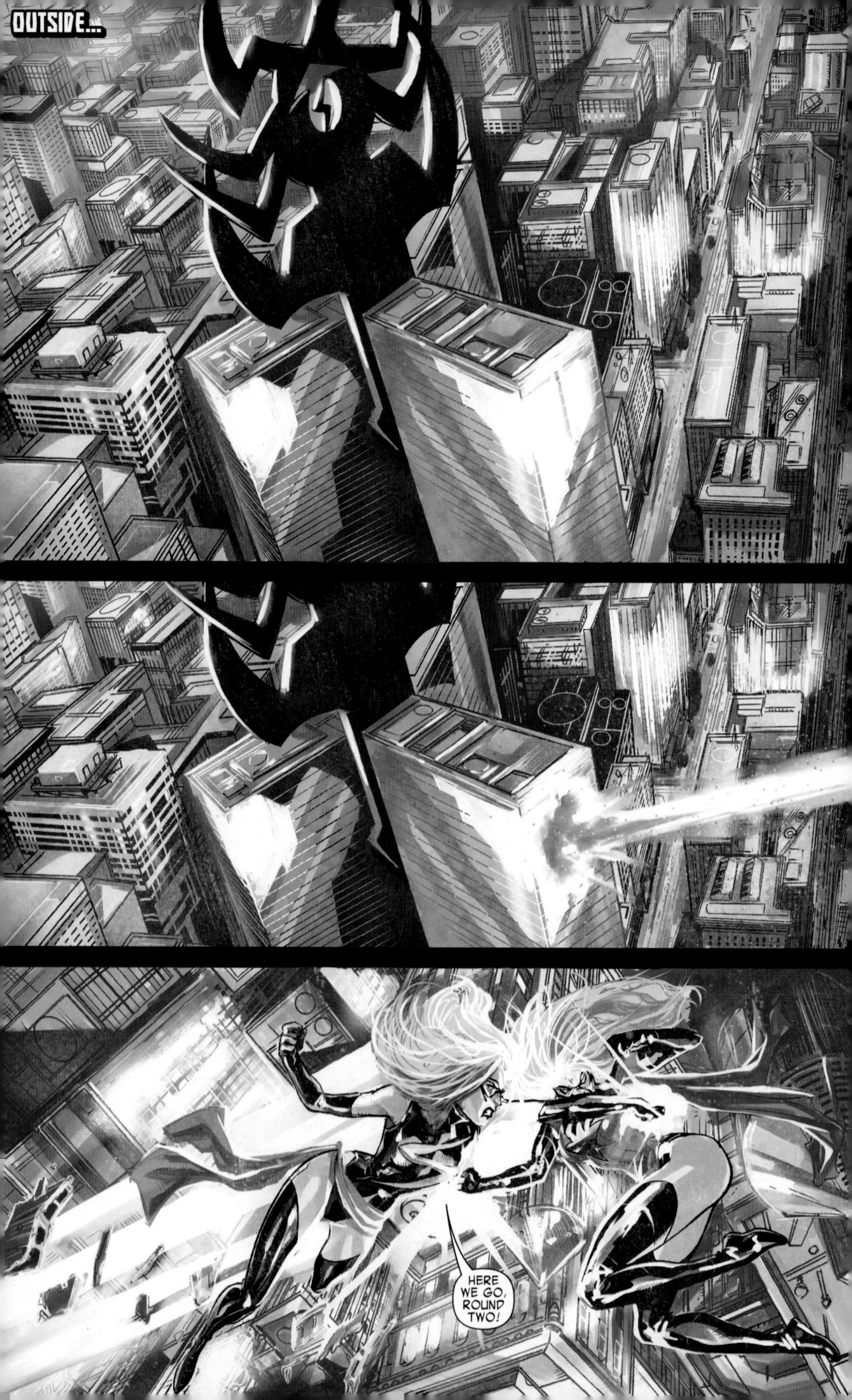
OUTSIDE...
HERE WE GO, ROUND TWO!

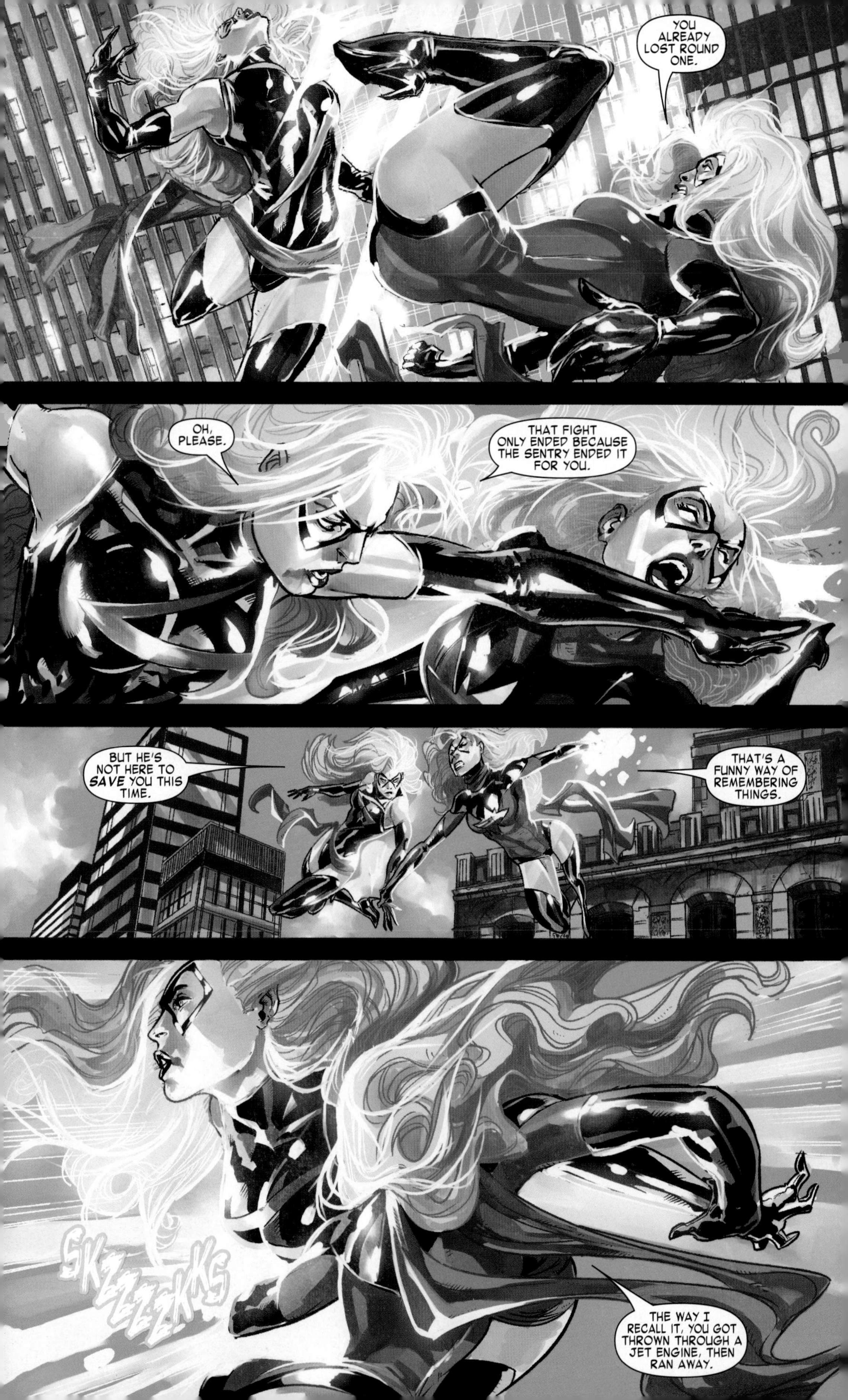
YOU ALREADY LOST ROUND ONE.
OH, PLEASE.
THAT FIGHT ONLY ENDED BECAUSE THE SENTRY ENDED IT FOR YOU.
BUT HE'S NOT HERE TO SAVE YOU THIS TIME.
THAT'S A FUNNY WAY OF REMEMBERING THINGS.
SKZZZZZKKS
THE WAY I RECALL IT, YOU GOT THROWN THROUGH A JET ENGINE, THEN RAN AWAY.

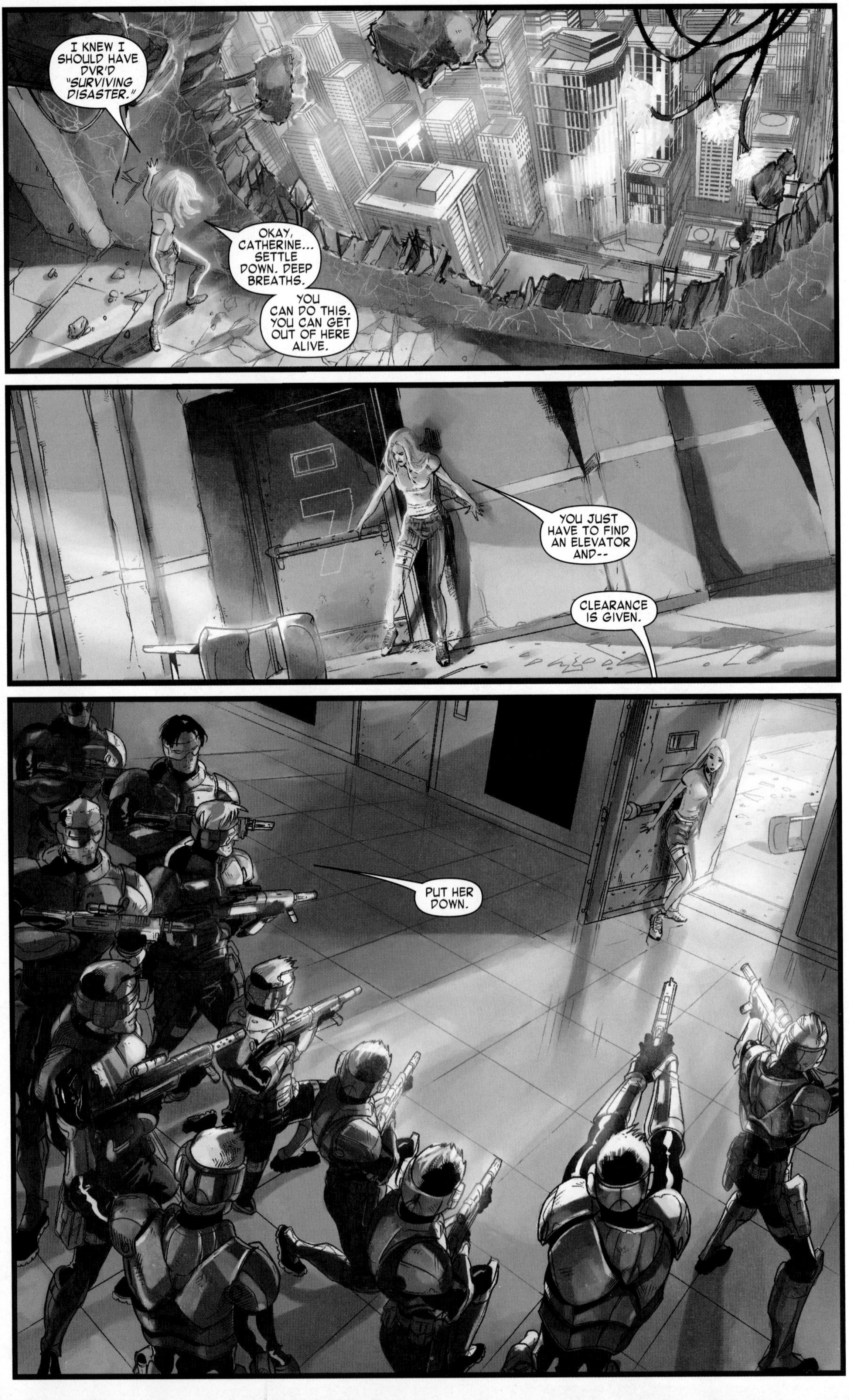
I KNEW I SHOULD HAVE DVR'D "SURVIVING DISASTER."
OKAY, CATHERINE... SETTLE DOWN. DEEP BREATHS.
YOU CAN DO THIS. YOU CAN GET OUT OF HERE ALIVE.
YOU JUST HAVE TO FIND AN ELEVATOR AND--
CLEARANCE IS GIVEN.
PUT HER DOWN.

GUNS. THEY'RE POINTING GUNS AT ME.

BUT THAT'S OKAY. I SUDDENLY KNOW HOW TO DEAL WITH THAT.

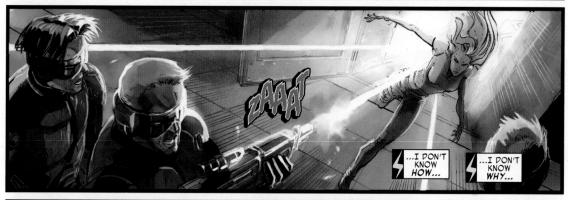

ZAAAT

...I DON'T KNOW HOW...

...I DON'T KNOW WHY...

KRAK

...BUT I KNOW HOW TO DEAL WITH THAT.

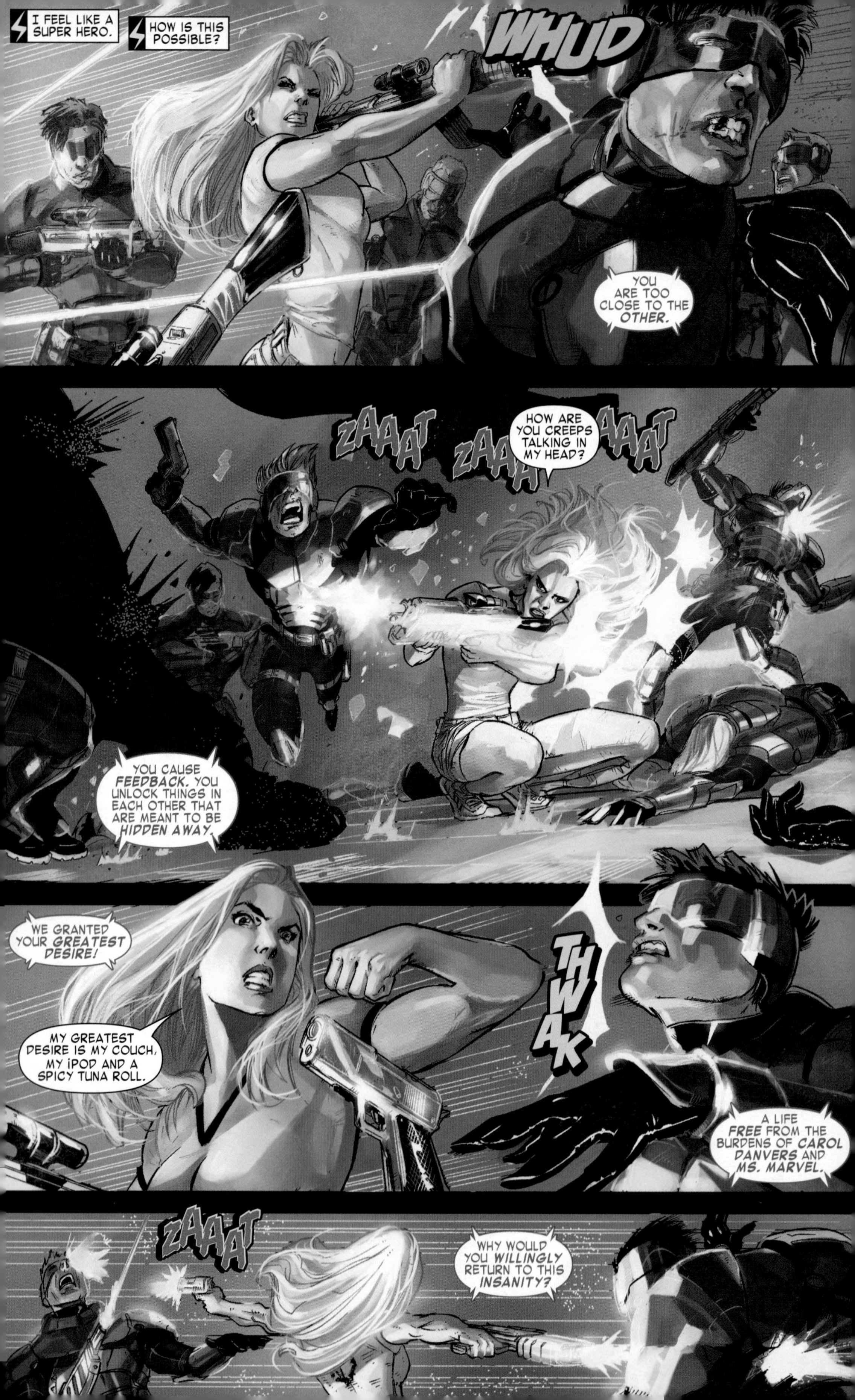
I FEEL LIKE A SUPER HERO.
HOW IS THIS POSSIBLE?
WHUD
YOU ARE TOO CLOSE TO THE OTHER.
ZAAAT
ZAAAT
HOW ARE YOU CREEPS TALKING IN MY HEAD?
AAAT
YOU CAUSE FEEDBACK. YOU UNLOCK THINGS IN EACH OTHER THAT ARE MEANT TO BE HIDDEN AWAY.
WE GRANTED YOUR GREATEST DESIRE!
MY GREATEST DESIRE IS MY COUCH, MY iPOD AND A SPICY TUNA ROLL.
THWAK
A LIFE FREE FROM THE BURDENS OF CAROL DANVERS AND MS. MARVEL.
ZAAAT
WHY WOULD YOU WILLINGLY RETURN TO THIS INSANITY?

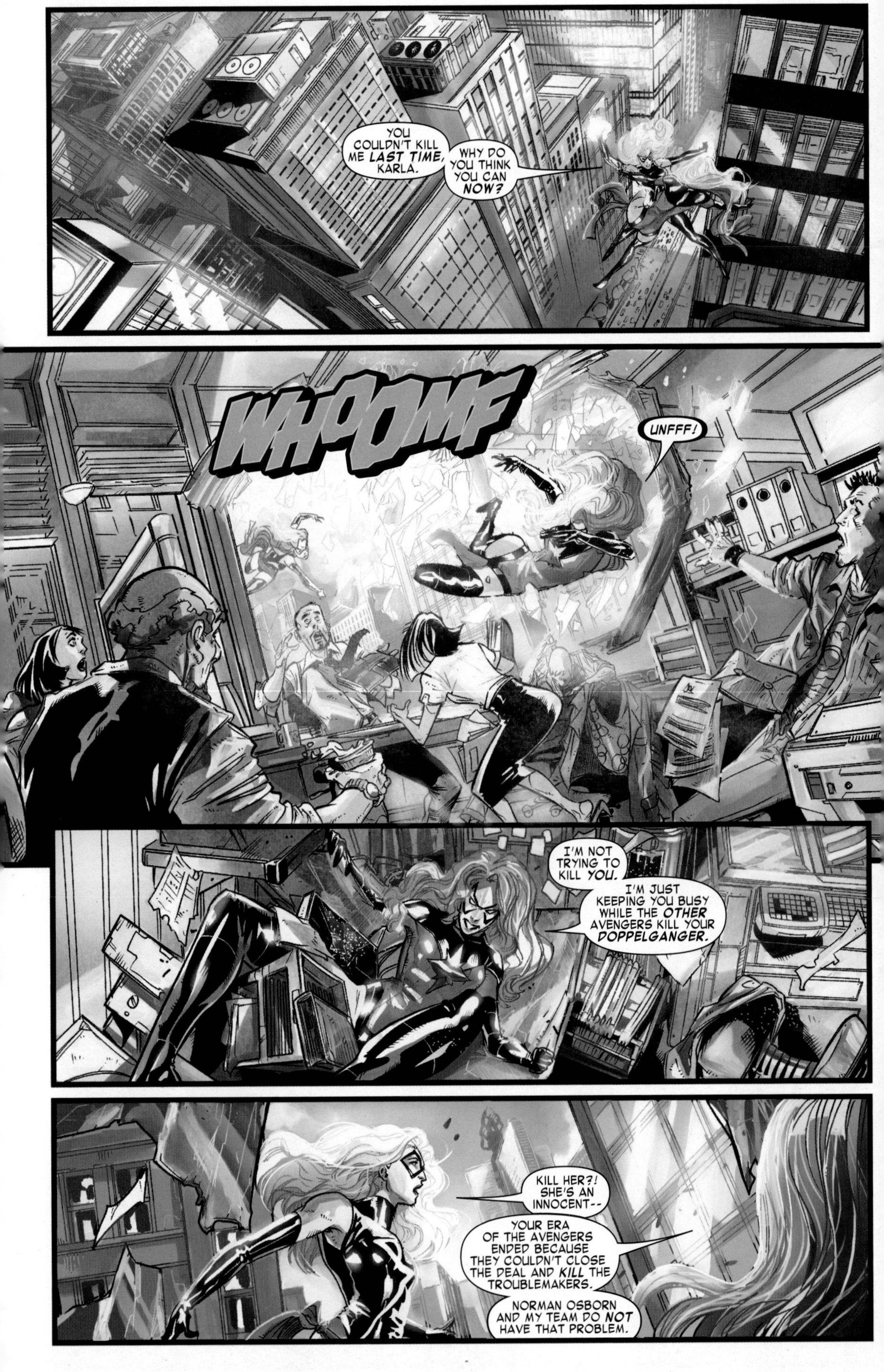
YOU COULDN'T KILL ME LAST TIME, KARLA.
WHY DO YOU THINK YOU CAN NOW?
WHOOMF
UNFFF!
I'M NOT TRYING TO KILL YOU.
I'M JUST KEEPING YOU BUSY WHILE THE OTHER AVENGERS KILL YOUR DOPPELGANGER.
KILL HER?! SHE'S AN INNOCENT--
YOUR ERA OF THE AVENGERS ENDED BECAUSE THEY COULDN'T CLOSE THE DEAL AND KILL THE TROUBLEMAKERS.
NORMAN OSBORN AND MY TEAM DO NOT HAVE THAT PROBLEM.

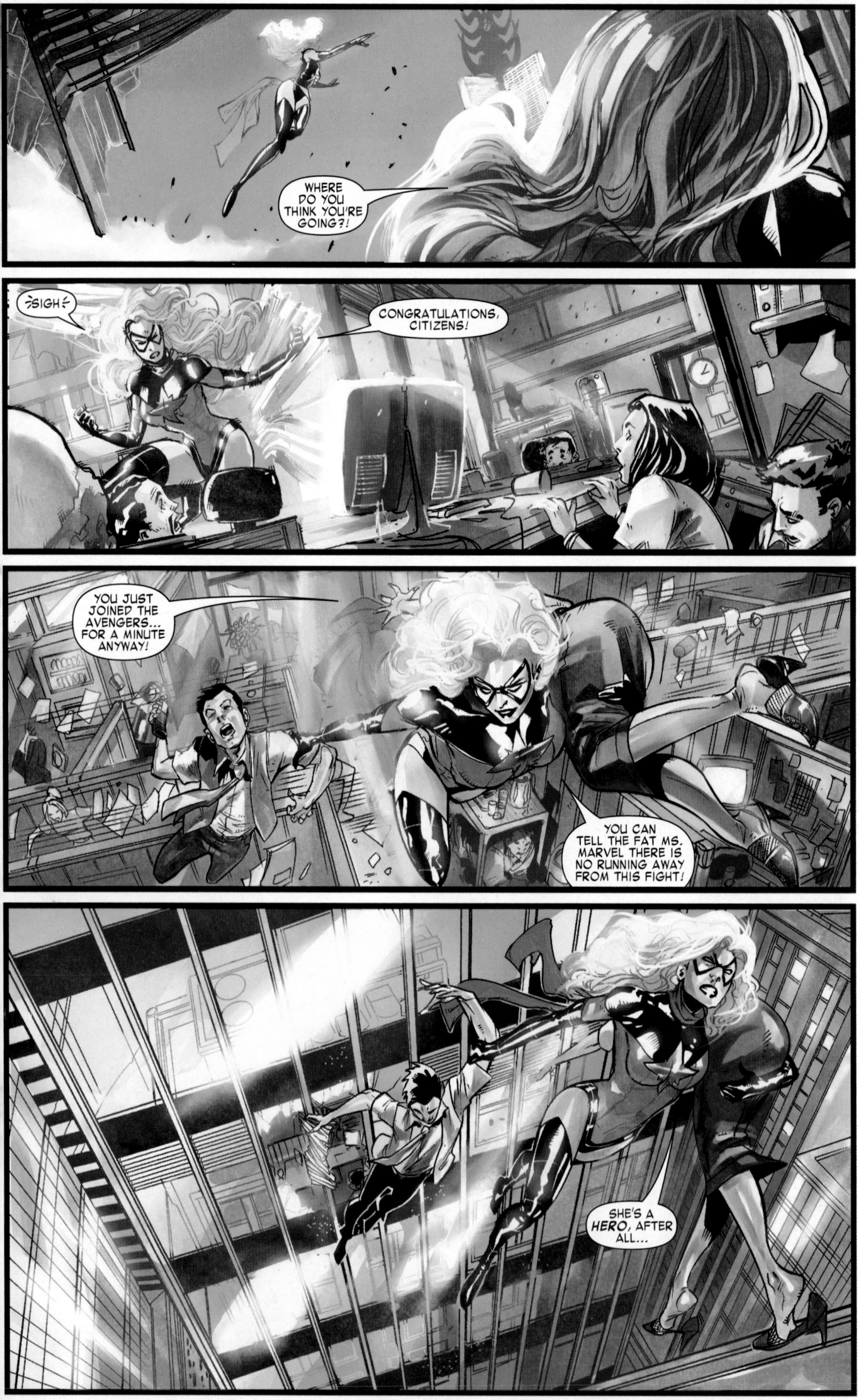
WHERE DO YOU THINK YOU'RE GOING?!
-SIGH-
CONGRATULATIONS, CITIZENS!
YOU JUST JOINED THE AVENGERS... FOR A MINUTE ANYWAY!
YOU CAN TELL THE FAT MS. MARVEL THERE IS NO RUNNING AWAY FROM THIS FIGHT!
SHE'S A HERO, AFTER ALL...

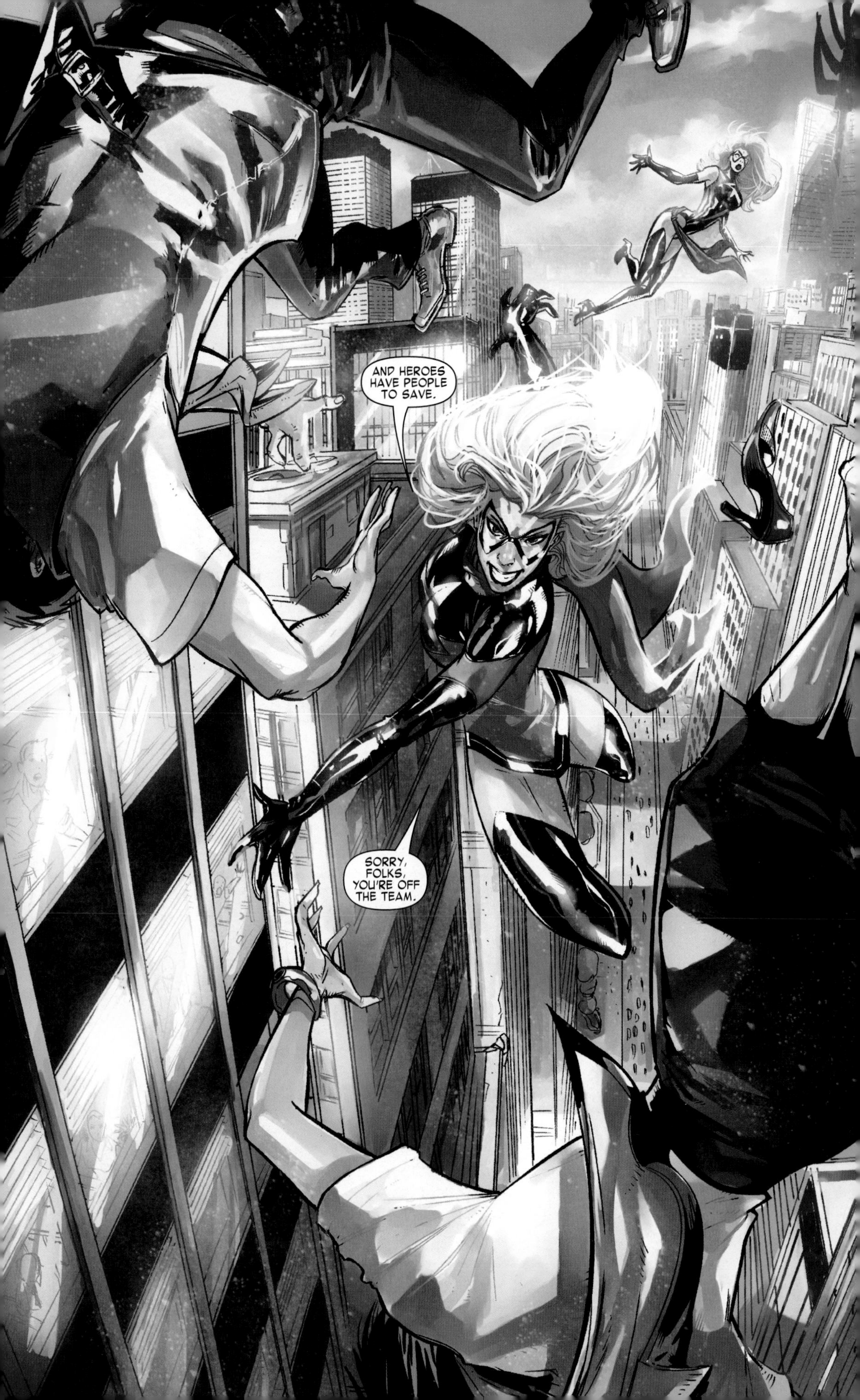
AND HEROES HAVE PEOPLE TO SAVE.
SORRY, FOLKS, YOU'RE OFF THE TEAM.

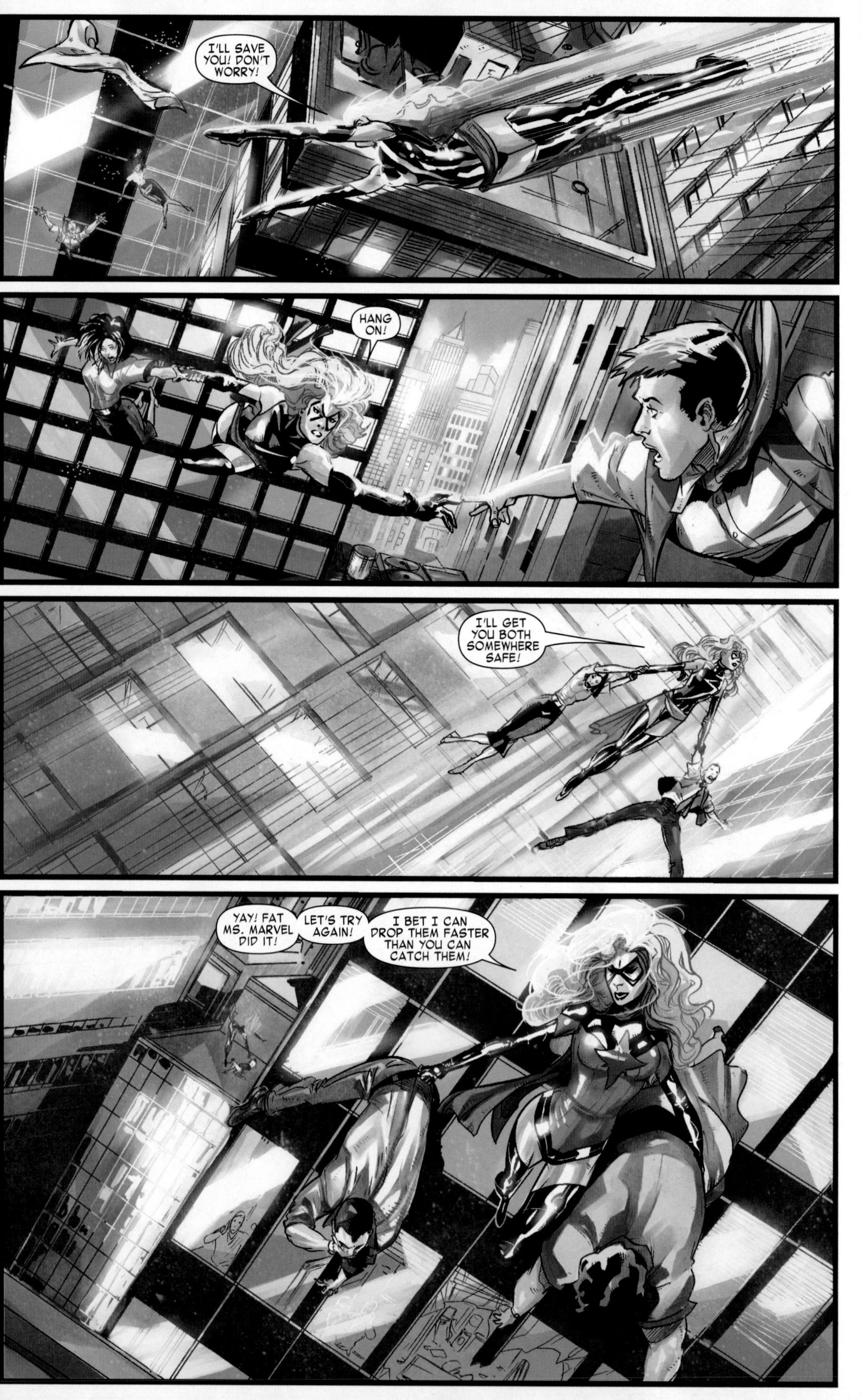
I'LL SAVE YOU! DON'T WORRY!
HANG ON!
I'LL GET YOU BOTH SOMEWHERE SAFE!
YAY! FAT MS. MARVEL DID IT!
LET'S TRY AGAIN!
I BET I CAN DROP THEM FASTER THAN YOU CAN CATCH THEM!

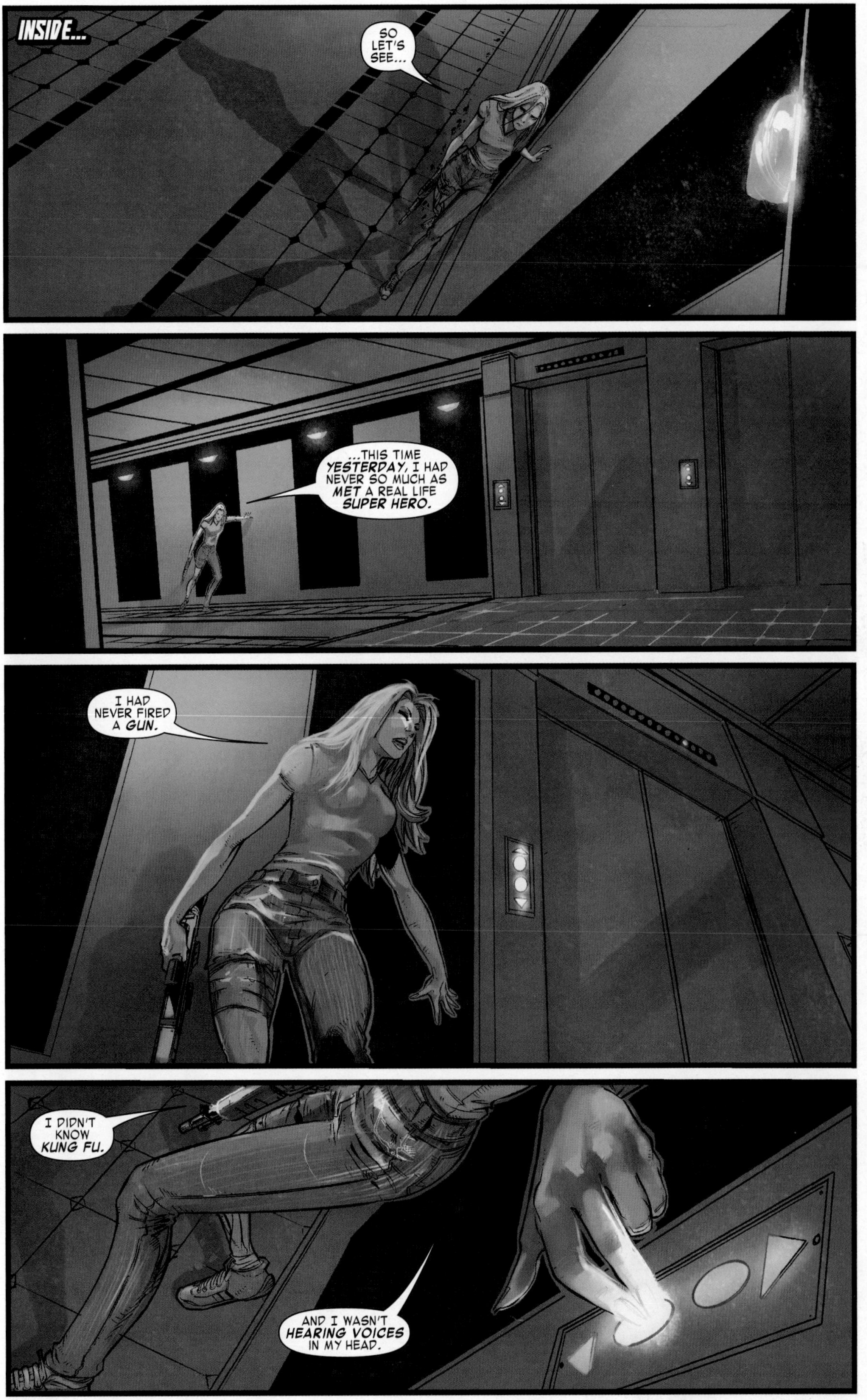
INSIDE...
SO LET'S SEE...
...THIS TIME YESTERDAY, I HAD NEVER SO MUCH AS MET A REAL LIFE SUPER HERO.
I HAD NEVER FIRED A GUN.
I DIDN'T KNOW KUNG FU.
AND I WASN'T HEARING VOICES IN MY HEAD.

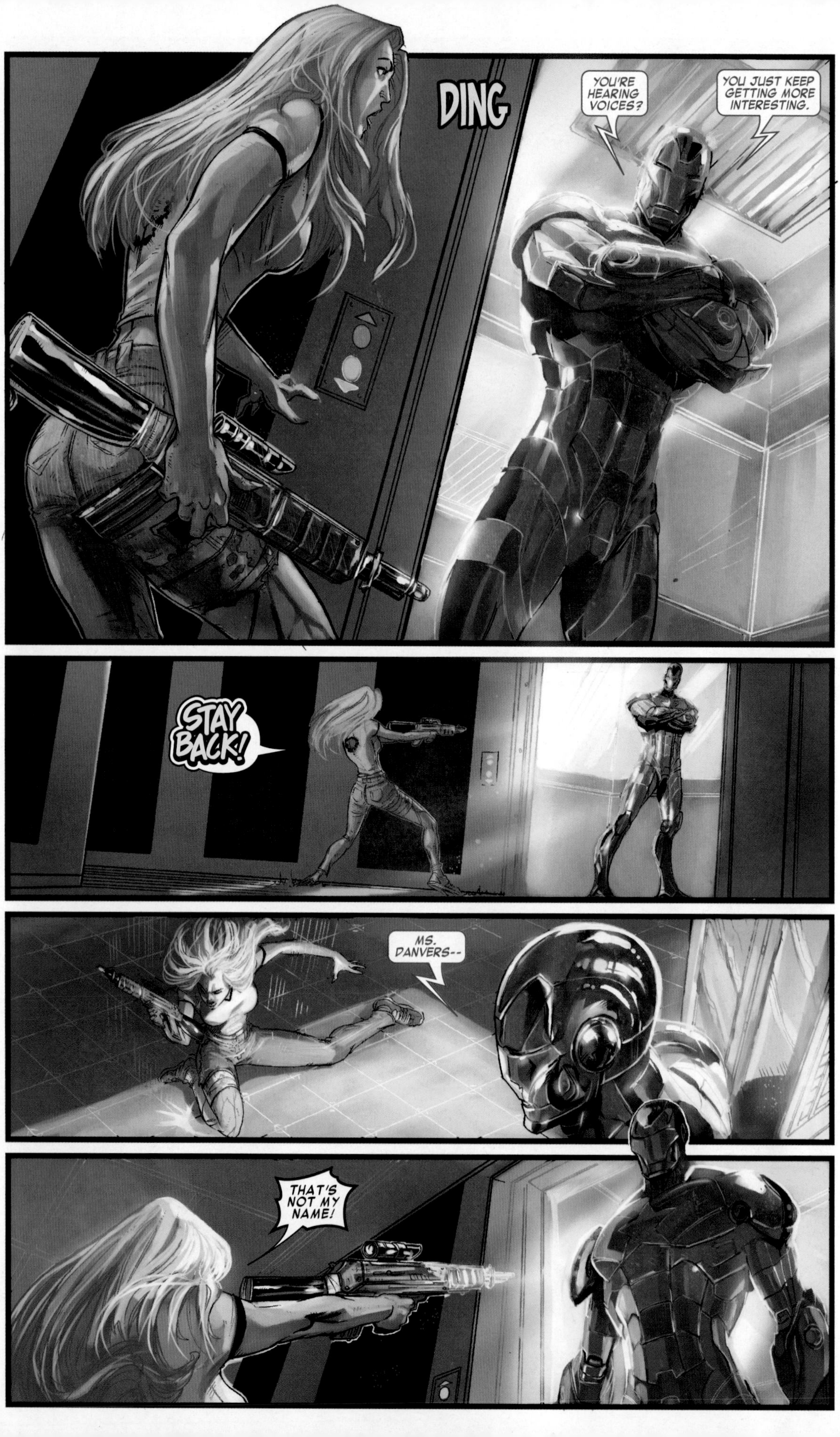
DING
YOU'RE HEARING VOICES?
YOU JUST KEEP GETTING MORE INTERESTING.
STAY BACK!
MS. DANVERS--
THAT'S NOT MY NAME!

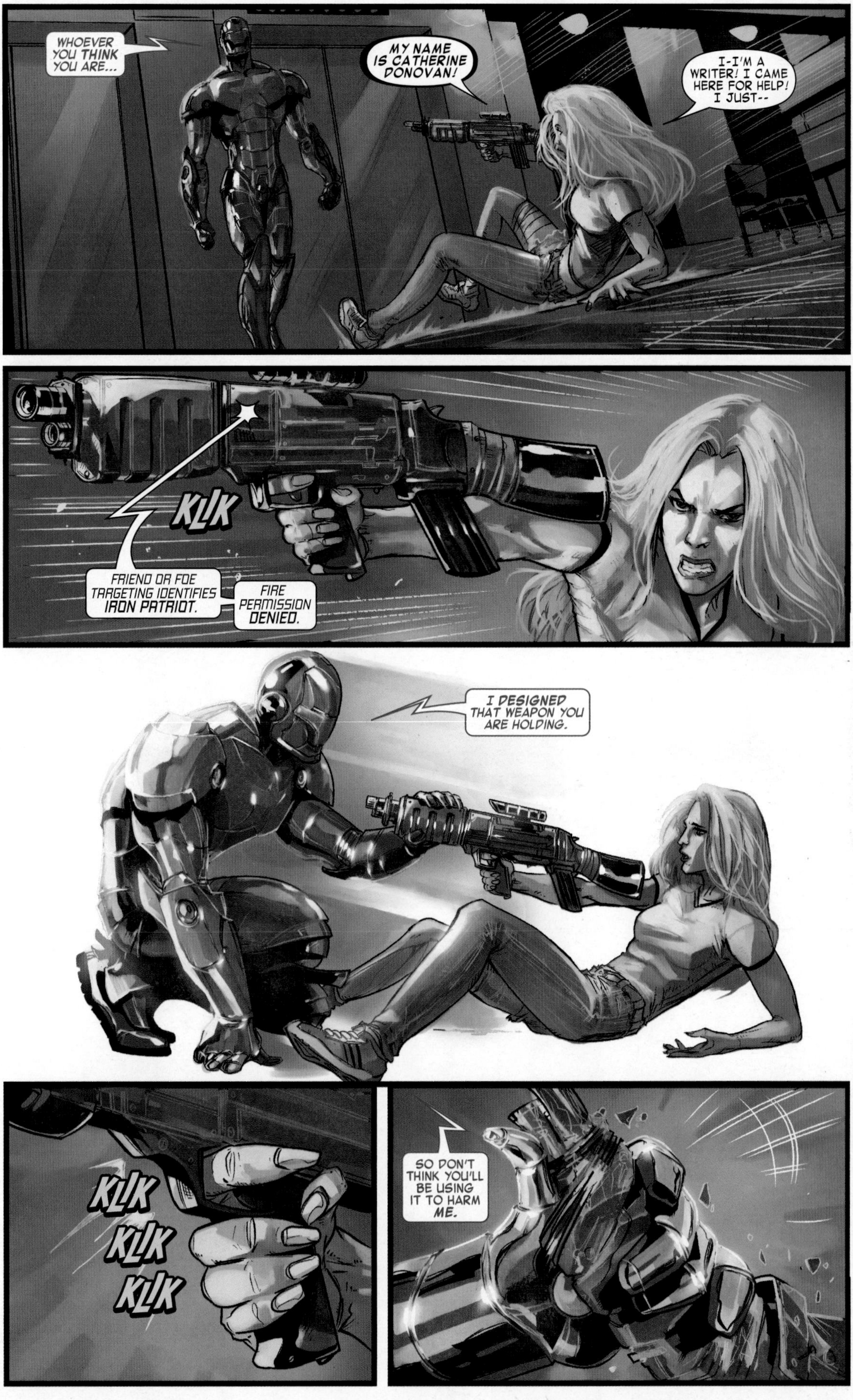
WHOEVER YOU THINK YOU ARE...
MY NAME IS CATHERINE DONOVAN!
I-I'M A WRITER! I CAME HERE FOR HELP! I JUST--
KLIK
FRIEND OR FOE TARGETING IDENTIFIES IRON PATRIOT.
FIRE PERMISSION DENIED.
I DESIGNED THAT WEAPON YOU ARE HOLDING.
KLIK
KLIK
KLIK
SO DON'T THINK YOU'LL BE USING IT TO HARM ME.

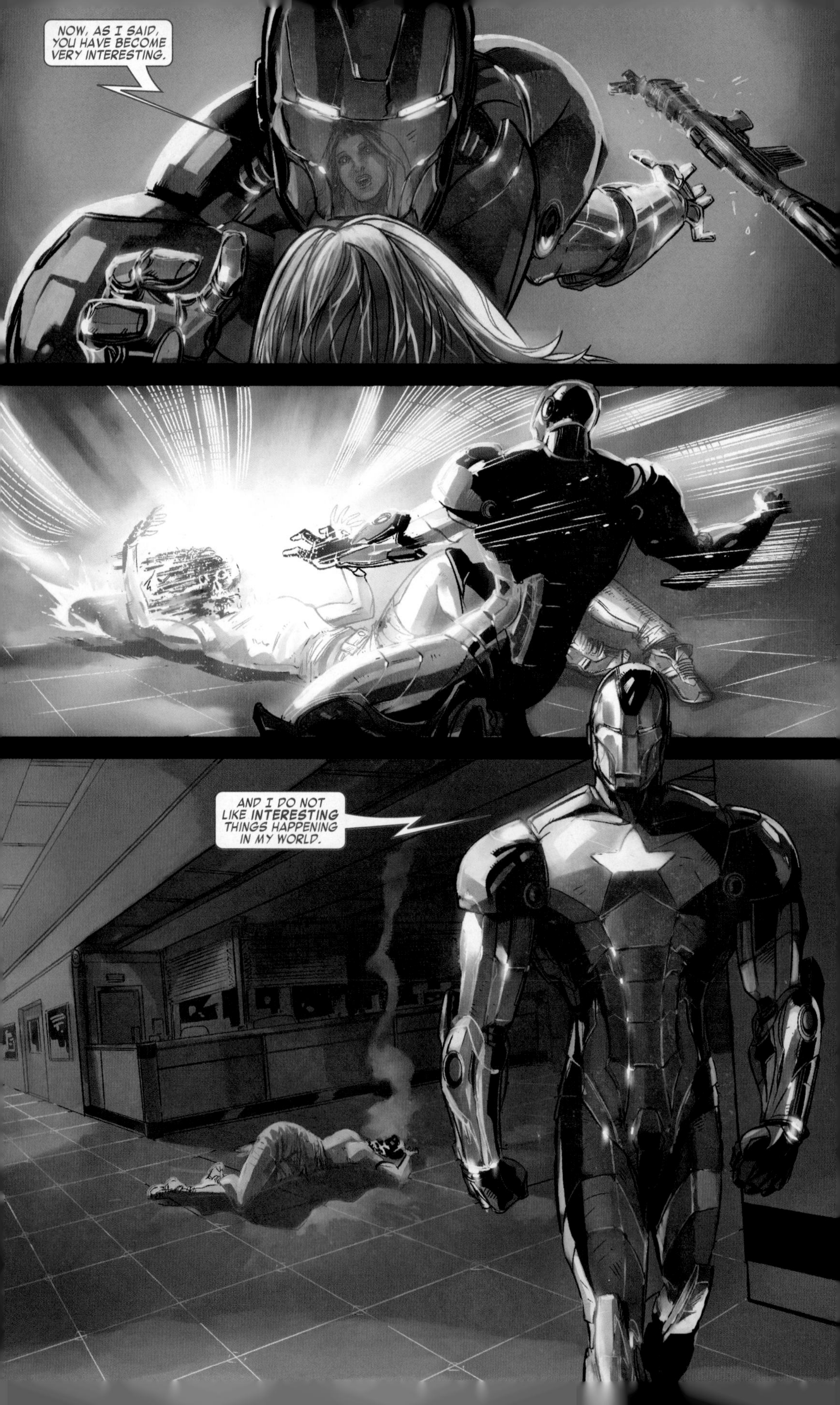
NOW, AS I SAID, YOU HAVE BECOME VERY INTERESTING.
AND I DO NOT LIKE INTERESTING THINGS HAPPENING IN MY WORLD.

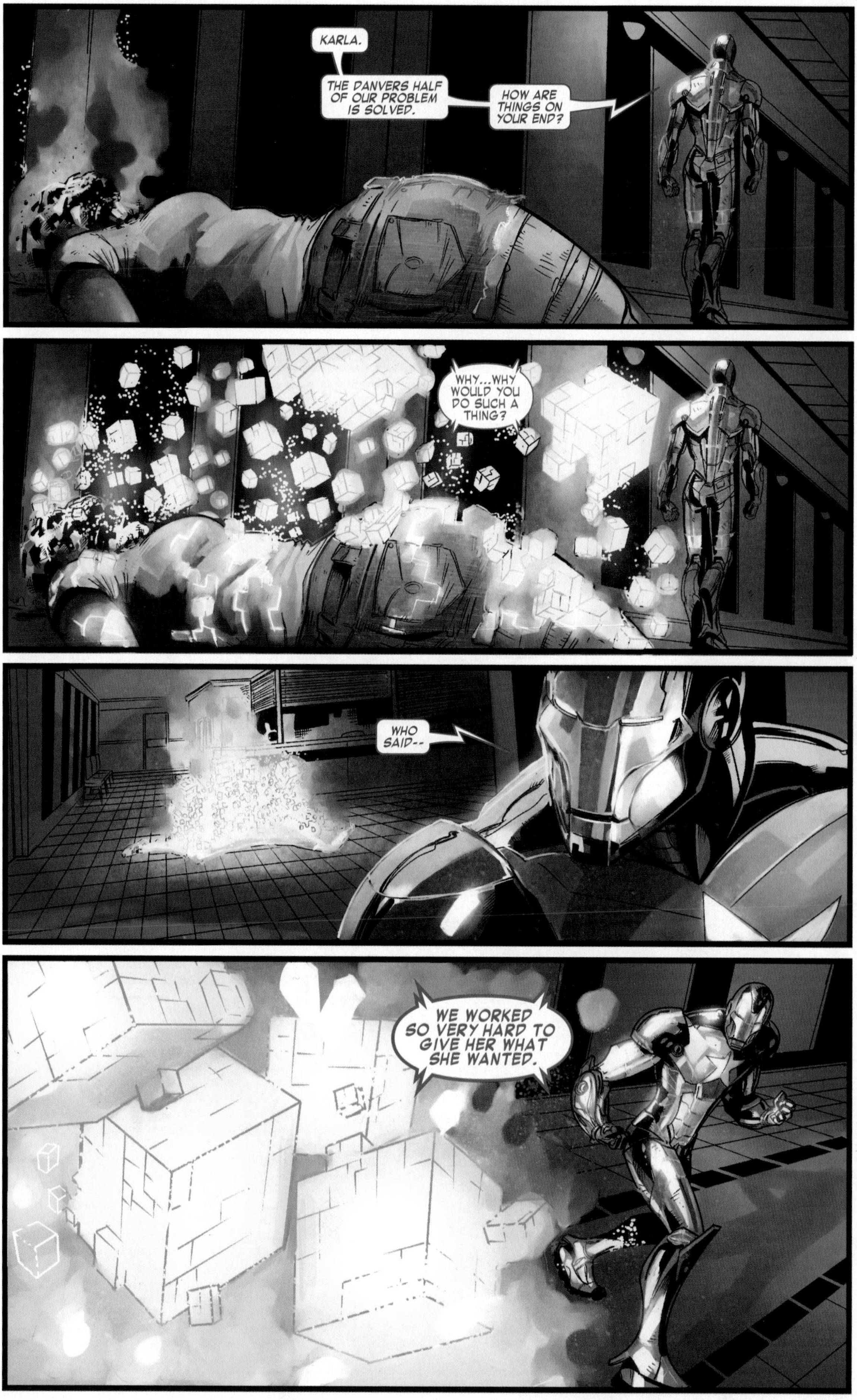
KARLA.
THE DANVERS HALF OF OUR PROBLEM IS SOLVED.
HOW ARE THINGS ON YOUR END?
WHY...WHY WOULD YOU DO SUCH A THING?
WHO SAID--
WE WORKED SO VERY HARD TO GIVE HER WHAT SHE WANTED.

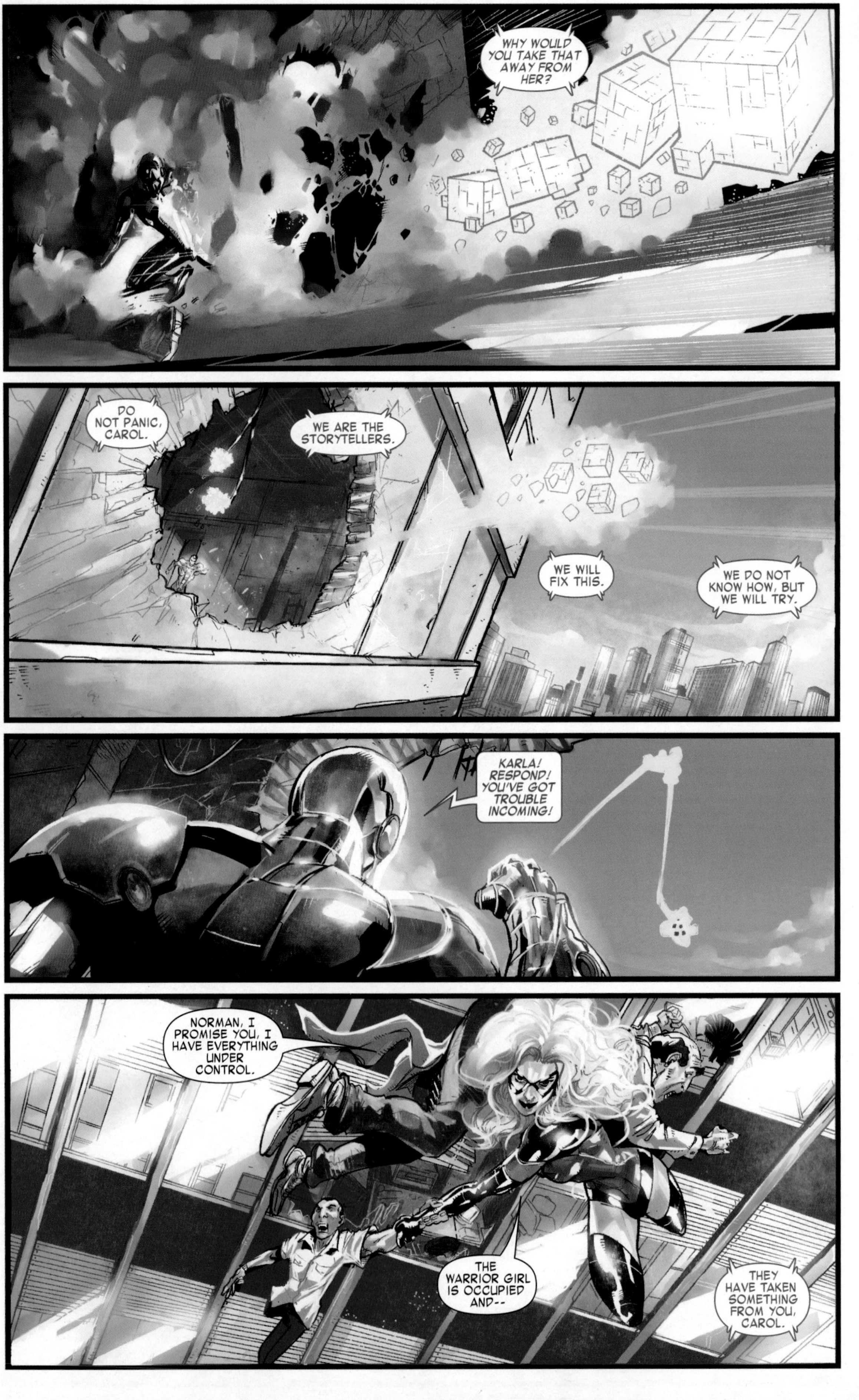
WHY WOULD YOU TAKE THAT AWAY FROM HER?
DO NOT PANIC, CAROL.
WE ARE THE STORYTELLERS.
WE WILL FIX THIS.
WE DO NOT KNOW HOW, BUT WE WILL TRY.
KARLA! RESPOND! YOU'VE GOT TROUBLE INCOMING!
NORMAN, I PROMISE YOU, I HAVE EVERYTHING UNDER CONTROL.
THE WARRIOR GIRL IS OCCUPIED AND--
THEY HAVE TAKEN SOMETHING FROM YOU, CAROL.

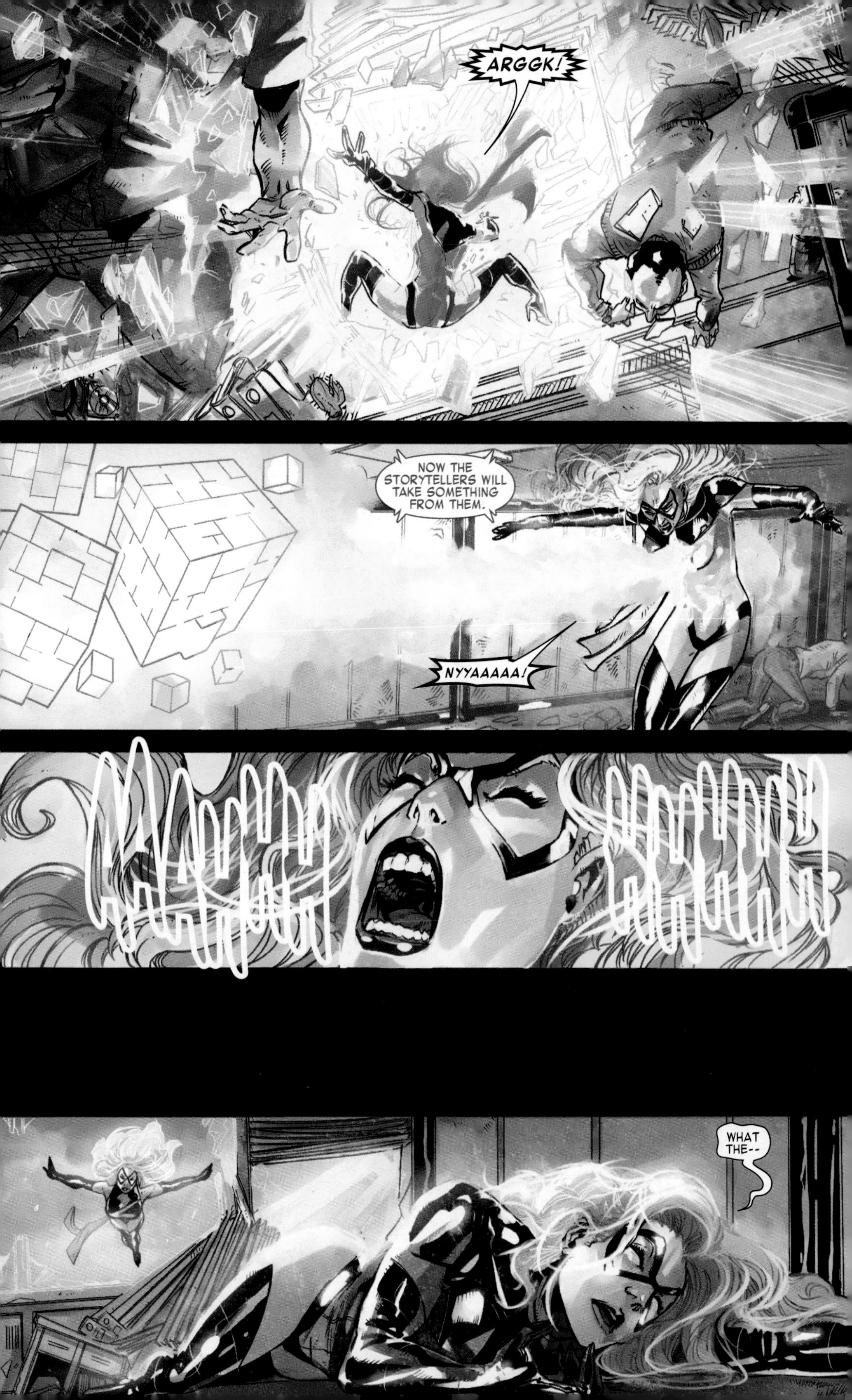
ARGGK!
NOW THE STORYTELLERS WILL TAKE SOMETHING FROM THEM.
NYYAAAAA!
WHAT THE--

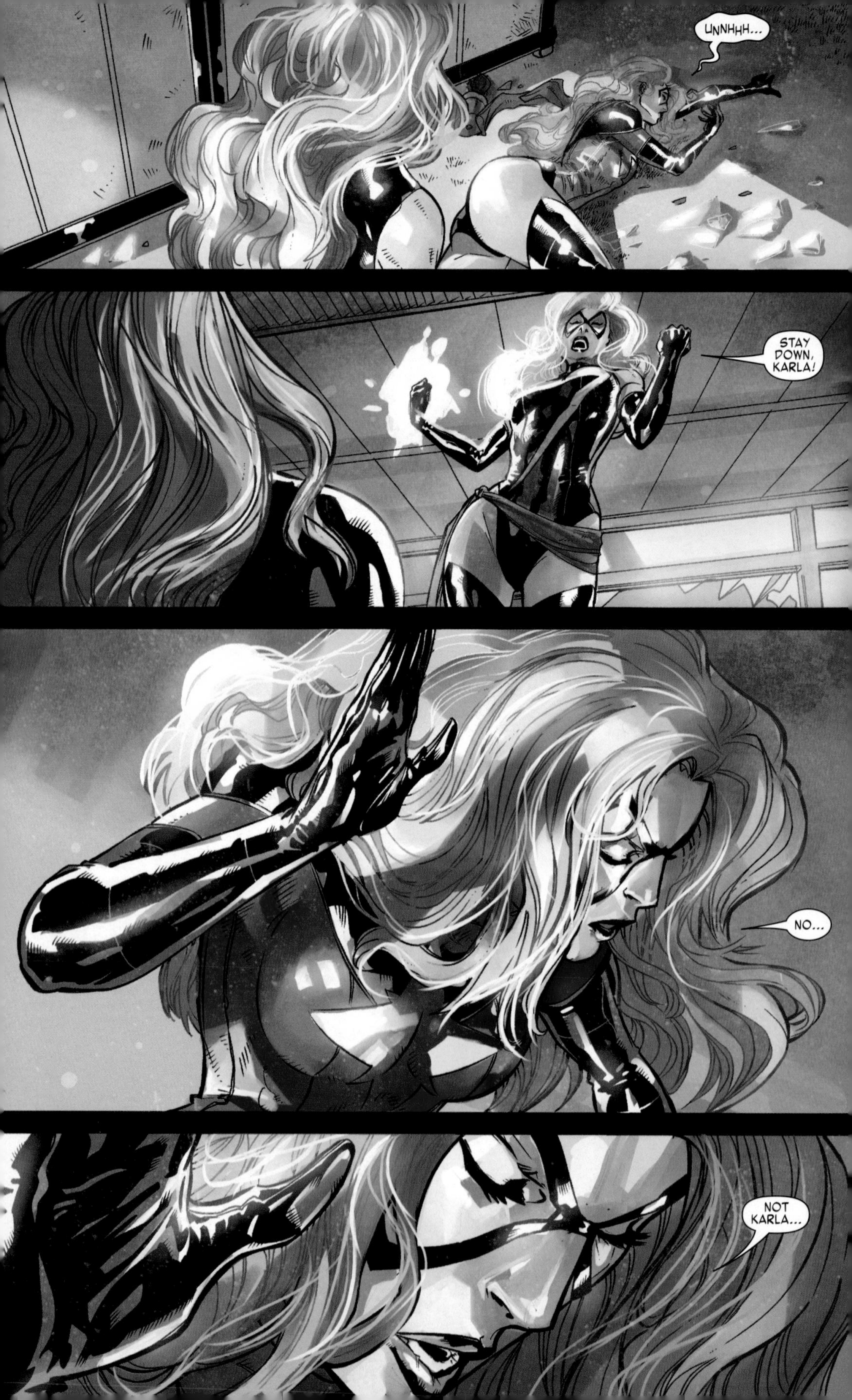
UNNHHH...
STAY DOWN, KARLA!
NO...
NOT KARLA...

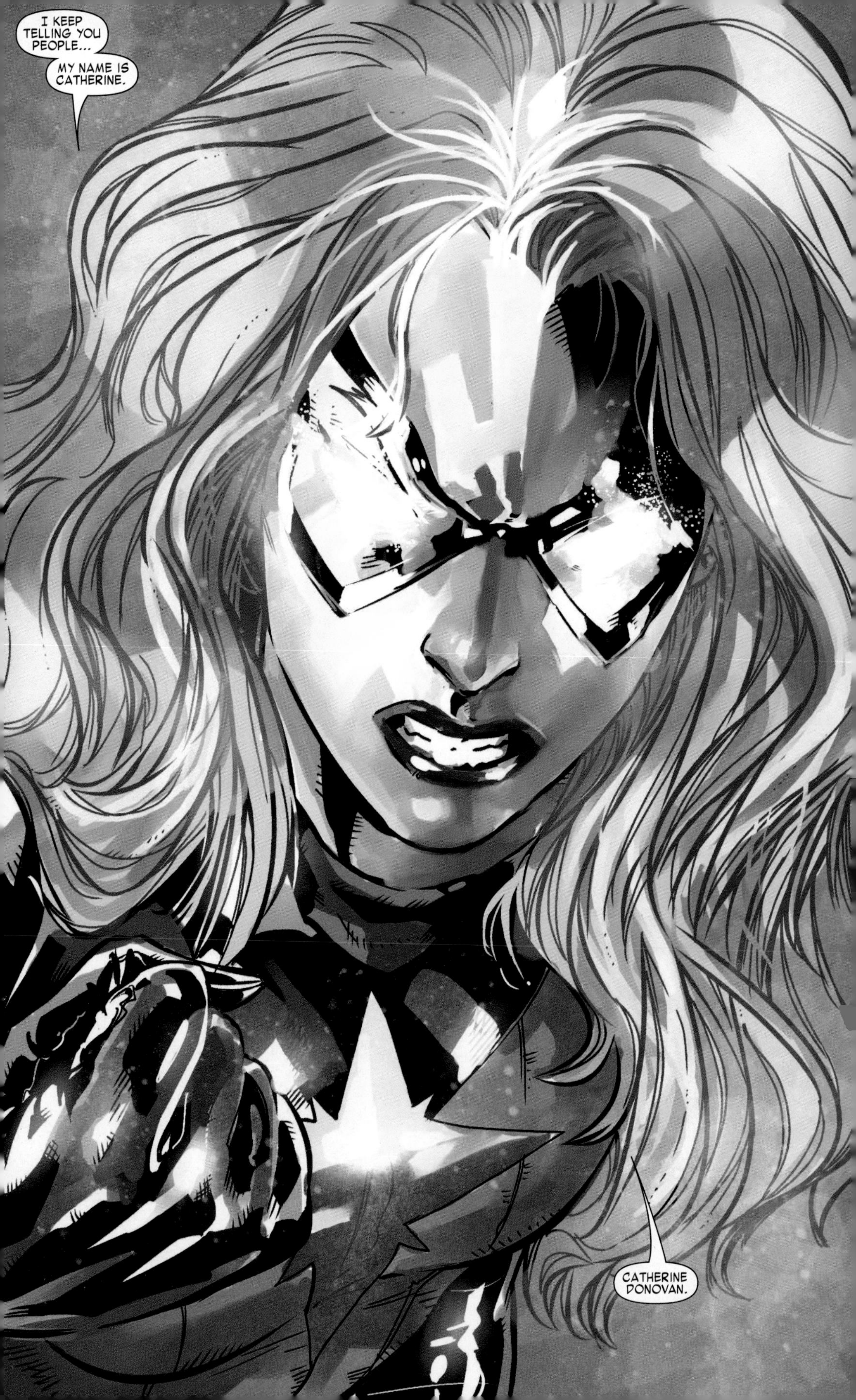
I KEEP TELLING YOU PEOPLE...
MY NAME IS CATHERINE.
CATHERINE DONOVAN.

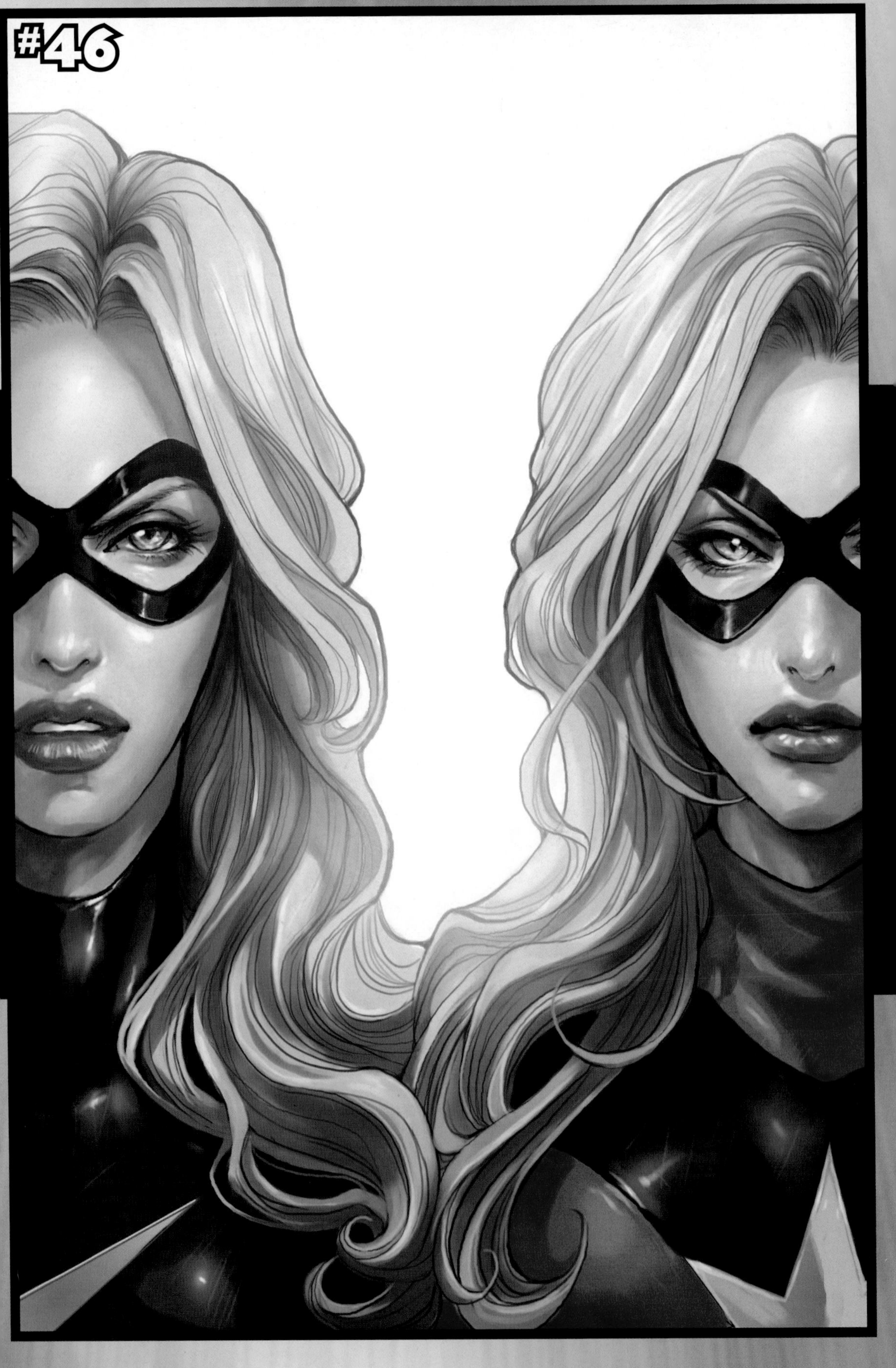
#46

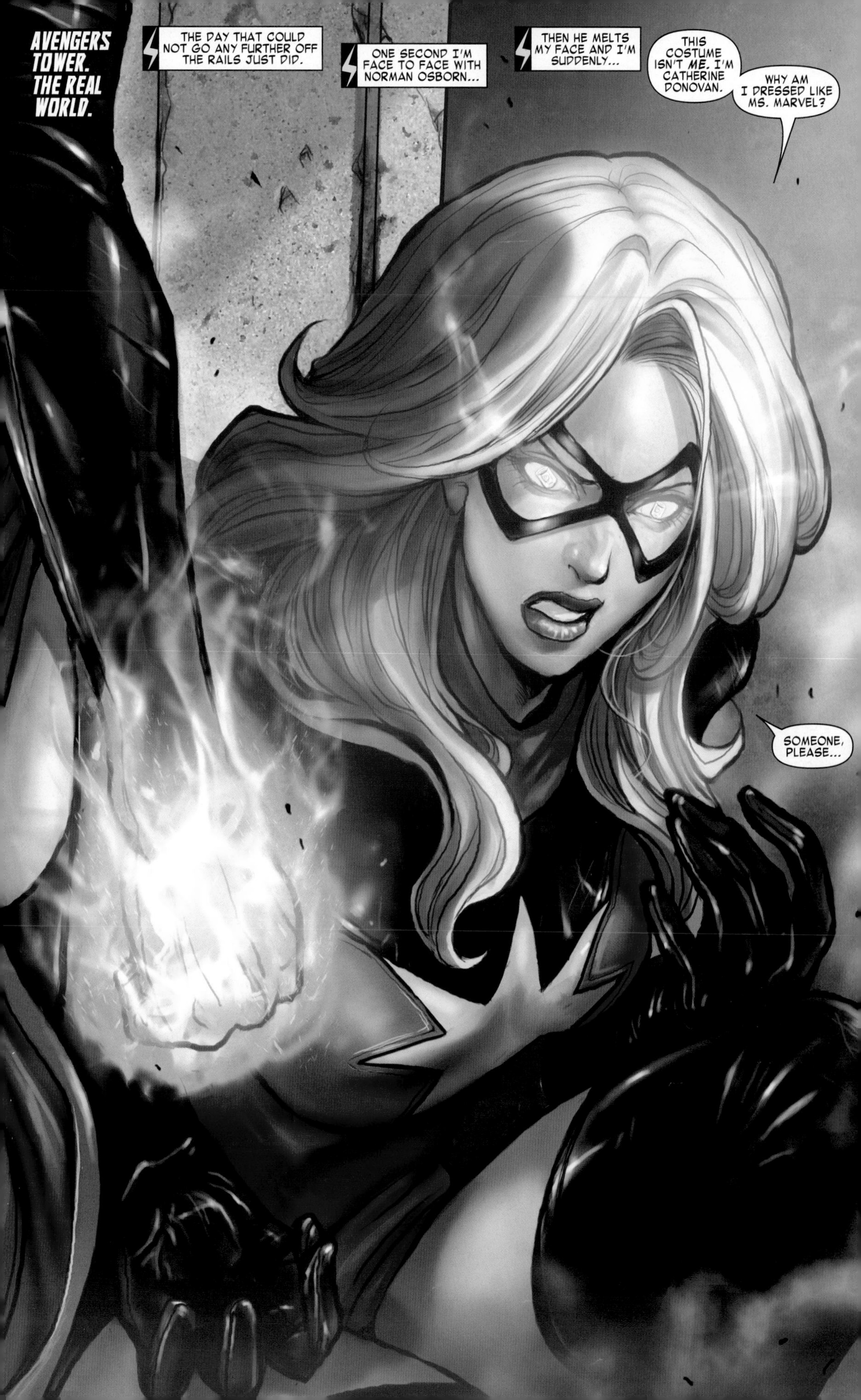
AVENGERS TOWER. THE REAL WORLD.
THE DAY THAT COULD NOT GO ANY FURTHER OFF THE RAILS JUST DID.
ONE SECOND I'M FACE TO FACE WITH NORMAN OSBORN...
THEN HE MELTS MY FACE AND I'M SUDDENLY...
THIS COSTUME ISN'T ME. I'M CATHERINE DONOVAN.
WHY AM I DRESSED LIKE MS. MARVEL?
SOMEONE, PLEASE...

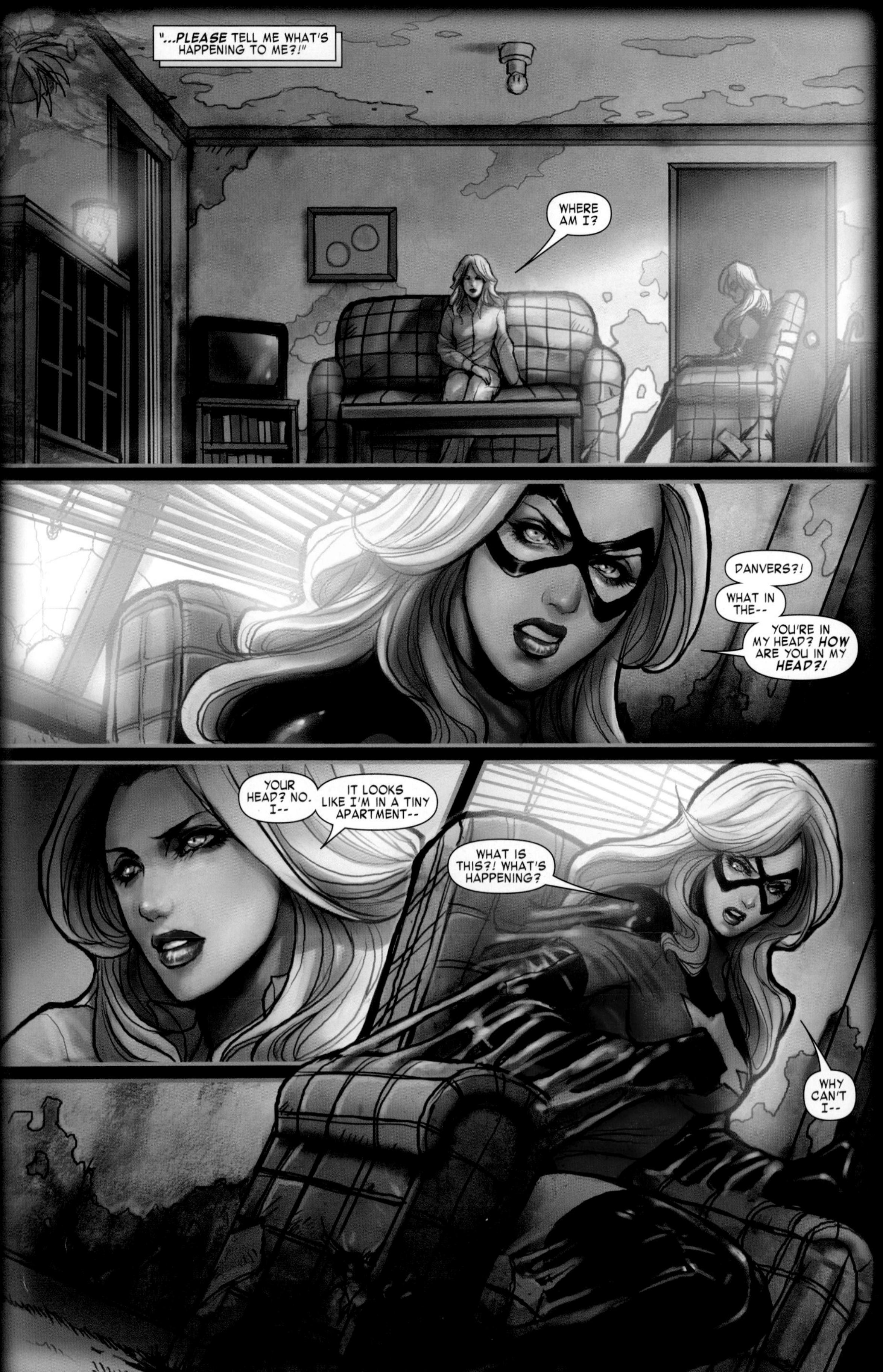
"...PLEASE TELL ME WHAT'S HAPPENING TO ME?!"
WHERE AM I?
DANVERS?!
WHAT IN THE--
YOU'RE IN MY HEAD? HOW ARE YOU IN MY HEAD?!
YOUR HEAD? NO. I--
IT LOOKS LIKE I'M IN A TINY APARTMENT--
WHAT IS THIS?! WHAT'S HAPPENING?
WHY CAN'T I--

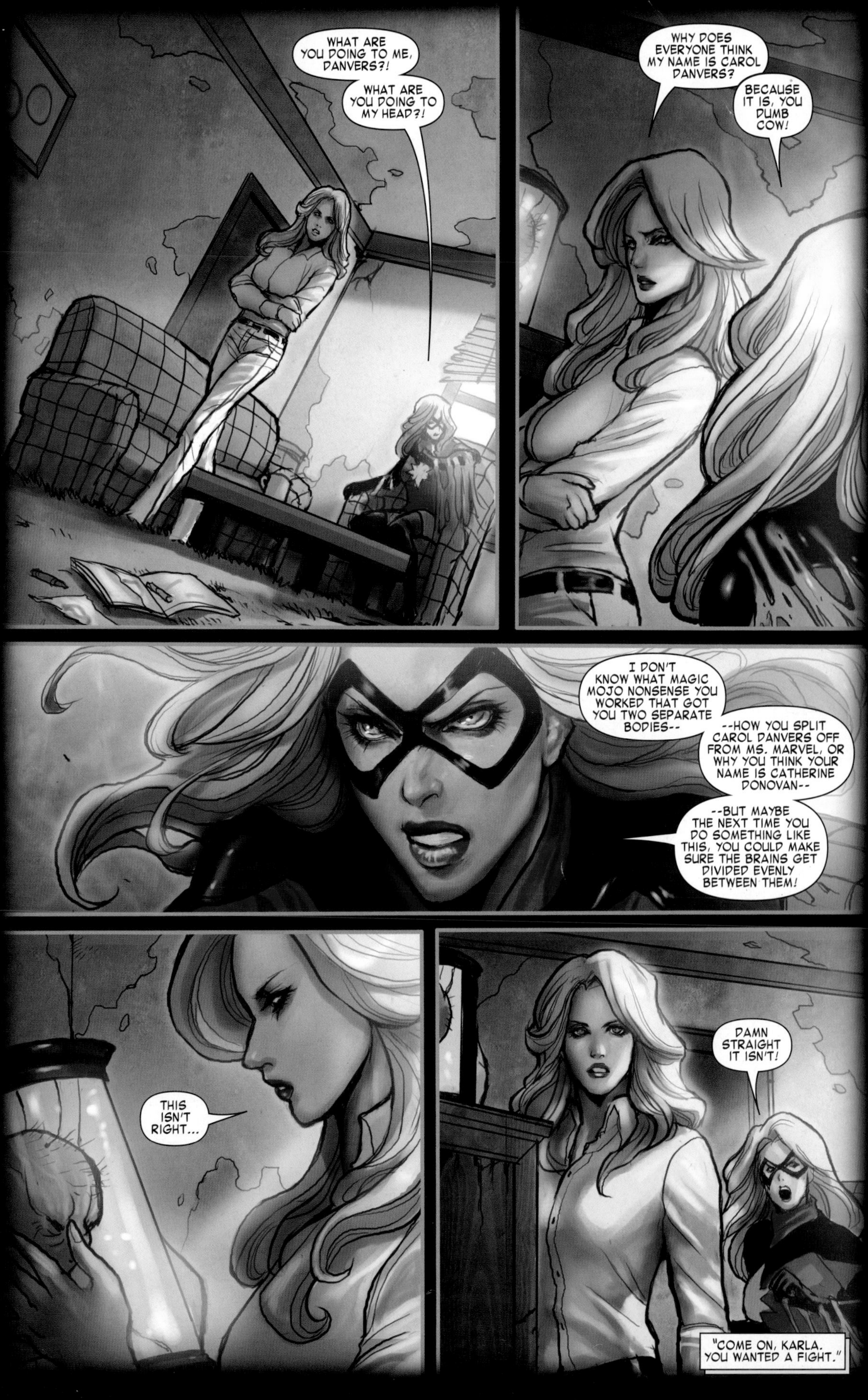
WHAT ARE YOU DOING TO ME, DANVERS?!
WHAT ARE YOU DOING TO MY HEAD?!
WHY DOES EVERYONE THINK MY NAME IS CAROL DANVERS?
BECAUSE IT IS, YOU DUMB COW!
I DON'T KNOW WHAT MAGIC MOJO NONSENSE YOU WORKED THAT GOT YOU TWO SEPARATE BODIES--
--HOW YOU SPLIT CAROL DANVERS OFF FROM MS. MARVEL, OR WHY YOU THINK YOUR NAME IS CATHERINE DONOVAN--
--BUT MAYBE THE NEXT TIME YOU DO SOMETHING LIKE THIS, YOU COULD MAKE SURE THE BRAINS GET DIVIDED EVENLY BETWEEN THEM!
THIS ISN'T RIGHT...
DAMN STRAIGHT IT ISN'T!
"COME ON, KARLA. YOU WANTED A FIGHT."

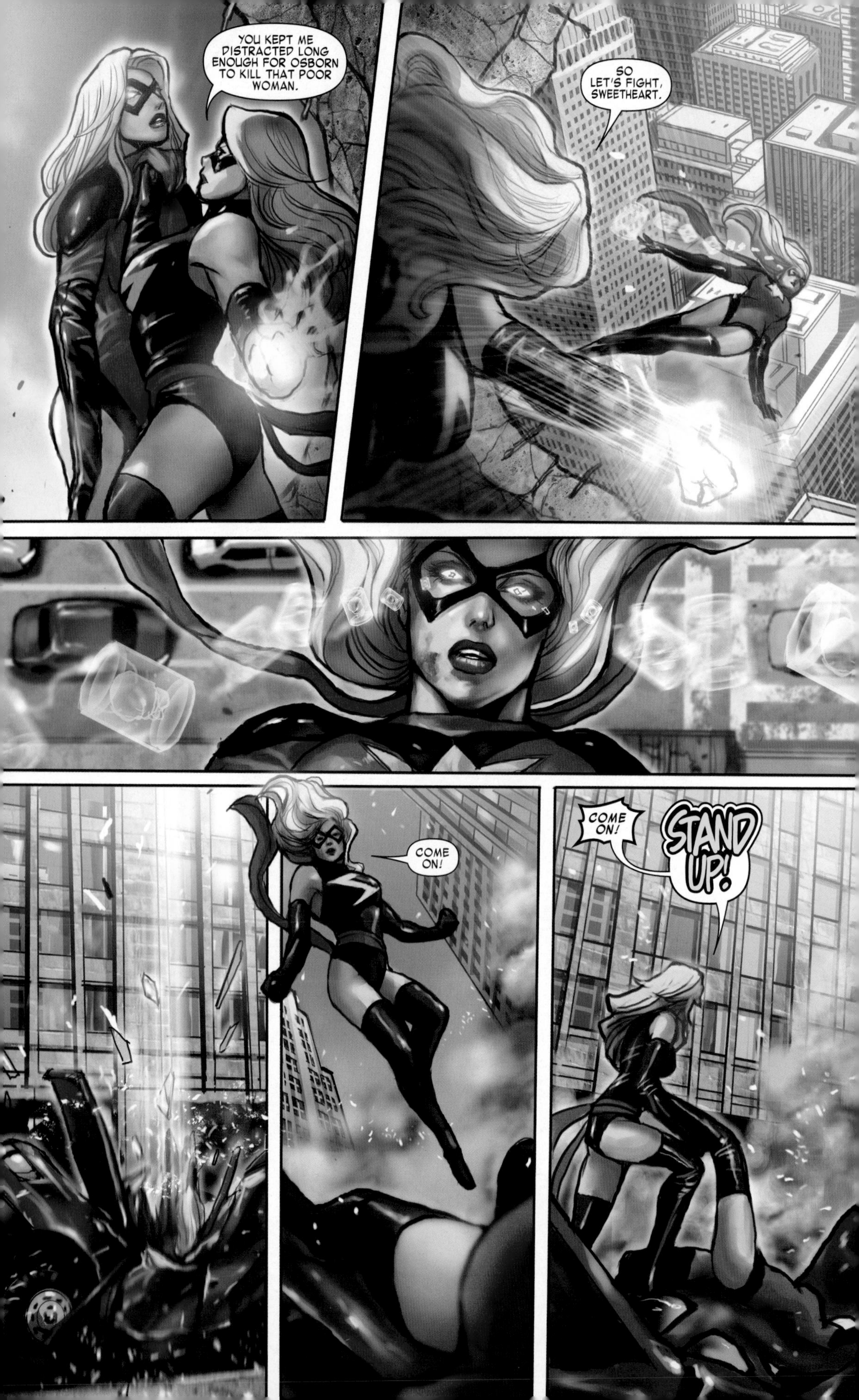
YOU KEPT ME DISTRACTED LONG ENOUGH FOR OSBORN TO KILL THAT POOR WOMAN.
SO LET'S FIGHT, SWEETHEART.
COME ON!
COME ON!
STAND UP!

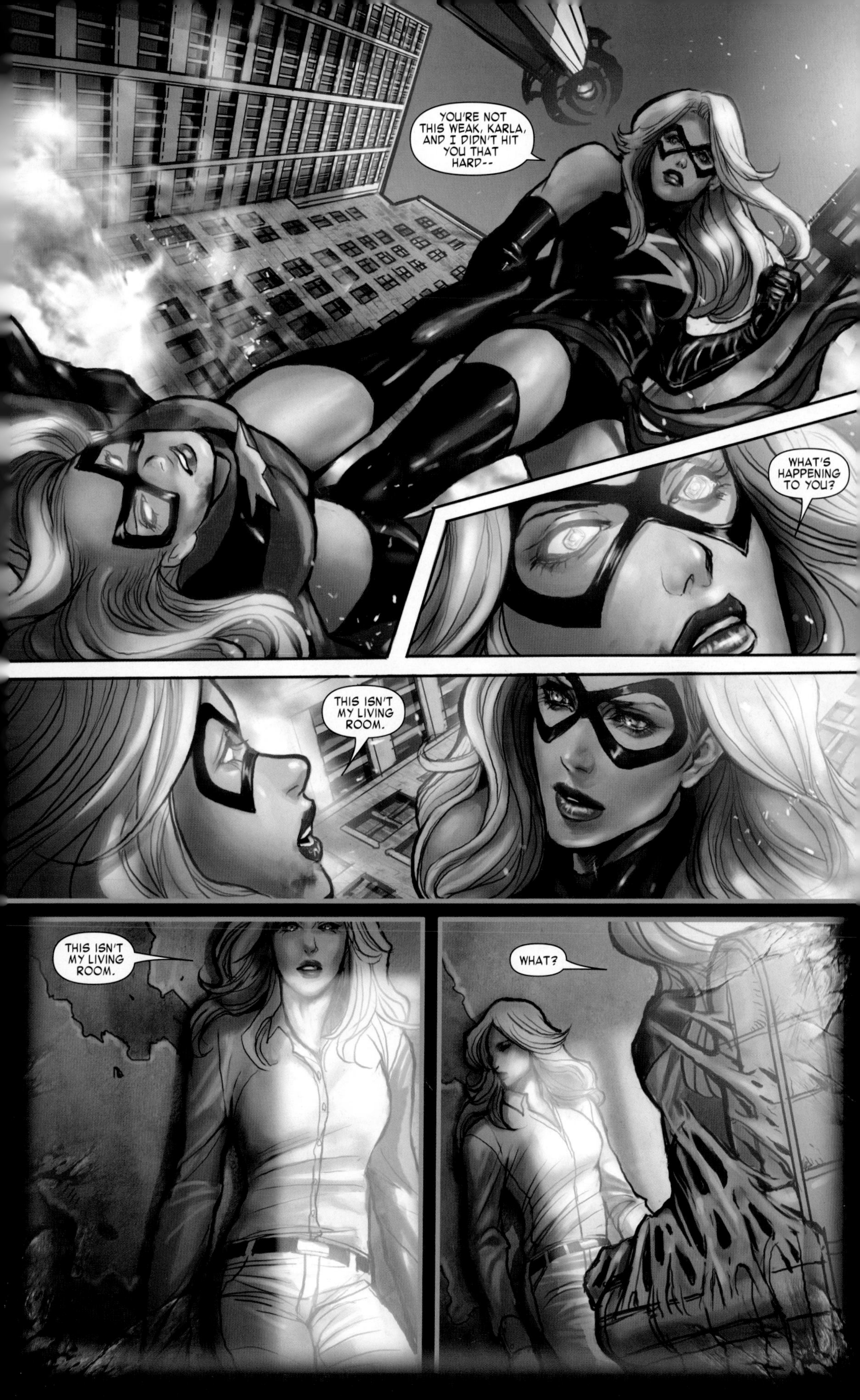
YOU'RE NOT THIS WEAK, KARLA, AND I DIDN'T HIT YOU THAT HARD--
WHAT'S HAPPENING TO YOU?
THIS ISN'T MY LIVING ROOM.
THIS ISN'T MY LIVING ROOM.
WHAT?

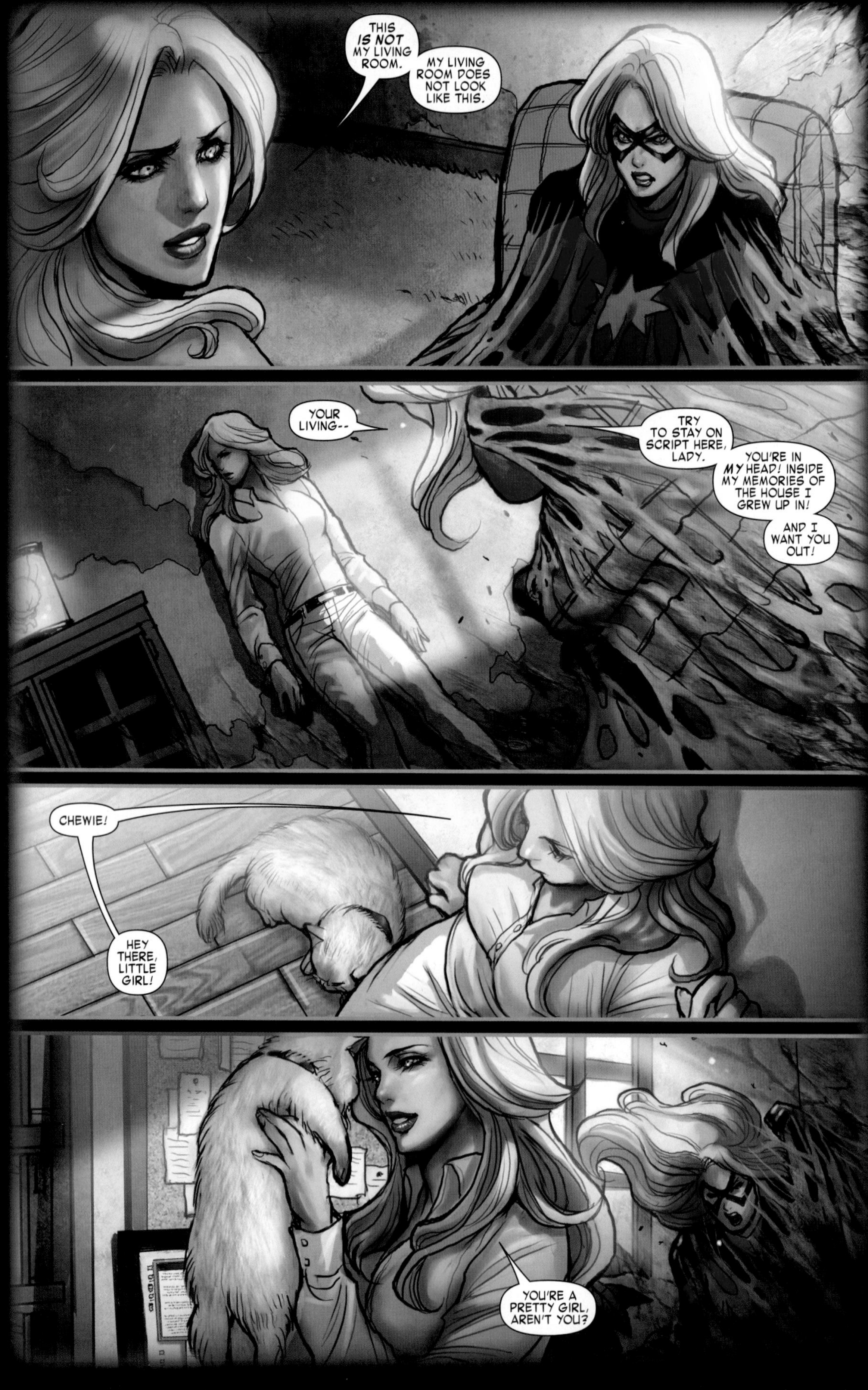
THIS IS NOT MY LIVING ROOM.
MY LIVING ROOM DOES NOT LOOK LIKE THIS.
YOUR LIVING--
TRY TO STAY ON SCRIPT HERE, LADY.
YOU'RE IN MY HEAD! INSIDE MY MEMORIES OF THE HOUSE I GREW UP IN!
AND I WANT YOU OUT!
CHEWIE!
HEY THERE, LITTLE GIRL!
YOU'RE A PRETTY GIRL, AREN'T YOU?

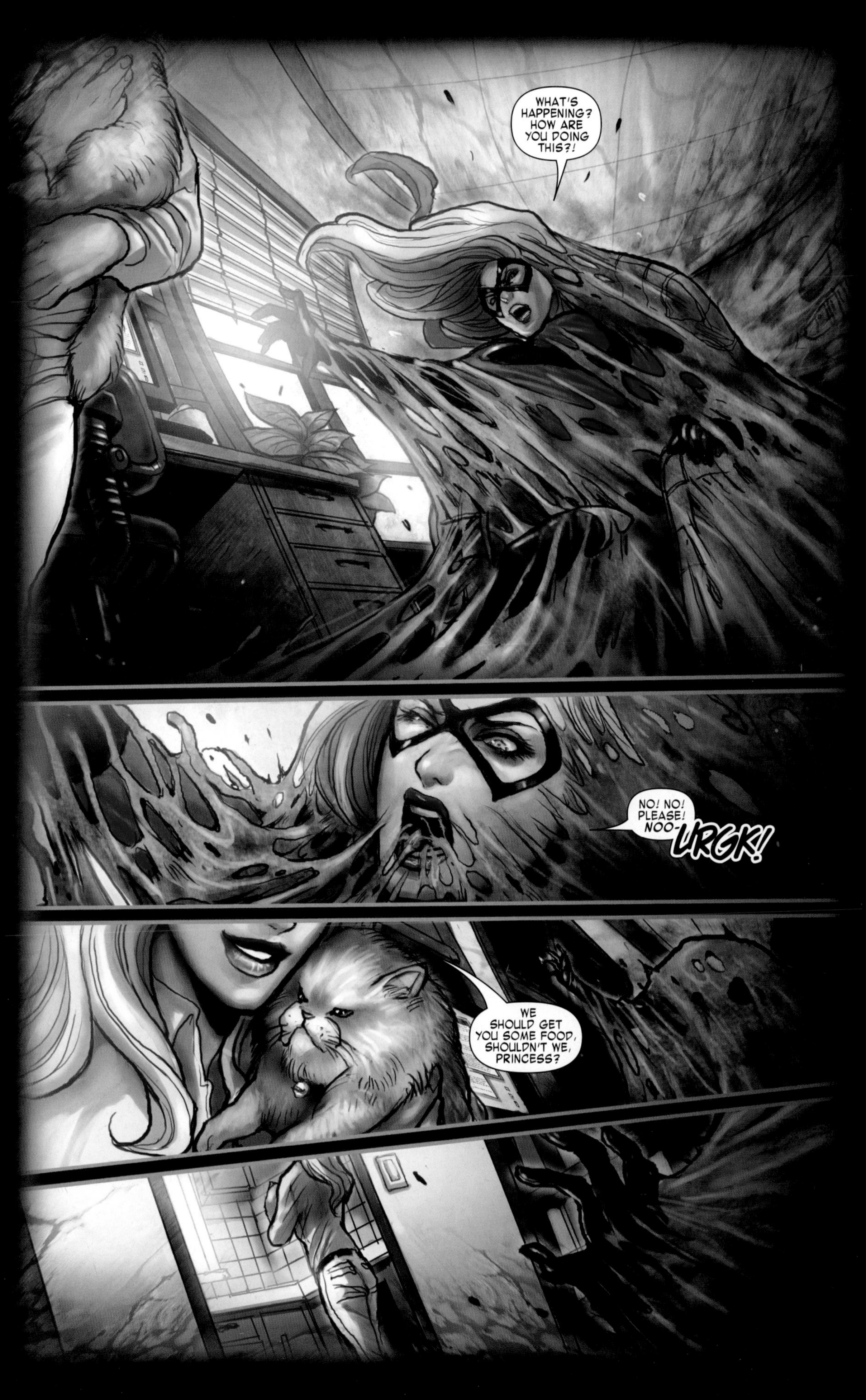
WHAT'S HAPPENING? HOW ARE YOU DOING THIS?!
NO! NO! PLEASE! NOO-URGK!
WE SHOULD GET YOU SOME FOOD, SHOULDN'T WE, PRINCESS?

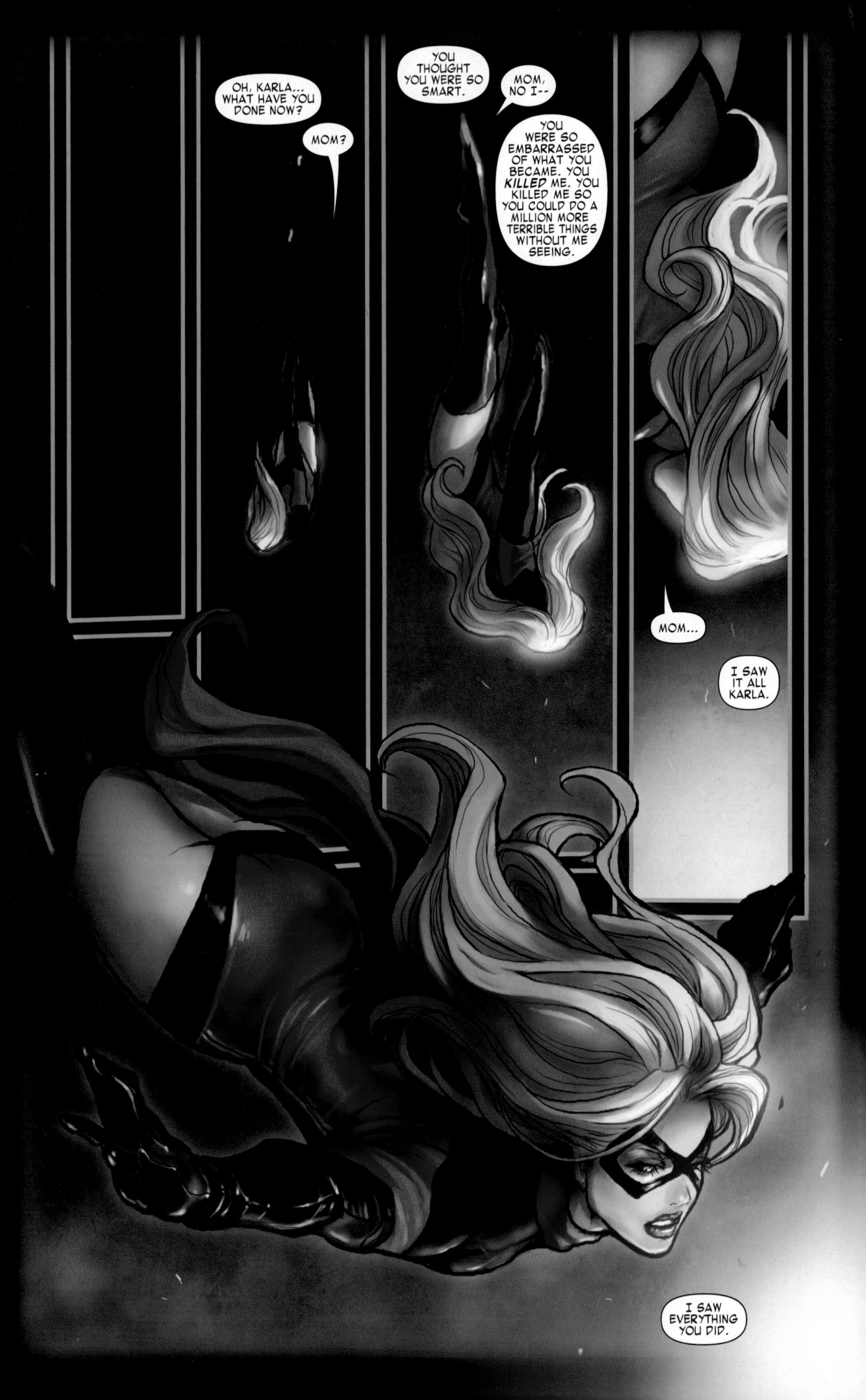
OH, KARLA... WHAT HAVE YOU DONE NOW?
MOM?
YOU THOUGHT YOU WERE SO SMART.
MOM, NO I--
YOU WERE SO EMBARRASSED OF WHAT YOU BECAME. YOU *KILLED* ME. YOU KILLED ME SO YOU COULD DO A MILLION MORE TERRIBLE THINGS WITHOUT ME SEEING.
MOM...
I SAW IT ALL KARLA.
I SAW EVERYTHING YOU DID.

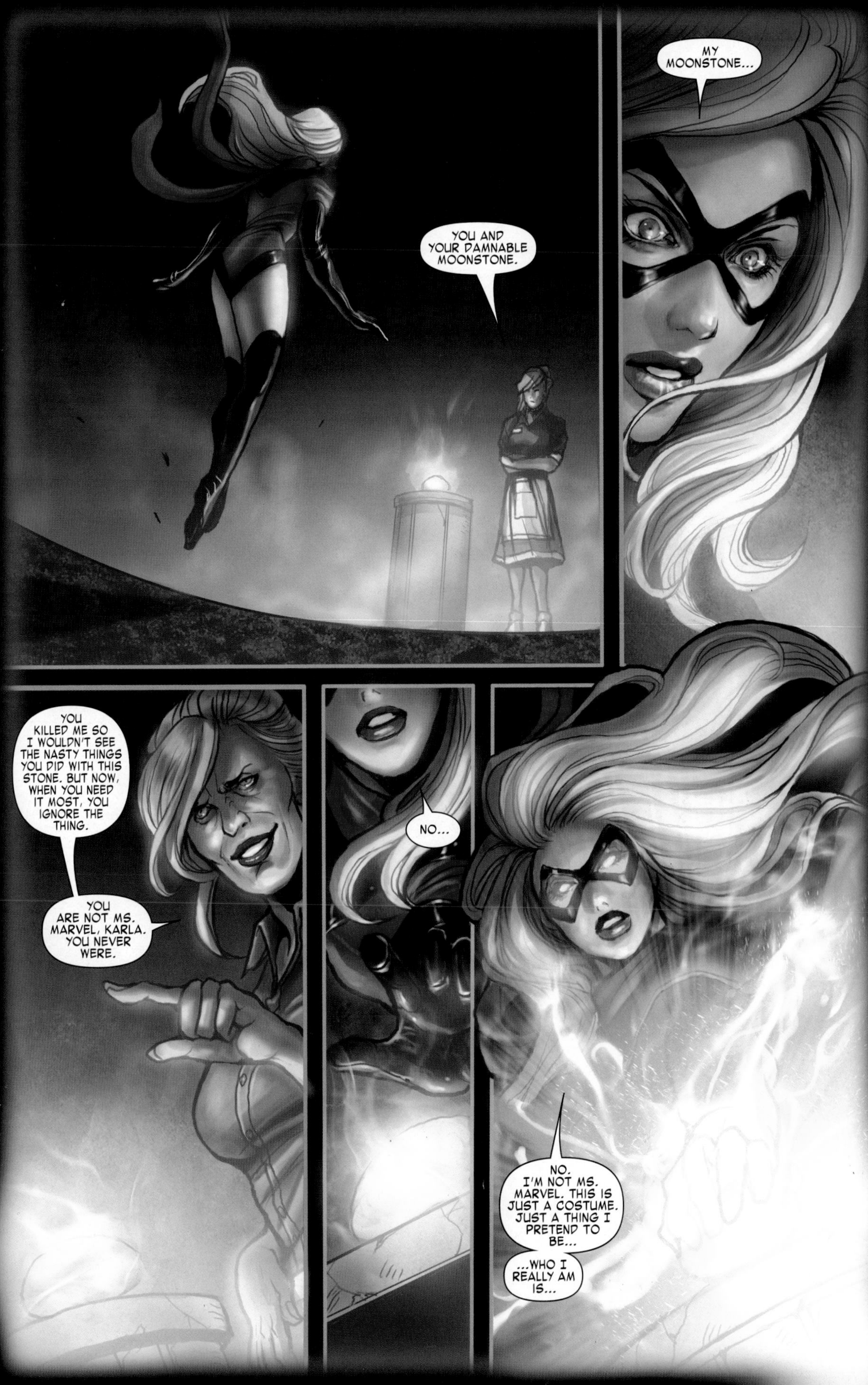
YOU AND YOUR DAMNABLE MOONSTONE.
MY MOONSTONE...
YOU KILLED ME SO I WOULDN'T SEE THE NASTY THINGS YOU DID WITH THIS STONE. BUT NOW, WHEN YOU NEED IT MOST, YOU IGNORE THE THING.
YOU ARE NOT MS. MARVEL, KARLA. YOU NEVER WERE.
NO...
NO. I'M NOT MS. MARVEL. THIS IS JUST A COSTUME. JUST A THING I PRETEND TO BE...
...WHO I REALLY AM IS...

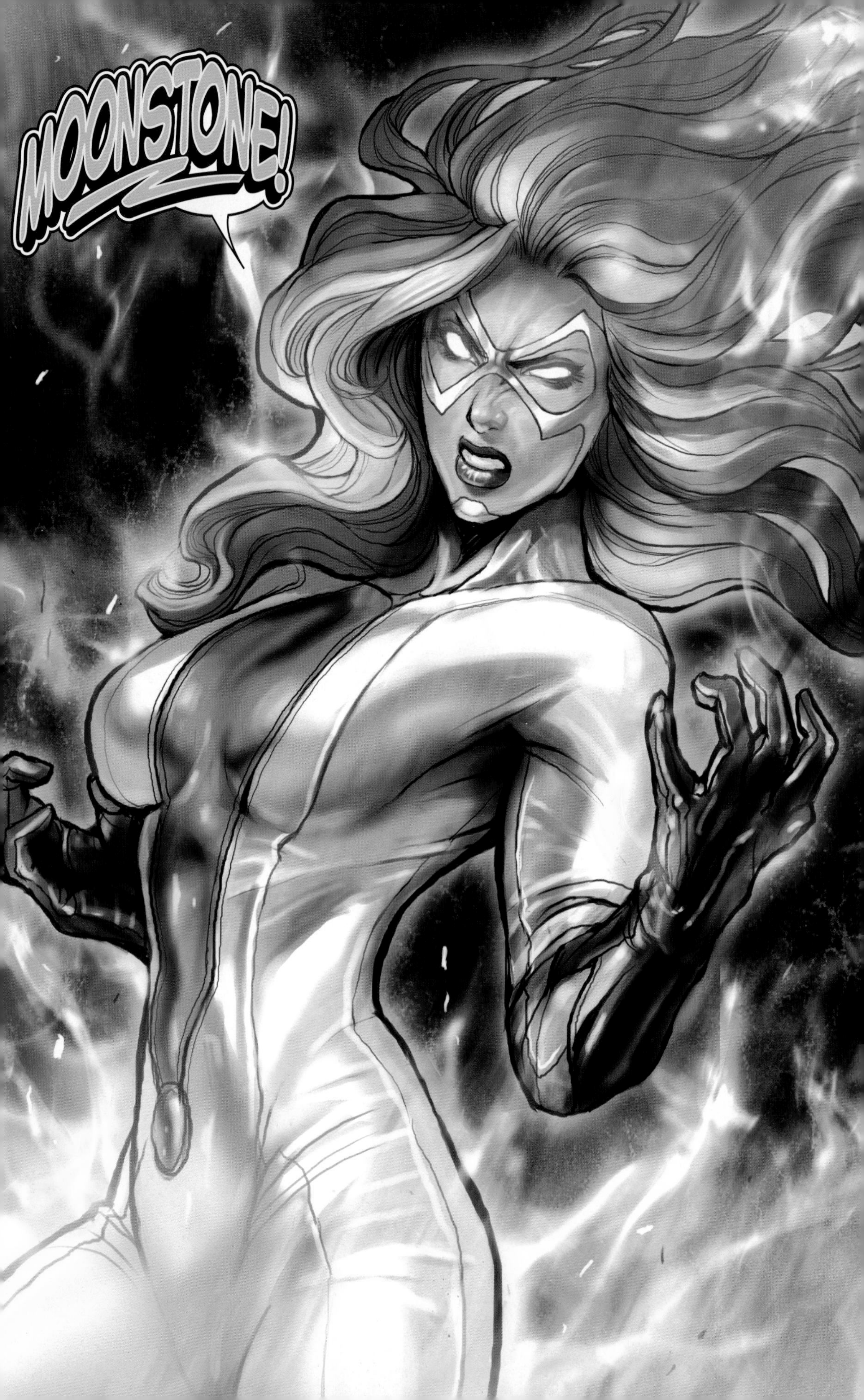
MOONSTONE!

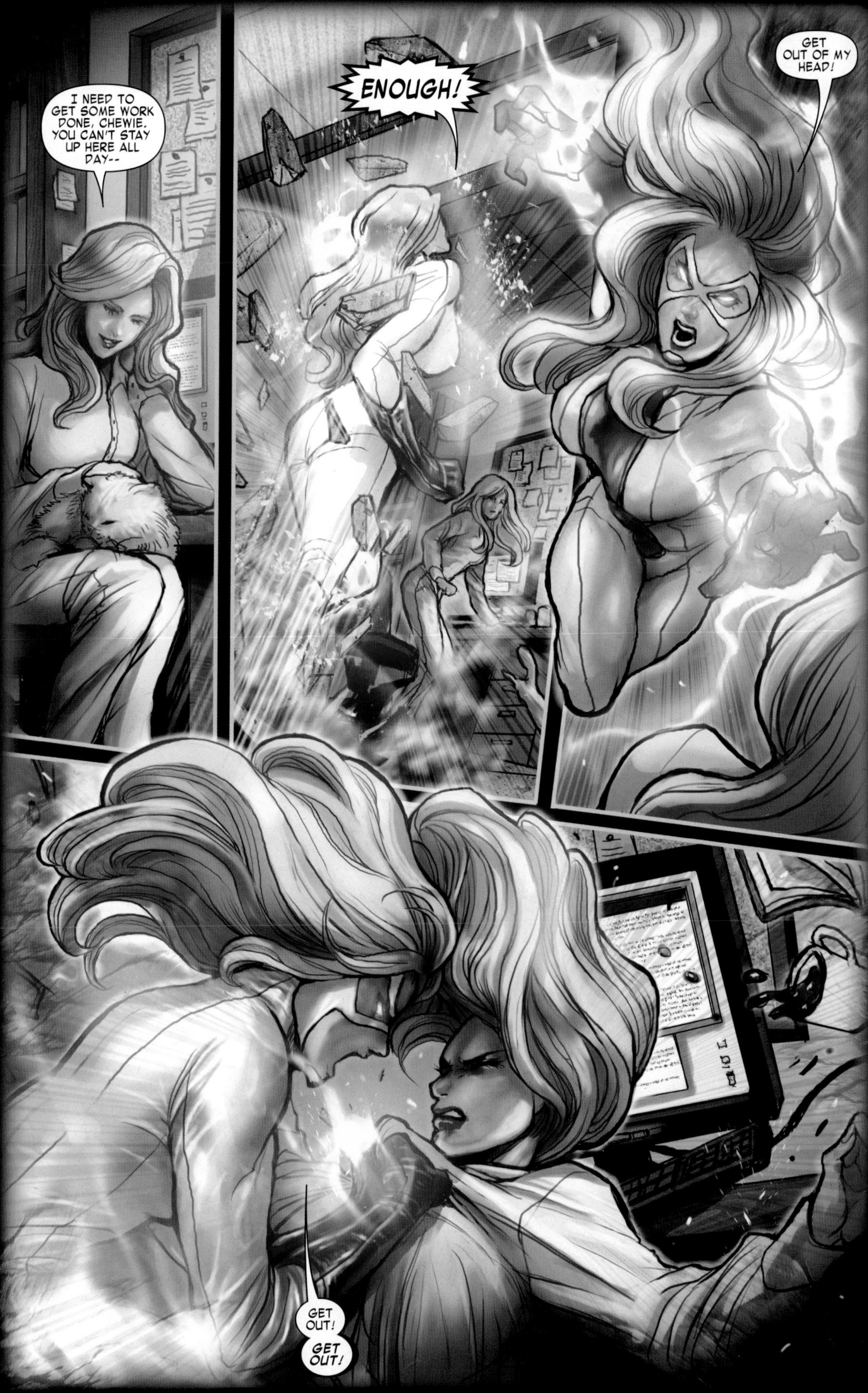
I NEED TO GET SOME WORK DONE, CHEWIE. YOU CAN'T STAY UP HERE ALL DAY--
ENOUGH!
GET OUT OF MY HEAD!
GET OUT!
GET OUT!

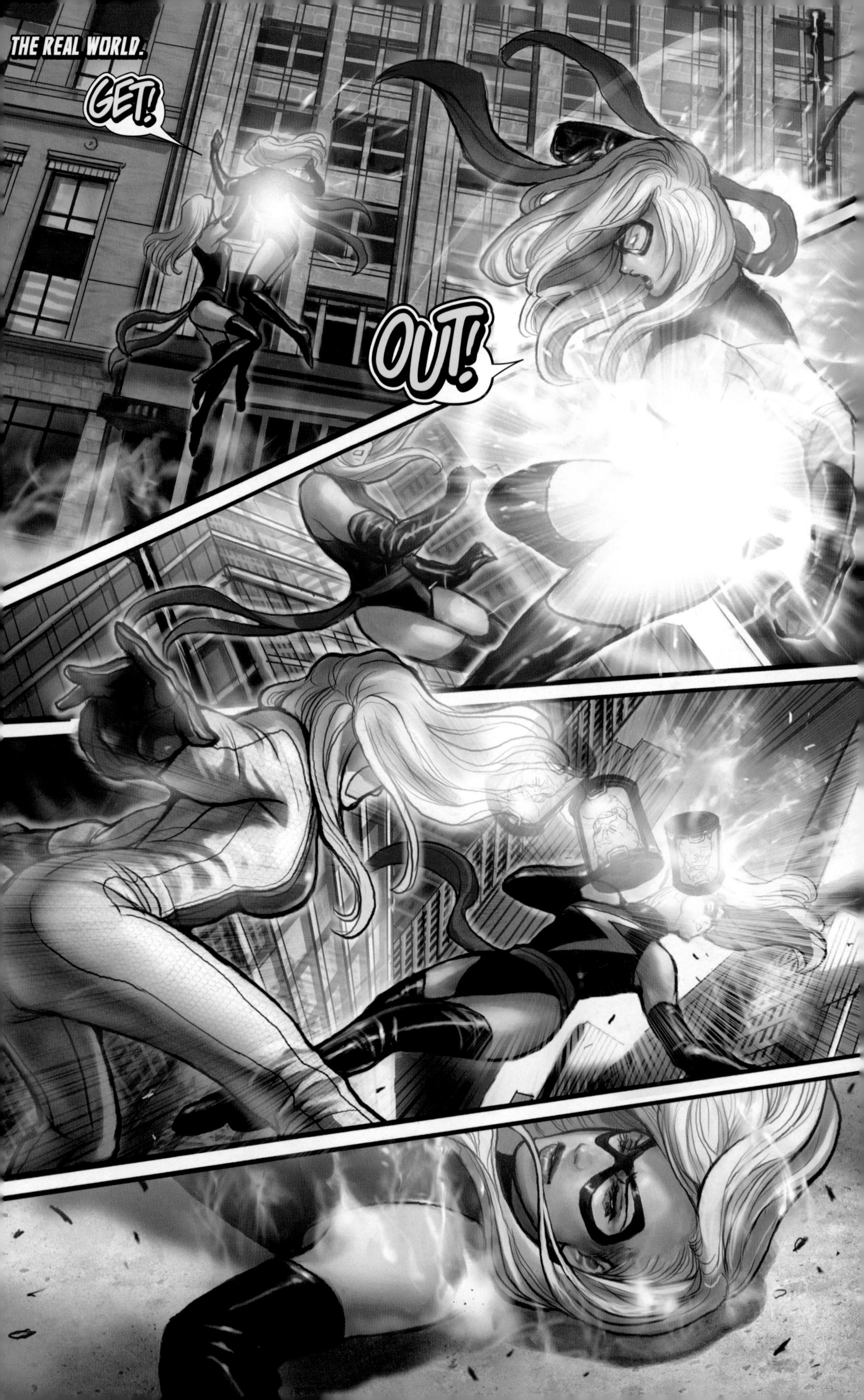
THE REAL WORLD.
GET!
OUT!

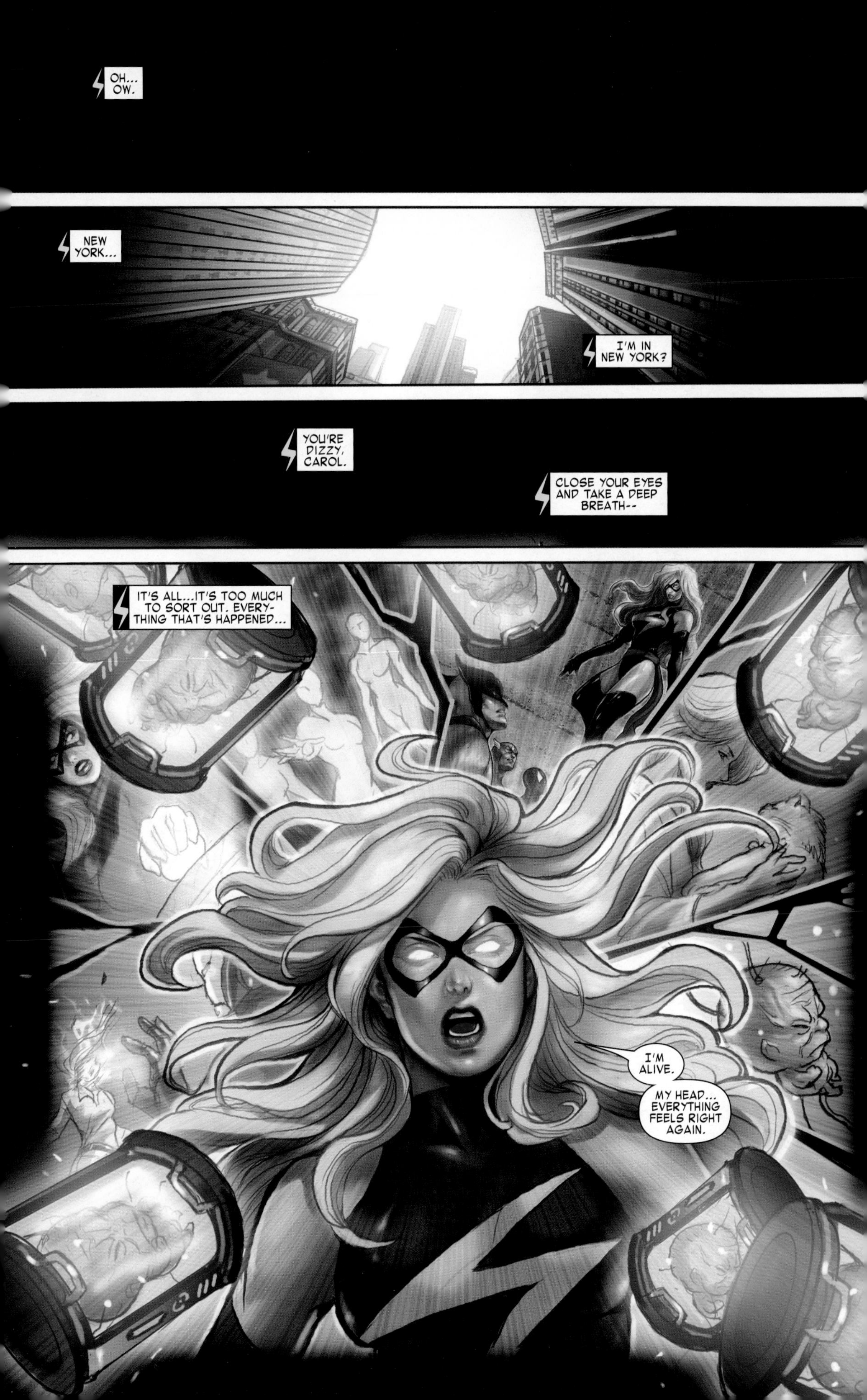
OH... OW.
NEW YORK...
I'M IN NEW YORK?
YOU'RE DIZZY, CAROL.
CLOSE YOUR EYES AND TAKE A DEEP BREATH--
IT'S ALL...IT'S TOO MUCH TO SORT OUT. EVERYTHING THAT'S HAPPENED...
I'M ALIVE.
MY HEAD... EVERYTHING FEELS RIGHT AGAIN.

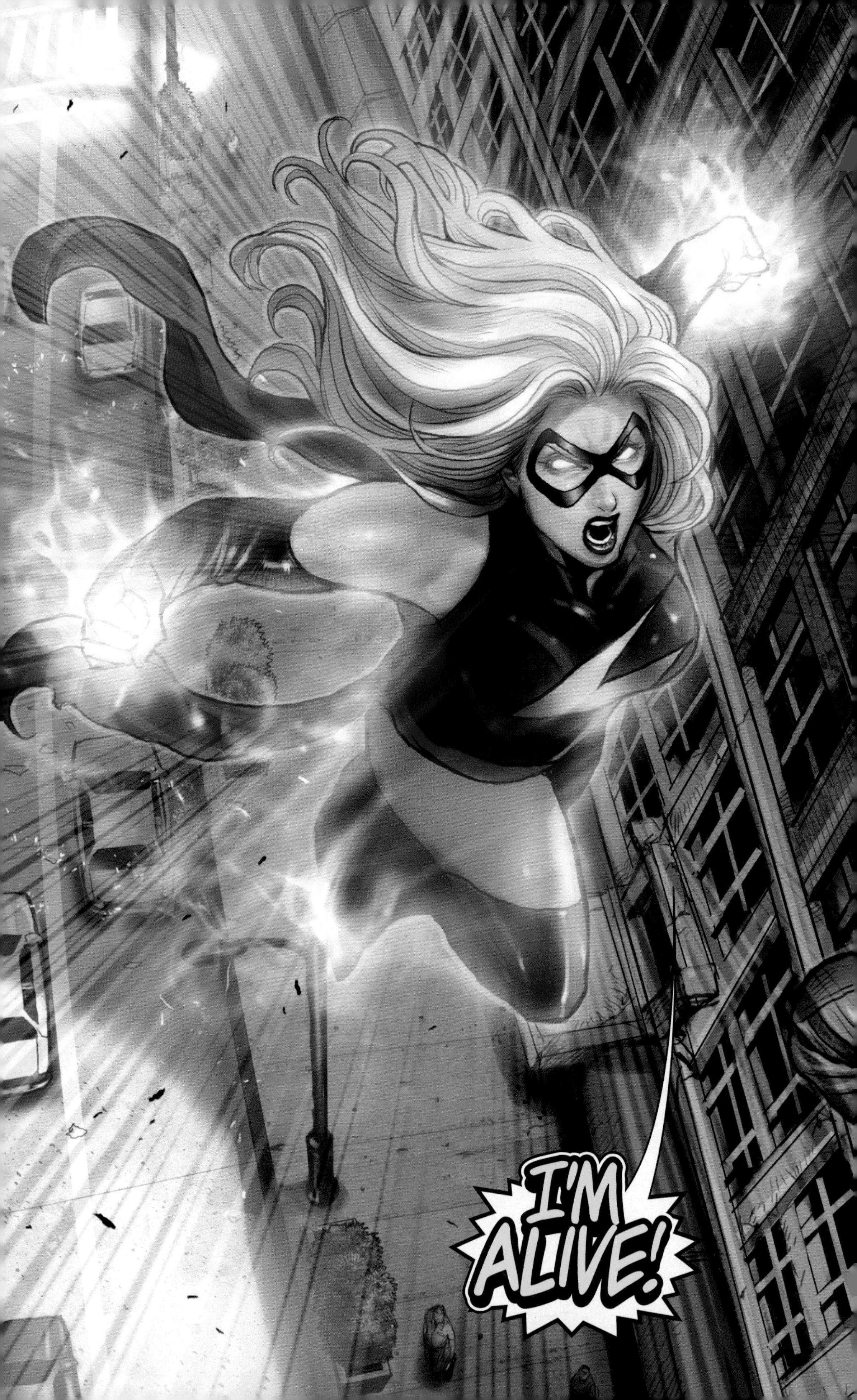
I'M ALIVE!

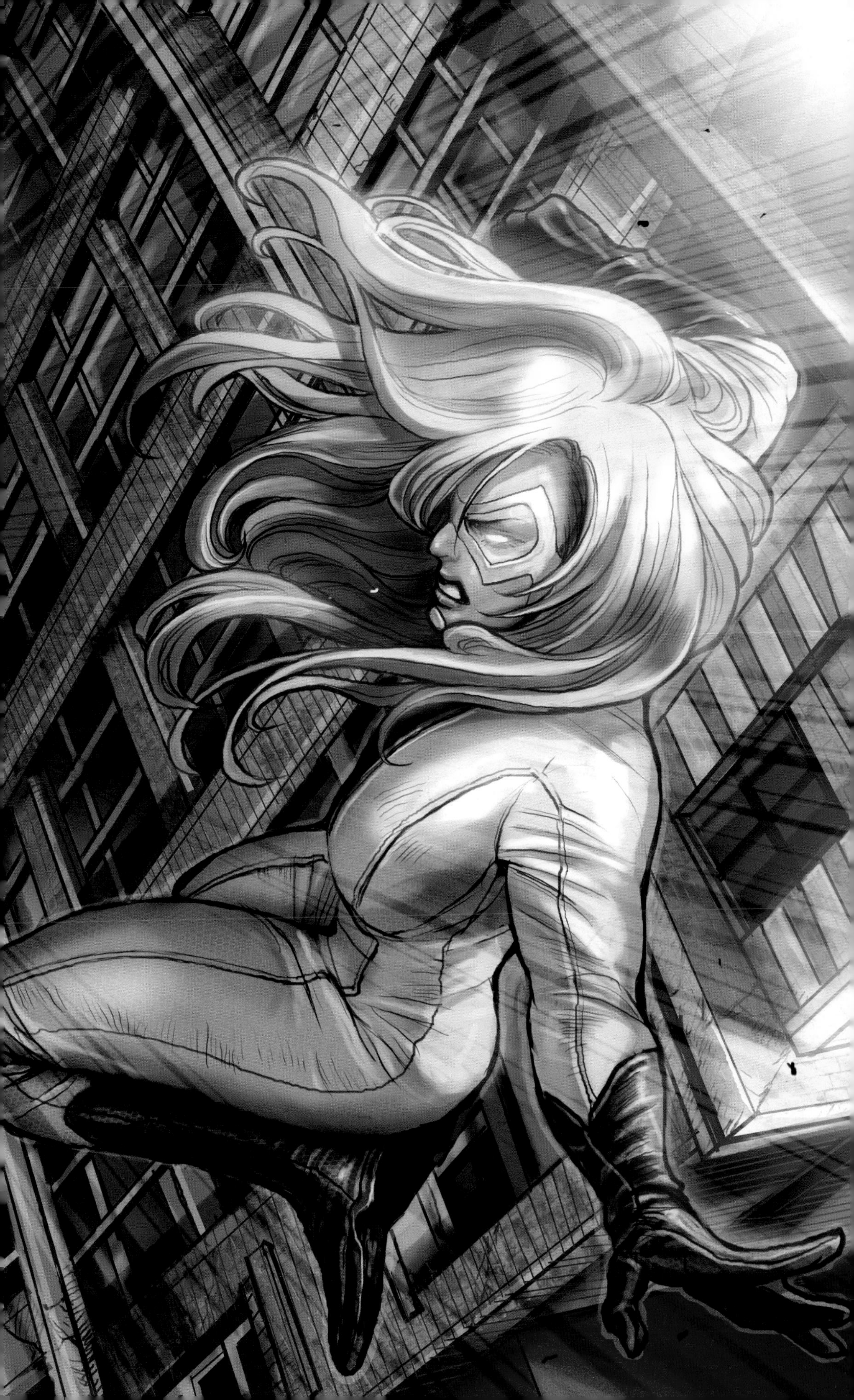

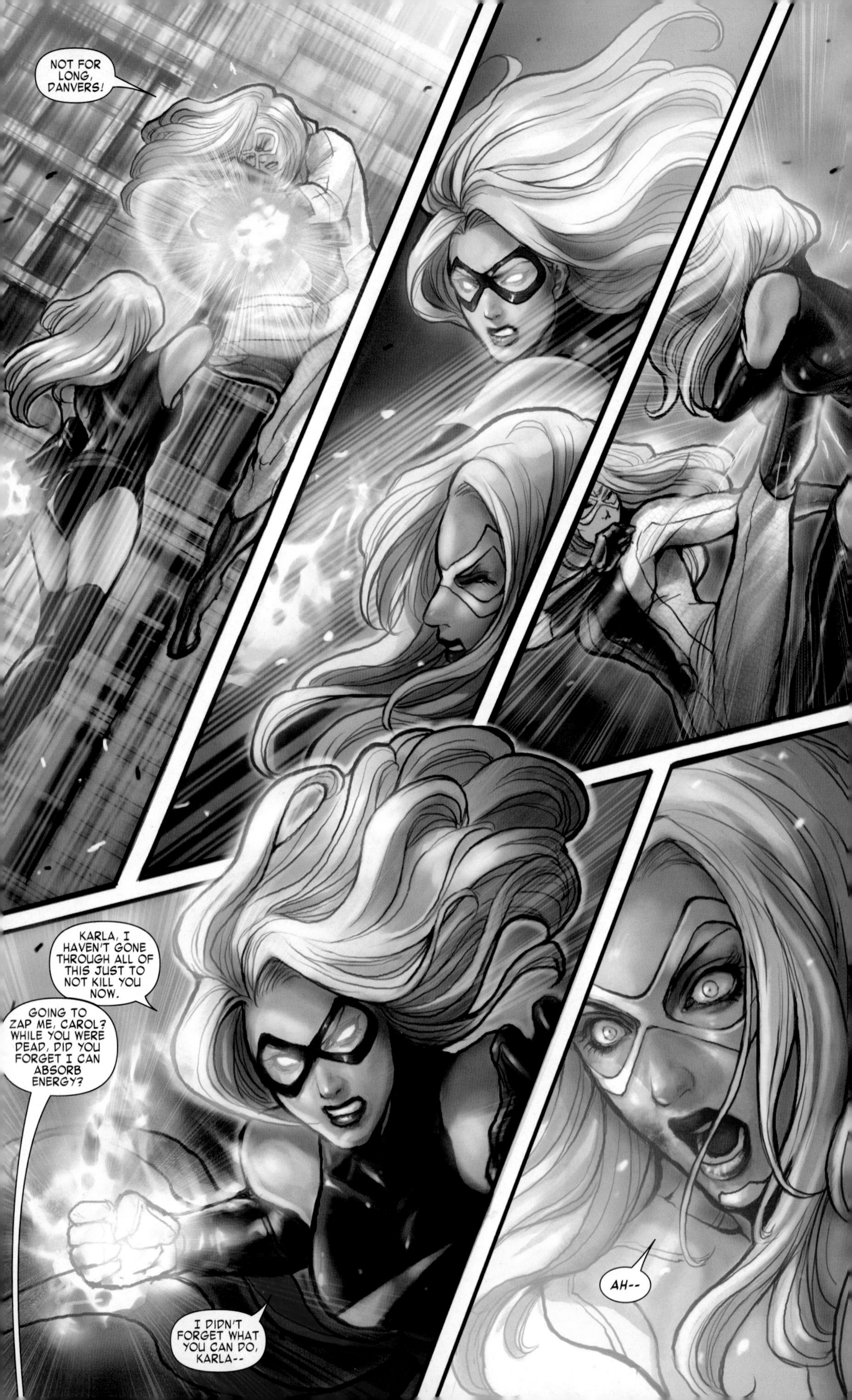
NOT FOR LONG, DANVERS!
KARLA, I HAVEN'T GONE THROUGH ALL OF THIS JUST TO NOT KILL YOU NOW.
GOING TO ZAP ME, CAROL? WHILE YOU WERE DEAD, DID YOU FORGET I CAN ABSORB ENERGY?
I DIDN'T FORGET WHAT YOU CAN DO, KARLA--
AH--

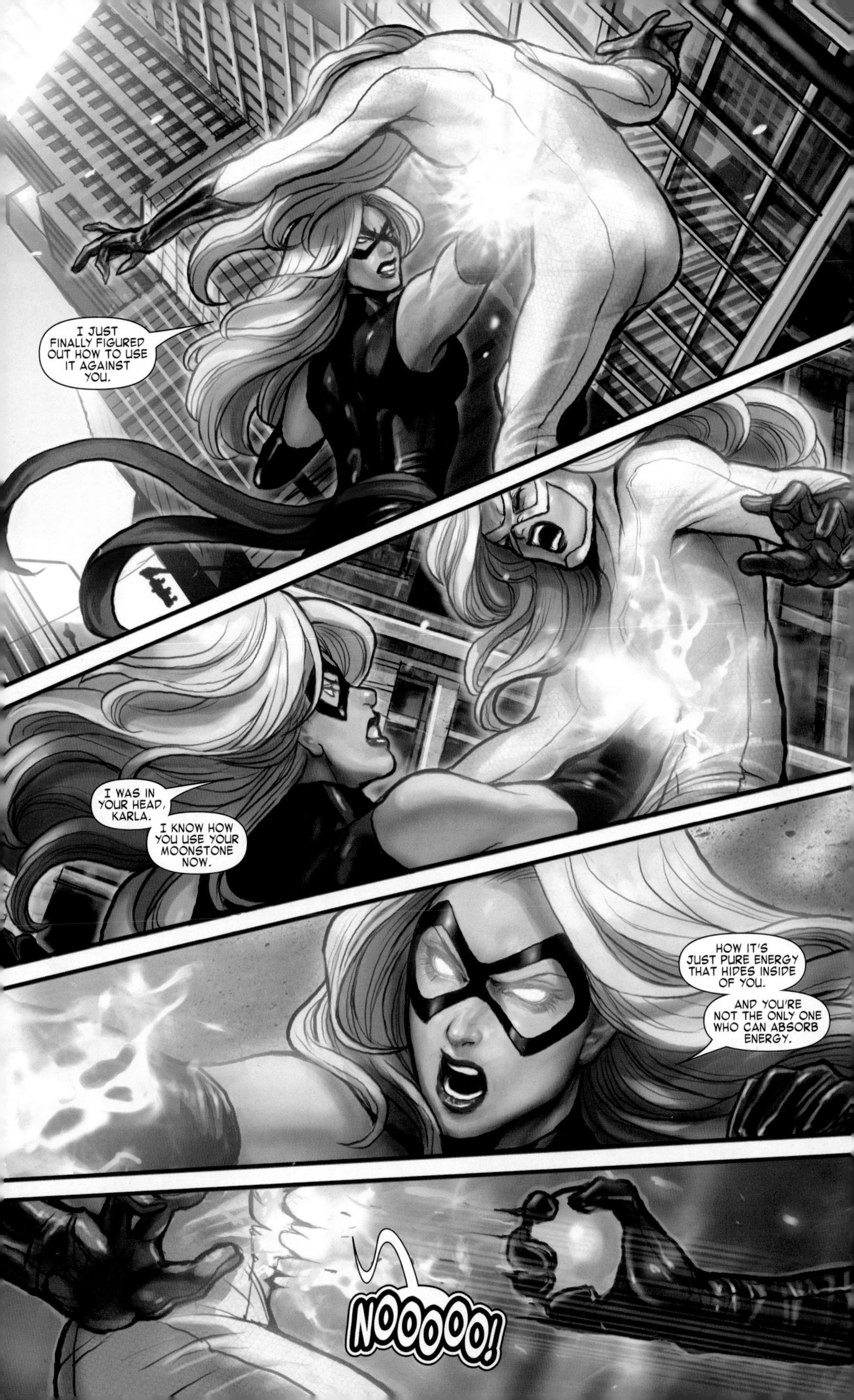
I JUST FINALLY FIGURED OUT HOW TO USE IT AGAINST YOU.
I WAS IN YOUR HEAD, KARLA.
I KNOW HOW YOU USE YOUR MOONSTONE NOW.
HOW IT'S JUST PURE ENERGY THAT HIDES INSIDE OF YOU.
AND YOU'RE NOT THE ONLY ONE WHO CAN ABSORB ENERGY.
NOOOOO!

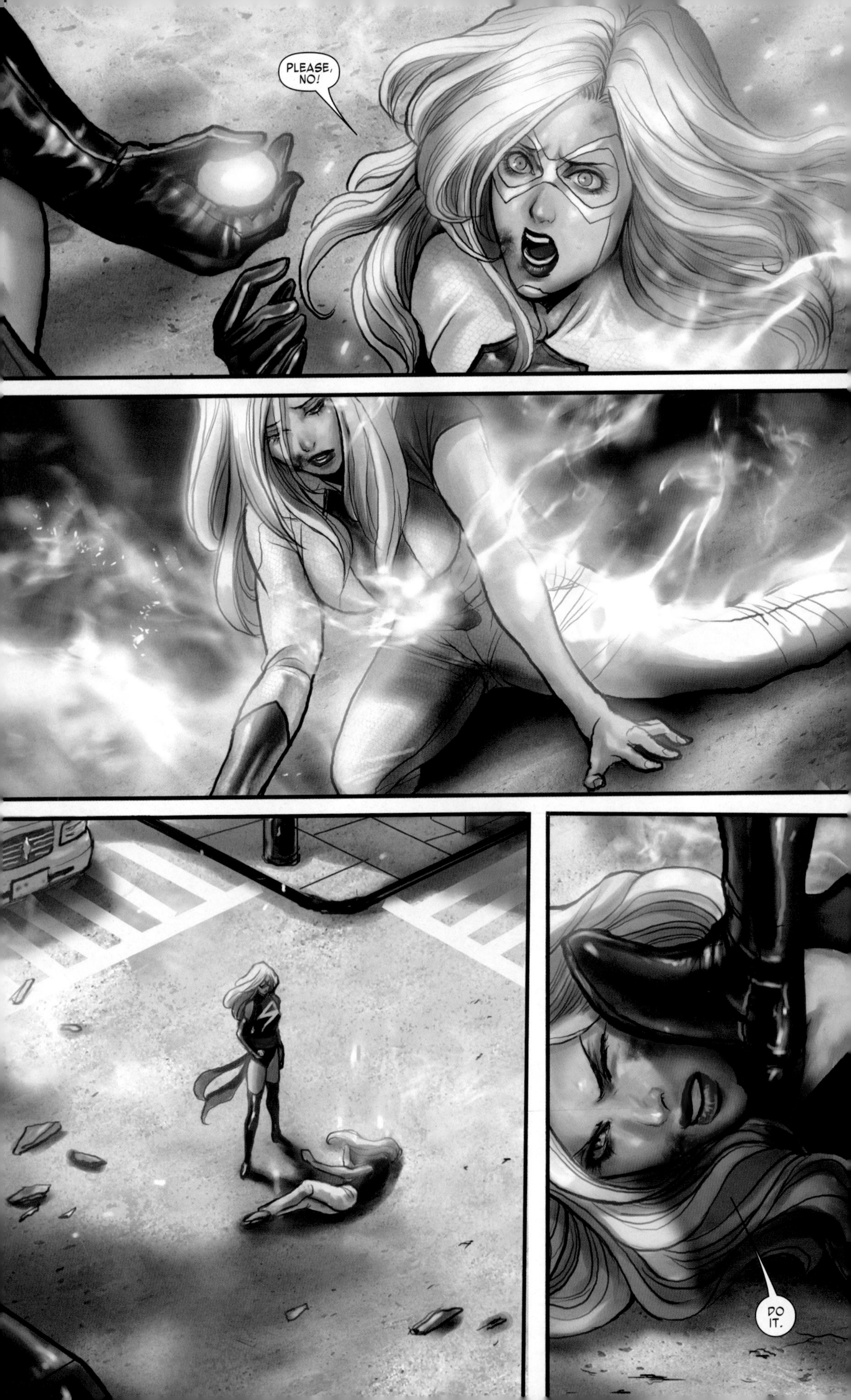
PLEASE, NO!
DO IT.

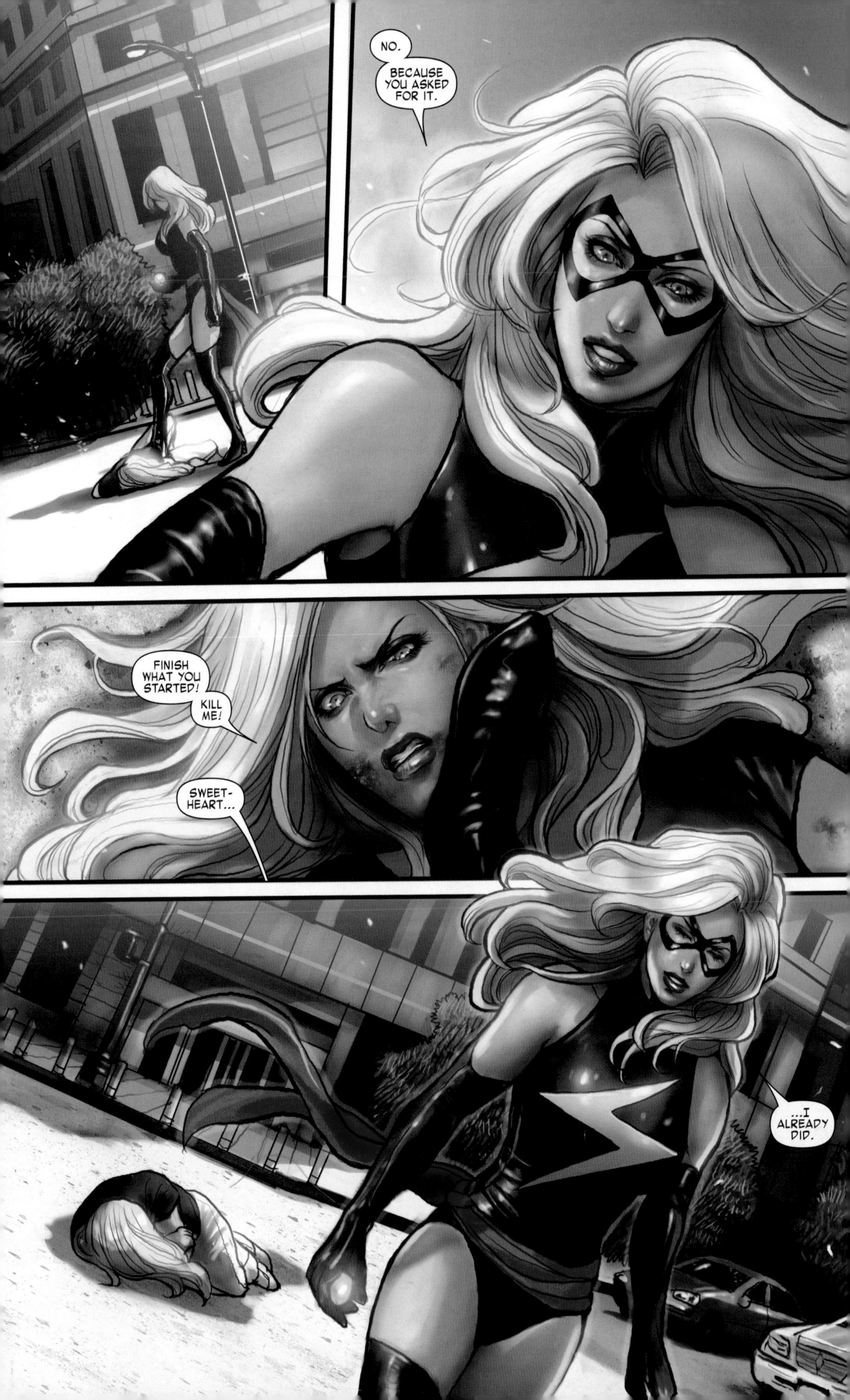
NO.
BECAUSE YOU ASKED FOR IT.
FINISH WHAT YOU STARTED!
KILL ME!
SWEET-HEART...
...I ALREADY DID.

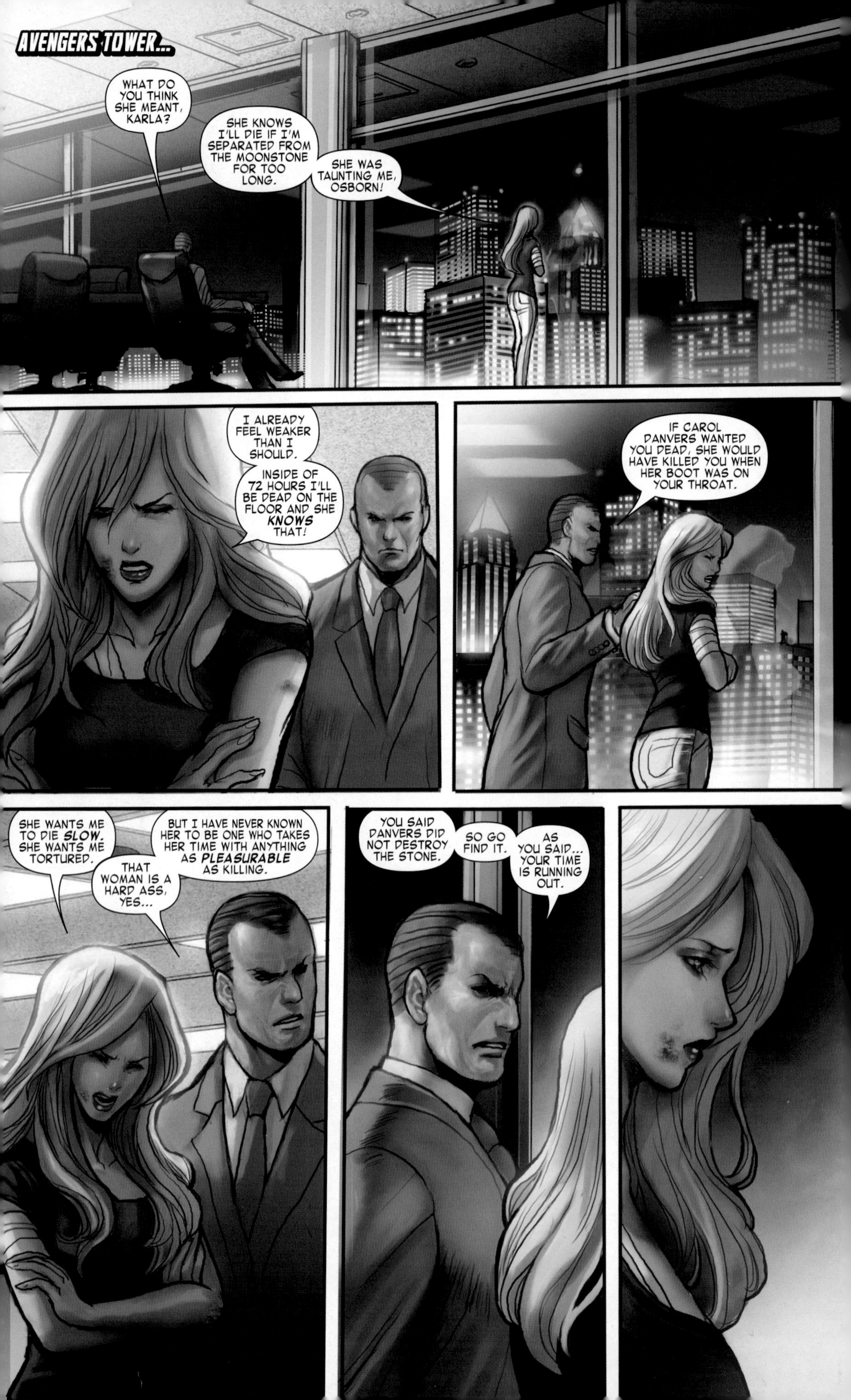
AVENGERS TOWER...
WHAT DO YOU THINK SHE MEANT, KARLA?
SHE KNOWS I'LL DIE IF I'M SEPARATED FROM THE MOONSTONE FOR TOO LONG.
SHE WAS TAUNTING ME, OSBORN!
I ALREADY FEEL WEAKER THAN I SHOULD.
INSIDE OF 72 HOURS I'LL BE DEAD ON THE FLOOR AND SHE *KNOWS* THAT!
IF CAROL DANVERS WANTED YOU DEAD, SHE WOULD HAVE KILLED YOU WHEN HER BOOT WAS ON YOUR THROAT.
SHE WANTS ME TO DIE *SLOW.* SHE WANTS ME TORTURED.
THAT WOMAN IS A HARD ASS, YES...
BUT I HAVE NEVER KNOWN HER TO BE ONE WHO TAKES HER TIME WITH ANYTHING AS *PLEASURABLE* AS KILLING.
YOU SAID DANVERS DID NOT DESTROY THE STONE.
SO GO FIND IT.
AS YOU SAID... YOUR TIME IS RUNNING OUT.

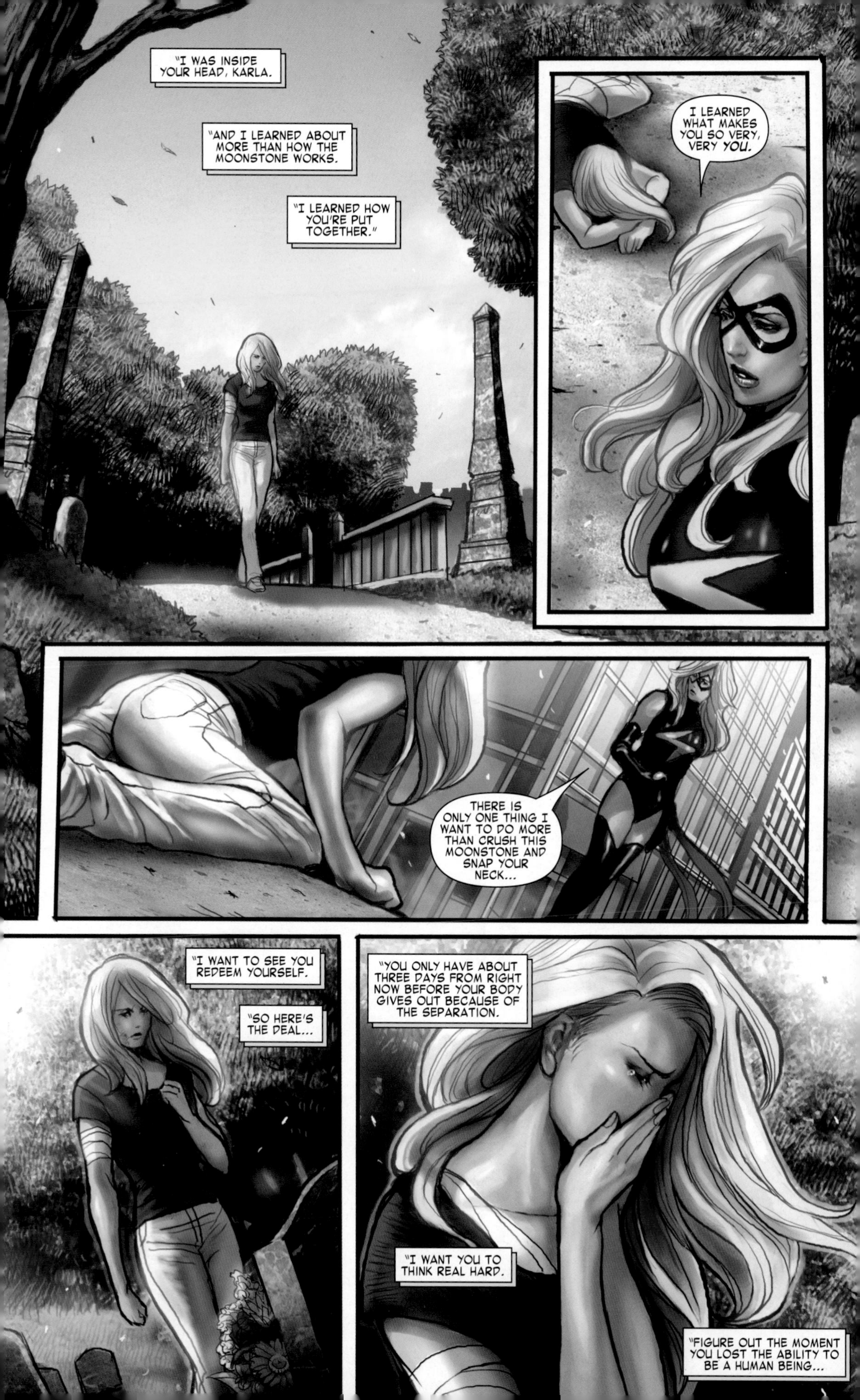
"I WAS INSIDE YOUR HEAD, KARLA.
"AND I LEARNED ABOUT MORE THAN HOW THE MOONSTONE WORKS.
"I LEARNED HOW YOU'RE PUT TOGETHER."
I LEARNED WHAT MAKES YOU SO VERY, VERY YOU.
THERE IS ONLY ONE THING I WANT TO DO MORE THAN CRUSH THIS MOONSTONE AND SNAP YOUR NECK...
"I WANT TO SEE YOU REDEEM YOURSELF.
"SO HERE'S THE DEAL...
"YOU ONLY HAVE ABOUT THREE DAYS FROM RIGHT NOW BEFORE YOUR BODY GIVES OUT BECAUSE OF THE SEPARATION.
"I WANT YOU TO THINK REAL HARD.
"FIGURE OUT THE MOMENT YOU LOST THE ABILITY TO BE A HUMAN BEING...

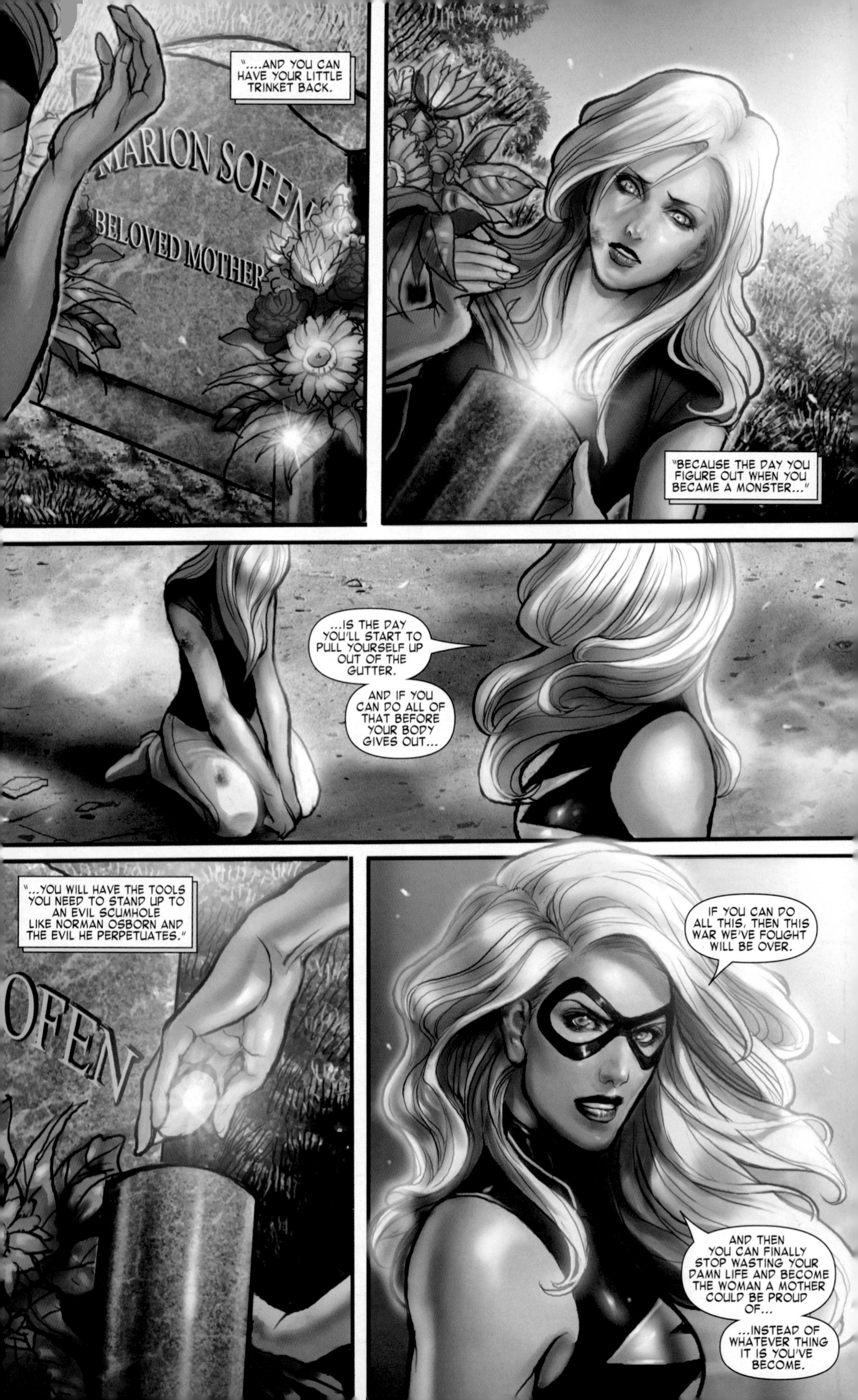
"....AND YOU CAN HAVE YOUR LITTLE TRINKET BACK.
MARION SOFEN
BELOVED MOTHER
"BECAUSE THE DAY YOU FIGURE OUT WHEN YOU BECAME A MONSTER..."
...IS THE DAY YOU'LL START TO PULL YOURSELF UP OUT OF THE GUTTER.
AND IF YOU CAN DO ALL OF THAT BEFORE YOUR BODY GIVES OUT...
"...YOU WILL HAVE THE TOOLS YOU NEED TO STAND UP TO AN EVIL SCUMHOLE LIKE NORMAN OSBORN AND THE EVIL HE PERPETUATES."
OFEN
IF YOU CAN DO ALL THIS, THEN THIS WAR WE'VE FOUGHT WILL BE OVER.
AND THEN YOU CAN FINALLY STOP WASTING YOUR DAMN LIFE AND BECOME THE WOMAN A MOTHER COULD BE PROUD OF...
...INSTEAD OF WHATEVER THING IT IS YOU'VE BECOME.

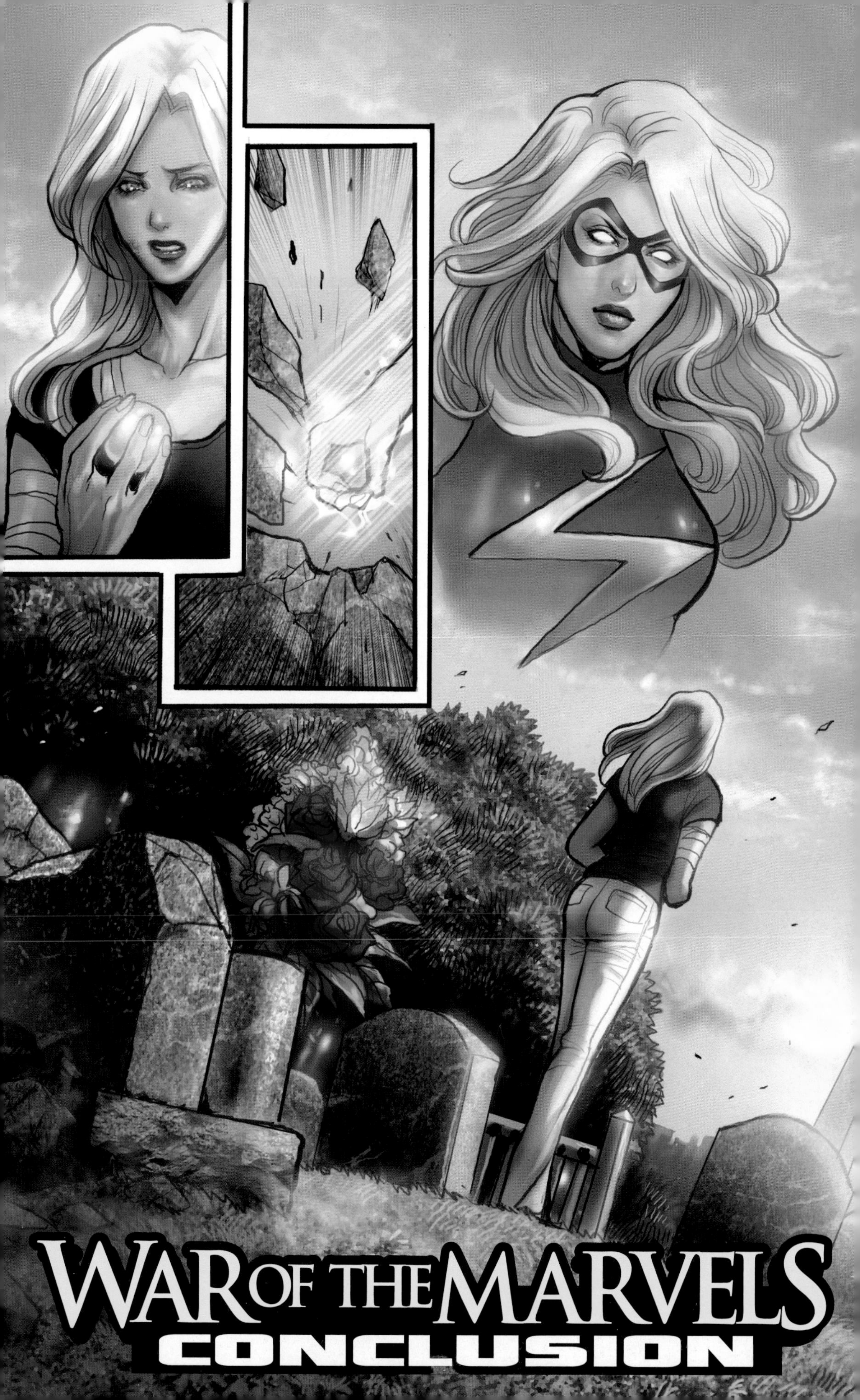
WAR OF THE MARVELS
CONCLUSION

#46

Zombie Variant by Sana Takeda

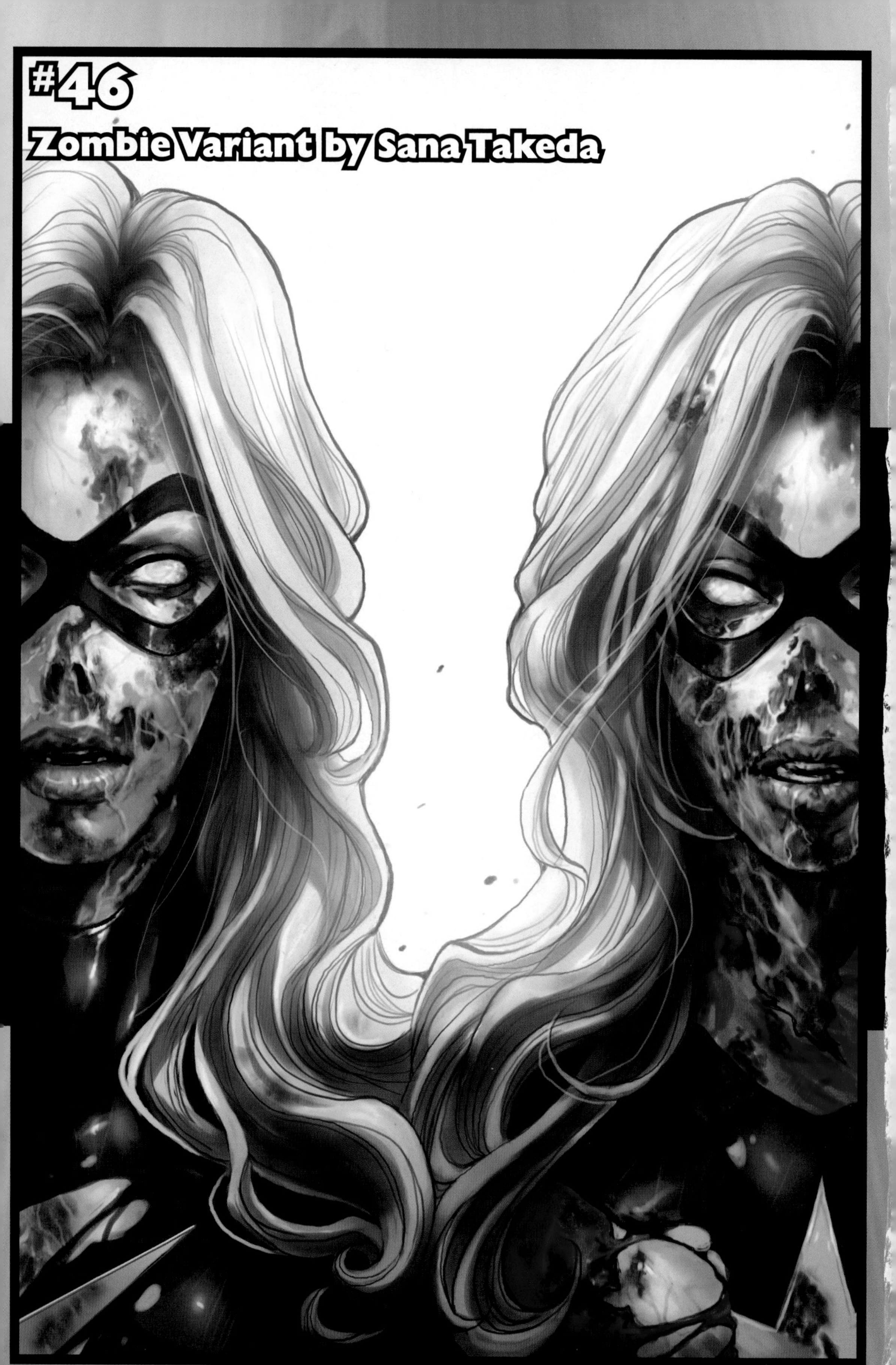

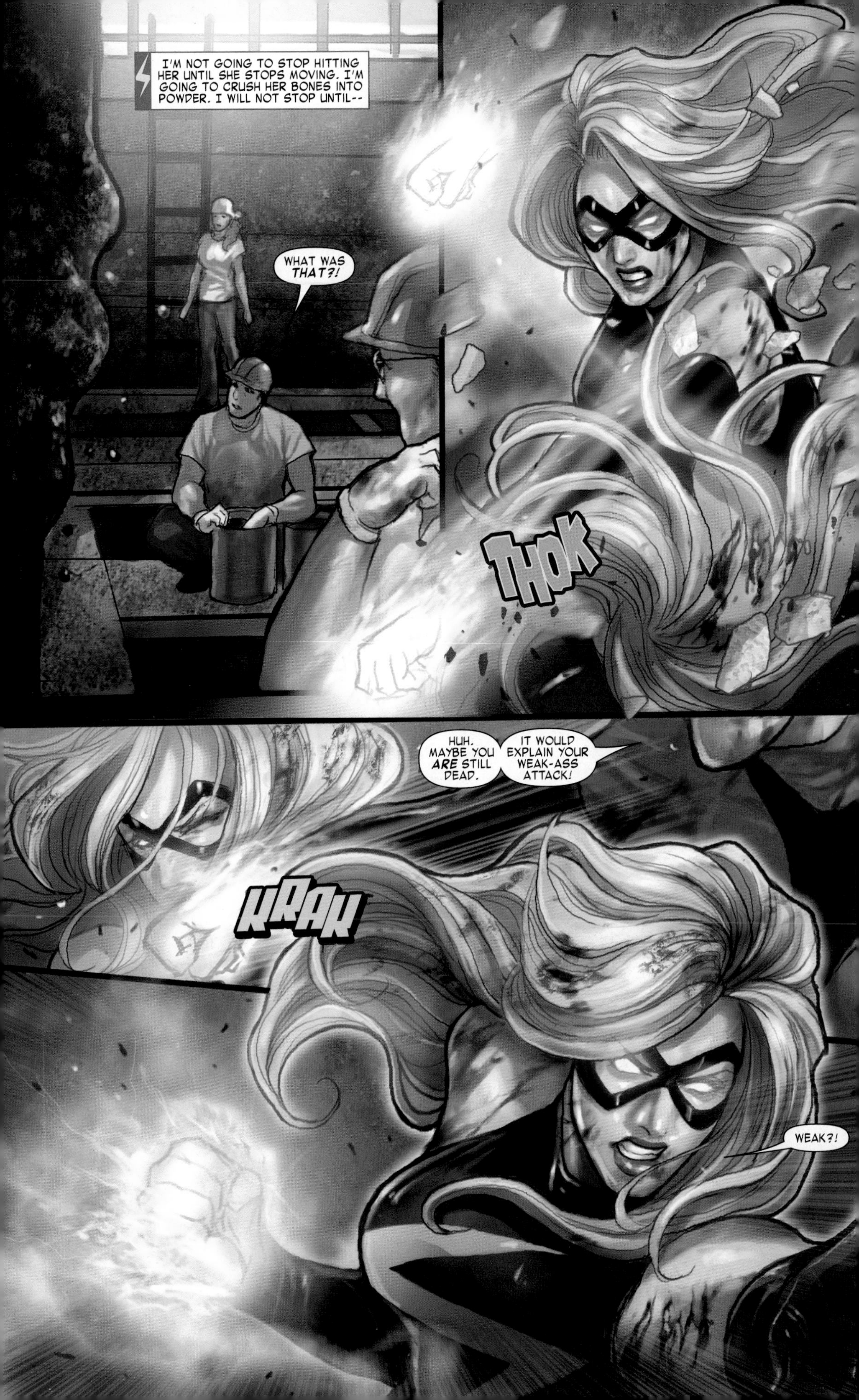
I'M NOT GOING TO STOP HITTING HER UNTIL SHE STOPS MOVING. I'M GOING TO CRUSH HER BONES INTO POWDER. I WILL NOT STOP UNTIL--
WHAT WAS THAT?!
THOK
HUH. MAYBE YOU ARE STILL DEAD.
IT WOULD EXPLAIN YOUR WEAK-ASS ATTACK!
KRAK
WEAK?!

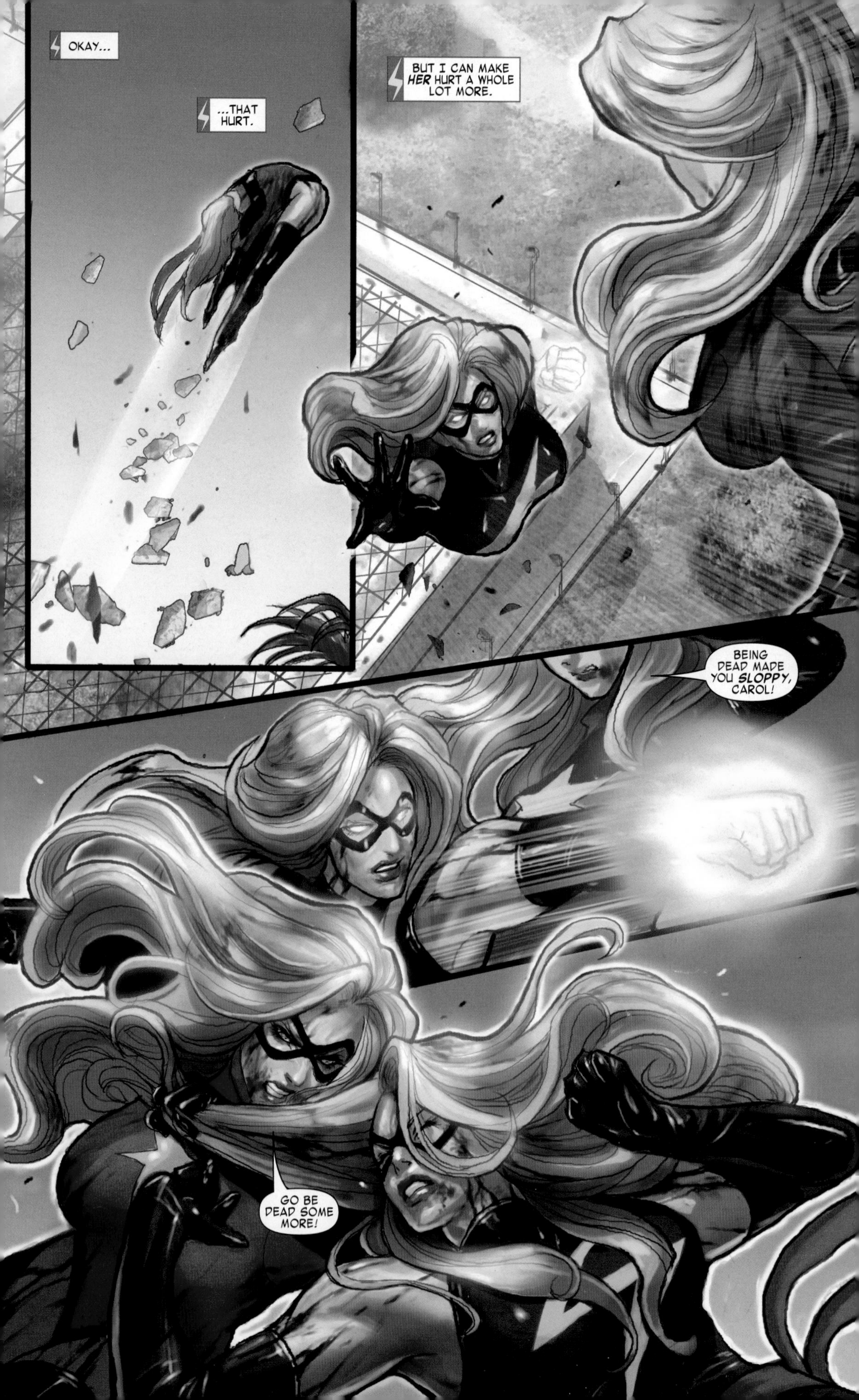
OKAY...
...THAT HURT.
BUT I CAN MAKE HER HURT A WHOLE LOT MORE.
BEING DEAD MADE YOU SLOPPY, CAROL!
GO BE DEAD SOME MORE!